T0305209

Leadership and Sexuality

JEPSON STUDIES IN LEADERSHIP

Series Editors: Kristin Bezio, George R. Goethals *and* Thad Williamson, *Jepson School of Leadership Studies, University of Richmond, USA*

Managing Editor: Elizabeth DeBusk-Maslanka

Jepson Studies in Leadership is dedicated to the interdisciplinary pursuit of important questions related to leadership. The series aims to publish the best work on leadership from such fields as economics, English, history, philosophy, political science, psychology and religion, and also contributions from management and organizational studies. In addition to monographs and edited collections on leadership, the series includes volumes that bring together influential scholars from multiple disciplines to think collectively about distinctive leadership themes in politics, science, civil society and corporate life. The books in the series are of interest to humanists and social scientists, as well as organizational theorists and instructors teaching in business, leadership and professional programs.

Titles in the series include:

Cultural Icons and Cultural Leadership
Edited by Peter Iver Kaufman and Kristin M.S. Bezio

Reconstruction and the Arc of Racial (in)Justice
Edited by Julian Maxwell Hayter and George R. Goethals

Leadership and Sexuality
Power, Principles and Processes
Edited by James K. Beggan and Scott T. Allison

Leadership and Sexuality

Power, Principles and Processes

Edited by

James K. Beggan

Department of Sociology, University of Louisville, USA

Scott T. Allison

Department of Psychology, University of Richmond, USA

JEPSON STUDIES IN LEADERSHIP

Cheltenham, UK • Northampton, MA, USA

Published by
Edward Elgar Publishing Limited
The Lypiatts
15 Lansdown Road
Cheltenham
Glos GL50 2JA
UK

Edward Elgar Publishing, Inc.
William Pratt House
9 Dewey Court
Northampton
Massachusetts 01060
USA

A catalogue record for this book
is available from the British Library

Library of Congress Control Number: 2017950480

This book is available electronically in the **Elgar**online
Business subject collection
DOI 10.4337/9781786438652

ISBN 978 1 78643 864 5 (cased)
ISBN 978 1 78643 865 2 (eBook)

Typeset by Columns Design XML Ltd, Reading

Printed and bound by CPI Group (UK) Ltd, Croydon, CR0 4YY

Contents

PART III   THE SEXUALITY OF LEADERS

Contributors

Scott T. Allison has authored numerous books, including *Heroes, Heroic Leadership*, and *Heroic Humility*. He is a professor of psychology at the University of Richmond, where he has published extensively on heroism and leadership. His other books include *Reel Heroes, Conceptions of Leadership, Frontiers in Spiritual Leadership*, and *Handbook of Heroism and Heroic Leadership*. His work has appeared in *USA Today*, the *New York Times*, the *Los Angeles Times, Slate Magazine, Psychology Today*, and the *Christian Science Monitor* and on National Public Radio, MSNBC, and CBS. He has received Richmond's Distinguished Educator Award and the Virginia Council of Higher Education's Outstanding Faculty Award.

James K. Beggan is a professor of sociology at the University of Louisville. He regularly teaches courses in human sexuality, the self and society, and statistics. He earned a BA from the State University of New York at Buffalo and a PhD from the University of California at Santa Barbara. His research interests include the representation of gender and sexuality in mass media, especially sexually explicit material, stigmatization with regard to physical characteristics, and psychological processes associated with serious leisure in the form of extreme fitness and social dancing.

Lucy Dwight is an assistant professor, clinical track, in CU Denver's School of Public Affairs, with expertise in quantitative research methods, race, and public policy. She has published on immigration and law enforcement policy. Her research interests include the interaction of race and gender, the role of religion in behavior, and the intersection of race and location in contributing to inequality.

Olivia Efthimiou is a transdisciplinary researcher at Murdoch University, Perth, and Associate Researcher at the Australian National Academy of Screen and Sound. Her current research focuses on the emerging field of heroism science, embodiment, transdisciplinarity, the philosophy of science, and creative play in social, locative, and mobile spaces. She is the creator and administrator of the website "Heroism science: Promoting the transdisciplinary study of heroism in the 21st century." She is editor of *Heroism Science*, the first crossdisciplinary journal dedicated to advancing heroism research.

Dr. Jeremy Fyke (PhD Purdue University) is an assistant professor in Communication Studies and Corporate Communication and a corporate trainer for the Center for Executive Education at Belmont University. His research topics include corporate social responsibility, conscious capitalism, consulting, leadership development, and ethics. His work has been published in the *International Journal of Strategic Communication, Business and Society Review, Human Relations, Journal of Applied Communication Research, and Journal of Business Ethics, among others. He is also lead editor of Cases in Organizational and Managerial Communication: Stretching Boundaries (Routledge, 2017).*

Sheila Huss is a senior instructor in the School of Public Affairs at the University of Colorado Denver (CU Denver). She earned her Master's in criminology from the University of South Florida and her PhD in Public Affairs from CU Denver. She teaches a wide variety of courses. Her research interests include quantitative methods, issues of social differentiation (race, class, gender, sexuality) and social justice, including environmental justice and capital punishment.

Kristen Lucas (PhD Purdue University) is an associate professor in the management department at the University of Louisville. Her research expertise centers on how communication—from micro-level interactions to broader social discourses—constructs organizations, gives meaning to careers, and influences the experience of dignity at work. She has published research in outlets such as *Journal of Management Studies, Organization Studies, Journal of Business Ethics, and Journal of Management Inquiry.*

Shaun Pichler (PhD Michigan State University) is an associate professor of management at the Mihaylo College of Business & Economics at California State University, Fullerton, where he teaches courses in organizational behavior and human resource management. Shaun has published in journals such as *Human Resource Management, Journal of Occupational & Organizational Psychology, Journal of Vocational Behavior, and Personnel Psychology,* among others. He is currently serving or has previously served on the editorial boards for journals such as *Academy of Management Review, Equality, Diversity & Inclusion: An International Journal, Human Resource Management, Journal of Occupational & Organizational Psychology, and Journal of Vocational Behavior.* His research has been covered by a variety of prominent national (e.g., Forbes) and local (e.g., O.C. Register) outlets and in the US Congress, as well as being cited in a number of policy reports and other outlets. He regularly consults on management and leadership topics for organizations in a variety of industries in Orange County and across the US.

Carrie Pitzulo is the author of *Bachelors and Bunnies: The Sexual Politics of Playboy*, and teaches American history at Colorado State University.

Charol Shakeshaft has been studying equity in schools for nearly four decades. She is the author of three books and more than 200 refereed articles and papers. Her research focuses on three strands: the intersection of gender and race in leadership, educator sexual misconduct, and the effectiveness of technology for learning, particularly for students of color. Dr. Shakeshaft received a $5.2 million grant to develop state-of-the-art principal preparation to include the first immersive, interactive, and web-enabled computer simulation for school administrators. She previously completed a three-year national study of the relationships between a school-based risk prevention program and risk behaviors of sixth to eighth-grade students. Dr. Shakeshaft was also the principal investigator on a three-year National Science Foundation project to promote interest in science careers among seventh and eighth-grade girls of color. Dr. Shakeshaft completed a report on educator sexual misconduct that was mandated by the US Senate and has formed the foundation for scholarship, policy, and legal remedies for prevention. Two earlier studies, also funded by the US Department of Education, examined responses to reports of educator sexual misconduct and sexual harassment in middle schools. She has just completed a study on the Standard of Care for the Prevention of Educator Sexual Misconduct and is currently completing a book on educator sexual misconduct. She was elected an AERA fellow in 2015 and also received the 2015 AERA Distinguished Contributions to Gender Equity in Education Research Award. Dr. Shakeshaft currently teaches graduate courses in research design, policy research methods, and gender and race equity at Virginia Commonwealth University.

William R. Stayton, M.Div, ThD, PhD is Professor, Series III, of Community Health & Preventive Medicine at Morehouse School of Medicine in Atlanta, GA. He is Professor Emeritus and former Director of the Center for Human Sexuality Studies at Widener University in Chester, PA. For 28 years he was on the faculty of the University of Pennsylvania. He is also an adjunct professor in the Human Sexuality Program at the University of Minnesota Medical School. He has received numerous awards from AASECT, SIECUS, and Widener University, and received the Gold Medal Award from the World Association for Sexual Health in Scotland in June 2011 for promoting dialogue with sexuality, medicine, and religion. Dr Stayton is an ordained minister in the American Baptist Churches, USA; a licensed clinical psychologist; and a certified sexuality, marriage, and family therapist and supervisor.

Maggie B. Stone is an assistant professor at Marshall University. She earned a PhD in applied sociology from the University of Louisville, in addition to a Master's degree in counseling psychology. She has worked for the Kentucky Department of Corrections, a community mental health services provider, and a variety of regional acute and long-term care medical facilities. The clients for whom she has provided services and assessments include marginalized populations such as the medically fragile, sex offenders, chronically mentally ill people, and developmentally challenged people. Today she continues her work with stigmatized persons through research on the sex industry, including exotic dance clubs, domestic adult sex work, and sex trafficking. Her studies focus on sexual health, legislative measures, stigma, and community initiatives. She teaches graduate and undergraduate courses in quantitative research methods, statistical analysis, and the sexualization and commodification of the body.

Bree Trisler is a PhD student in critical media studies at the University of Minnesota, Twin Cities. Bree received her BA at the University of Wisconsin-La Crosse and her MA at Marquette University in Communication Studies. Her research interests include exploring the political possibilities and consequences of memes and bringing together the cultural and historical conditions leading to the "Trump era."

Dr. Emma Turley is a senior lecturer in psychology at Manchester Metropolitan University, UK. She has a diverse range of research interests, including gender, sexualities, adult playfulness, well-being, and women's health. Emma's other special areas of interest include qualitative methodologies, especially phenomenological psychology and experiential research, and the use of innovative research methods. When she is not working, Emma enjoys reading crime fiction and is currently learning to speak French.

Introduction
Sexuality in leadership: A long-neglected topic with vast implications for individuals and society

James K. Beggan and Scott T. Allison

Sexual opportunities can be construed as a reward for achieving a leadership role (Baumeister, 2010). For some species of animals, social dominance is the sole basis for sexual access to mates (Dixson, 2015). One way that social dominance expresses itself is through leadership. Although becoming a leader may afford sexual opportunities, it is also true that in the twenty-first century, rather than being seen as a benefit, sexuality can be viewed as potential liability for leaders, as people have become more sensitive to issues related to gender, sexual orientation, sexual behavior, and sexual harassment.

There is no shortage of evidence demonstrating that great leaders sometimes have poor judgment when it comes to issues of sexuality (Gamson, 2001). Even a quick glance at the newspapers or history books reveals how many careers have been ruined or irrevocably altered because of sex. Bill Clinton's entire tenure as president can be reduced to a punch line about oral sex. Technically, although guilty of marital infidelity, Bill Clinton's crime with regard to Monica Lewinsky related not to the affair, but to the charges of perjury that stemmed from lying about the affair. Of course, he only lied because he knew there would be a scandal if the affair caught the attention of the media. His perceived wrongdoing stemmed from both the fact that he was married and that Lewinsky was a low-level intern, with far less power than the President of the United States. Elliot Spitzer and Anthony Weiner lost their jobs because of a weakness for prostitutes and sexting, respectively. Retired four-star general and director of the CIA David Petraeus resigned after news of a long-time affair with his biographer became public. Beloved entertainer, civil rights activist, and television surrogate father Bill Cosby had his entire life and career upended after allegations of years of sexual misconduct. Donald Trump's presidential race was marred, but ultimately not derailed, by comments he had made years before the election about how being a celebrity entitled him, in his opinion, to make inappropriate sexual advances toward women.

The problems that are created as a result of sex are more systemic than the bad judgment of a few well-positioned leaders. The US military has repeatedly failed to adequately address issues of sexual harassment and sexual assault in its ranks. The Catholic Church turned a blind eye to years of sexual abuse by priests. Fox News became notorious because of a climate of sexual harassment that existed, manifested by the behavior of Fox News CEO Roger Ailes and talk-show host Bill O'Reilly.

In looking at the details of these kinds of cases, we repeatedly ask ourselves two questions: Why do unarguably intelligent and successful leaders put themselves into these kinds of situations? And why are we, as members of the constituency, continually surprised by these revelations? Shouldn't we expect it by now?

Although the question of why rich and powerful men (we are not being sexist here—it is more often men than women) risk their careers by engaging in illicit sexual activity is an interesting one, we suggest that the connection between leadership and sexuality is much more important, complex, and broad than the phenomenon of a sex scandal. Sexual leadership can be viewed as operating at both macro and micro levels. Issues related to sexual leadership come into play when a nation decides in favor of or against an abstinence-only policy with regard to sexual education, the Supreme Court rules in favor of gay marriage, or a husband and wife decide whether to try a new sexual position. Sexual leadership also comes into play in gray and black markets. What leadership dynamics are involved in recruiting, motivating, and managing women who work as strippers, or as prostitutes? The purpose of this edited volume is to explore the largely ignored relationship between sexuality and leadership.

We approach leadership and sexuality from two perspectives. As social scientists, we would like to better understand the way in which human sexuality affects leadership and followership processes. How do sexual dynamics influence how leaders do their jobs? How do sexual dynamics hinder or help with leadership processes? To what degree should leaders initiate policies that address sexual issues? An additional goal is to take on the role of social engineers and apply our knowledge to problems that leaders face with regard to controlling the expression of human sexuality. Ineffective leadership with regard to sexuality can ruin lives. Would better efforts at social engineering ameliorate these problems, and with it create a reduction in human suffering caused by leaders who poorly handle problems associated with leadership and sexuality?

Our seemingly never-ending surprise that our leaders engage in covert sexual practices or make errors in judgment about issues in a sexual domain can be explained partly by recognizing that it seems almost everyone has trouble talking about sexuality. Even science, or, more accurately, the people who do science, presumably operate through the lens of value-free and objective thinking, yet scholars themselves have issues with sexuality. Social scientists who study sexuality feel their careers are marginalized by more mainstream members of their disciplines (Irvine, 2014). For example, it is more difficult to fund research on sexual science, unless it has a clear medical purpose such as disease prevention.

The focus of this volume is on how power, principles, and processes influence the way that sexuality exerts an influence on leadership and followership. We consider power as the ability to influence an outcome to occur, more specifically with regard to the ability to control resources and others (Stuppy & Mead, 2017). Leadership and sexuality can both be understood in terms of the expression of power (Parker, Barbosa, & Aggleton, 2000). Leaders exert influence over followers. People who can influence others often step into leadership roles. Sexual attractiveness can be a means of exerting social influence over another, that is, acting as a leader. Leader status is a characteristic that many people find sexually attractive. Leaders' ability to control others can come about through legitimate as well as illegitimate means. It is typically well within an employer's authority to fire a worker for coming to work late. *Quid pro quo* sexual relations, on the other hand, are outside the permissible.

A principle can refer to a moral belief about what is right or wrong. Moral judgments decidedly come into play when we evaluate our own and others' sexuality and sexual behavior. Beliefs about sexuality and leadership are often prescriptive in tone, rather than descriptive of what has actually happened or did occur. Principles related to sexuality are often difficult to uphold. Perhaps the clearest instance has to do with the sanctity of marriage. Although marriage is a relationship freely entered into between two consenting adults who *a priori* promise to make a lifelong commitment to each other ("in sickness and in health and until death do us part"), a significant percentage of marriages end in divorce. Despite some complexities involved in making an estimate (Kennedy & Ruggles, 2014), an estimate of 50 percent seems reasonable for the United States (Politifact New Jersey, 2012). One of the key elements of traditional marriages is sexual fidelity. Although statistics vary depending on the source, 30–70 percent of men report at least one instance of marital infidelity; about 20–68 percent of women report at least one instance (Thompson & O'Sullivan, 2016).

The third concept that is important to consider is the processes involved in understanding the relationship between sexuality and leadership. The processes involved in sexuality can range from micro-processes that last just a few seconds or minutes to macro-level evolutionary processes that have taken literally millions of years to play out. The act of judging someone sexually attractive might take only a second, but factors that influence what processes go into that judgment might have evolved across millions of years.

With regard to sexuality and leadership, we consider principles to be expressed through several prominent theories of sexuality. Sexuality can be viewed as a product of biology, as a psychological process, and as a sociological phenomenon. Biological theories can either focus on the actual process of having sex, as in the case of Masters and Johnson (1966), who studied the stages of sexual arousal, or they can focus on how evolutionary pressures have shaped the way sexual behavior is played out (Buss, 2015). Evolutionary psychology or sociobiology tends to look at the ways in which mate selection processes have evolved over time.

Another class of theories is psychological and focuses on the way people develop certain preferences. A classic example is learning theory, which can be used to consider the way in which an attraction to certain types of stimulation is reinforced (Hogben & Byrne, 1998). Social exchange theory views sexual behavior in terms of the way people evaluate the costs and benefits of a relationship (Cook, Cheshire, Rice, & Nakagawa, 2013). Like economics, social exchange theory assumes that actors are (at least mostly) rational actors who try to maximize their potential benefits.

The final approach we consider is sociological and focuses on the way the meaning of sexual activity is socially constructed. A prominent sociological theory of human sexuality is called sexual scripting theory (Simon & Gagnon, 2003). According to sexual scripting, the most important factor involved in sexuality is the meaning that we as human beings apply to sex. The conceptual basis for sexual scripting theory is symbolic interactionism, which focuses on how people use symbols— predominantly language—to create meaning (Longmore, 1998). From a social constructionist point of view, the importance and nature of sexuality is derived from how we, as a collective culture, choose to see it. Sexual scripts operate at cultural, interpersonal, and intrapersonal levels (Simon & Gagnon, 2003). At the cultural level, sexual scripts reflect the influence of social institutions such as religion, the law, and mass media. Interpersonal scripts refer to how two or more people negotiate meaning with regard to sexual behaviors. Intrapersonal scripts refer to how an individual feels about sexual activities, feelings, or beliefs. Different levels of sexual scripts can be consistent or inconsistent with each other. Consider, for example, kissing. Most people find kissing a pleasurable prelude to sexual activity, and as a result it is not too hard to find other people who might be willing to engage in kissing. Society tends to see kissing as a gesture consistent with both romance and sexuality.

In other instances, there can be conflict between different levels of sexual scripts. As a prominent example, in 2003 when Arnold Schwarzenegger was running for governor of California, a scandal broke because of allegations that he had sexually harassed women (Cohn, Hall, & Welkos, 2003). After an initial denial, he eventually apologized for the behavior, which had taken place as early as the 1970s and 1980s. The meaning of his actions changed between the end of the twentieth and the beginning of the twenty-first centuries. Womanizing behavior was once not only condoned but, to some, considered heroic for a man in a leadership role. Norms of acceptable leader behavior have shifted and men have been slow to adjust. Donald Trump is a classic example of a male whose sexual misconduct horrified millions of Americans while drawing apathetic responses from millions of others (including some women) who cling to the anachronism that "boys will be boys" (Freedman, 2013).

THE INVENTION OF SEX

At its most basic level, sex, invented about a billion years ago, is about the exchange of genetic material (Dabhoiwala, 2012). Although the origins of sex can be debated, it can be argued that sex evolved because it created greater variation in offspring, allowed the more rapid spread of beneficial traits, and discouraged the proliferation of harmful traits. In modern society, we have dressed up and romanticized sex so that it appears to involve abstract concepts such as love, beauty, and fidelity but in reality, in its raw form, sex is about influence, coercion, and quite literally survival. Those organisms that managed to have sex and reproduce continued to exist and climb the evolutionary ladder. Those that did not disappeared and now only exist in the fossil record.

Organisms could gain a competitive advantage in two ways (Buss, 1995; Buss & Schmidt, 1993). Most people know about *natural selection*, that is, that traits that allow an individual to better adapt to their environment will be selected for and will over time increase in the population. For humans, being stronger, faster, and more intelligent provided an advantage in terms of living long enough first to reproduce and second to help one's offspring live long enough to become self-sufficient and then also reproduce. Fewer people recognize the role that *sexual selection* plays. Sexual selection involves a potential mate expressing a greater willingness to mate with someone on the basis of a trait that person possesses. Organisms that develop traits which those of the opposite sex find more appealing will end up with a greater number of possible mating opportunities. As a result, they will have more children and those descendants will be more likely to have that attractive trait, thus creating a self-reinforcing cycle.

There is a strong association between leadership and sexual success. In some species of animals, the ability to engage in sexual behavior is restricted to only a leader, the alpha male. Leaders can be viewed as positive deviants, in that they are more successful than average. They have more authority than the average member of the species. The link between leadership and sexual access creates a powerful incentive for males to try to become leaders. The desire for sex and the fear of not being able to acquire sex is a powerful motivation that causes people, especially men, to take risks, and can lead to great accomplishment but can also result in great misfortune (Baumeister, 2010). Sexual attractiveness is both a cause and a consequence of leadership. "Power is the ultimate aphrodisiac," Henry Kissinger once observed. This quote carries two meanings. The first might be that being in power increases a person's interest in sex. The second is that people want to have sex with people who wield power.

The characteristics that make someone a good leader may carry over into their sexual desires, beliefs, or actions they are willing to take. A problem occurs when the same trait has different implications in the sexual world. For example, the traits implied in the phrases "I won't take no for an answer" or "I won't give up" are good attributes for a leader but not for a sex partner. The challenge for many leaders is to differentiate leadership attributes that contribute to effective leadership and those that inflate one's sense of entitlement to sexuality.

THE MISMATCH BETWEEN THE MODERN AND ANCIENT WORLDS

In ancient times, one important aspect of leadership was that it provided access to sexual reproductive opportunities. This may be one of the underlying problems with regard to translating certain principles of leadership to modern society. Mismatches between modern and ancestral environments can occur because we must recognize the concept of an environment of evolutionary adaptation (Vugt & Ronay, 2014). The world that existed when a trait or behavior emerged may not be the same world in which humans live today. Even though the modern world has changed dramatically since ancient times, we as human beings have not evolved as quickly. The assumption of sociobiology is that our hardware, which has evolved over thousands of generations, still exerts an influence on our behavior, even though the influence may no longer be as adaptive.

Culture has helped create mismatches between what is considered appropriate behavior and what preferences might be expressed by evolutionary forces. As noted by MacCannell (2000, p. 249), "Avowed sexualness is, of course, the biggest 'no no' for leader and follower alike" for modern democratic groups. MacCannell argued that the Bill Clinton–Monica Lewinsky affair can be understood as a conflict between Bill Clinton's belief that his sex life should be kept private and the group's belief that their leader should be asexual. The influence of culture can take many forms, ranging from legal or moral proscriptions to the creation of social or technological inventions designed to contain—or liberate—behavior.

Mismatches can occur for a wide range of reasons. In some cases, there can be a conflict between a desire or preference that may be based on an evolutionary imperative and a restraint that has been placed on people on the basis of societal norms or laws. There can also be a conflict that results from the application of one set of norms or rules in contrast to another set. Both Arnold Schwarzenegger and Donald Trump seemed to be using a "rank has its privileges" motto, a rule that was parodied years earlier in the Mel Brooks song *It's Good to be the King*. This outdated view of the perks of leadership nonetheless still holds sway in some quarters today. Over periods of time, different rules gain dominance. Conflicts can emerge when rules appropriate to one era are applied in a different one.

Sexual areas tend to create a moral panic which can lead to the imposition of rules, laws, and regulations that may, on the surface, seem like a good idea, but make less sense once they are put into practice. Abstinence-only education has been deemed a failure (Santelli, Ott, Lyon, Rogers, Summers, & Schleifer, 2006) but was motivated by the belief that any other form of sexual education (such as safer-sex methods of disease or pregnancy prevention) would then increase young adults' tendencies to have sex. Registries for sex offenders, which lead to permanent stigma and have not been shown to produce a reduction in further offending (Agan, 2011), seem contrary to the notion that after a criminal serves his or her time, he or she should enjoy a clean slate to try to be a productive citizen.

Despite many advances consistent with a liberal agenda that stresses openness, tolerance, and acceptance, in some ways the climate with regard to sexuality has become more repressive and fearful. There is a growing acceptance of sexual orientations and identities that deviate from hetero-sexual and biologically based. The legalization of gay marriage and support of the rights of transgender people come to mind. At the same time, in the age of the internet and viral videos, where an offended person's first response is often to become outraged and post an angry screed, leaders feel confused and defensive about attitudes toward sexuality.

Mismatches with regard to leaders in the modern and ancient worlds can interfere with leaders' abilities to function effectively, as well as our expectations about them. We have trouble distinguishing between our leaders' personal lives and the tasks they need to perform to function effectively in their role as leaders. This difficulty seems especially relevant when traits or behaviors associated with leadership translate over to domains of sexuality. In her analysis of the Bill Clinton scandal with regard to Monica Lewinsky, MacCannell (2000) noted that the public's attitudes toward Clinton were influenced by an implicit belief that leaders' sex lives belonged in the realm of unspoken territory.

DEALING WITH MISMATCHES: THE DISTINCTION BETWEEN PRACTICE AND REALITY

In the spring of 2017, we conducted a Google Scholar search for "sexual leadership" which produced only 43 hits. Few of them seemed relevant to our academic goals. Although scholars and policy makers have certainly examined issues related to leadership as well as issues related to sexuality, there has been a notable failure to carry out research under a conceptual umbrella of *sexual leadership*. Leadership scholars and sex-ology researchers have not fully addressed problems leaders face at the intersection of human sexual and leadership concerns, despite numerous instances of leaders acting in unethical and even illegal ways with regard to sexual matters. As public awareness about sexually related abuses of leaders has increased, government laws and regulations have increased the culpability of leaders who fail to respond properly to issues involving sexual malfeasance. For example, the Title IX Clery Act requires universities to investigate instances of sexual harassment and carries the threat of fines up to $35,000 for the failure to do so.

The tremendous variety in the ways people express their sexuality can create conflicts between individuals, groups, and institutions. Although it is tempting to embrace diversity and defend individuals' right to express their sexuality in any way they see fit, certain expressions can be problematic for society and for individuals within society. If we think of ethics as an attempt to create a system of recommendations for how people should live, or a way to distinguish right from wrong, sexual ethics can be viewed as guiding principles for how people should express or restrain their sexual feelings. At one end of the spectrum are sexually related behaviors that most people abhor, such as sexual violence. The other end would include activities that most individuals would see as acceptable, such as sexual activity between consenting married adults. In between those extremes is a large range of behaviors and expressions of sexuality about which people may have strong differences in opinion. These areas could include debates about the appropriate age of consent, the morality of premarital intercourse or infidelity, sexual activity between coworkers, sexual orientation, and the ethics of being consumers or providers of sexual services, such as prostitution.

We suggest that where there is debate, those in disagreement turn to their leaders to establish guiding principles or to enact and enforce rules and laws to govern the expression of sexuality. Leaders have a duty to provide for the well-being of their constituents, with *well-being* broadly defined to include a consideration of the physical, mental, moral, and spiritual health aspects of sexuality. What is the role of leaders with regard to sexuality? How leaders deal with sexually related issues can influence how they and their organizations are seen by both constituents and outsiders. What we require or demand from leaders with regard to sexuality depends on how we view sexuality. Are sexual desires something we should fight against or succumb to? Should we see sexuality as an outgrowth of our base, animal nature? If so, we need our leaders to protect us from ourselves. A leader can be seen as a moral compass who models appropriate behavior for us by fighting temptation or by creating systems and institutions that assist us in fighting those temptations. Paradoxically, it is also possible to see leaders as those individuals who have challenged outdated beliefs about sexuality and, in the process, allowed us to progress as a society. In other words, some leaders may tempt us to reject the *status quo* and broaden our definition of acceptable sexual behavior.

OVERVIEW OF THIS VOLUME: LEADERSHIP AND SEXUALITY

In this book, we distinguish among three categories with regard to sexuality and leadership: (1) sexual leaders; (2) leaders who encounter issues related to sexuality; and (3) the sexuality of leaders. We further suggest that leaders need to address issues of well-being by using three distinct strategies: protection, exemplification, and growth. In the present volume, contributing authors address the strategies these types of leaders use to guide their constituents.

Sexual leaders are those leaders who aid individuals in creating and adhering to guiding principles that directly promote sexual well-being. In some instances, these leaders are geared toward *protection*. For example, policy makers who guide organizations such as Planned Parenthood operate as sexual leaders who are trying to protect their constituents from unwanted pregnancy, sexually transmitted infections, or sexually related assault. In their examination of the history of Planned Parenthood, Sheila Huss and Lucy Dwight discuss how the organization can be viewed as part of a century-long struggle to provide women with an ability to control their own reproductive processes in a way that is free from the threat of criminality or social sanction. The formation of Planned Parenthood began with the pioneering efforts of Margaret Sanger and the organization has seen numerous legal challenges that have included landmark Supreme Court decisions and which continue to this day, with the recent efforts of President Donald Trump to restrict funding to domestic and international agencies that perform abortion or even promote it as an option.

Other sexual leaders can adopt an *exemplification* strategy and attempt to serve as models for appropriate behavior in a sexual domain. Church officials are viewed as exemplars as sexual leaders by acting as a moral compass for their parishioners. In his autobiographical analysis of the challenges associated with bridging the gap between religion and sexuality, William Stayton combines his more than 50 years of personal experience as an educator with a discussion of science-based efforts to develop training methods to help clergy to become more adept at providing sexually related counseling.

Growth leaders operate like transformational leaders in that they attempt to introduce evolutionary changes in our views of sexual behavior. Sex researchers such as Kinsey and Masters and Johnson can be viewed as growth-oriented leaders because their research findings influenced people to think about human sexuality in new ways. Publishers such as Hugh Hefner, Bob Guccione, and Larry Flynt addressed issues of sexuality through their magazines *Playboy*, *Penthouse*, and *Hustler*. In her analysis of Hugh Hefner as someone who might, at first pass, be seen merely as a staunch defender of hedonism, Carrie Pitzulo makes the argument that he was more than a playboy. He was also an icon and leader because of the way he used his magazine to advance a sexually liberal philosophy that included much more than the agenda of hetero-sexual white males. Starting in *Playboy*'s early years, Hugh Hefner—through the medium of his magazine—was also a champion of gay rights and an advocate of women's reproductive rights, in the form of both contraception and abortion. As a counterpoint to Hefner, whose influence has been strongly established over the decades since he founded *Playboy*, James Beggan uses a qualitative method known as autoethnography to examine the case of a high school student whose protest march for the Free the Nipple movement can be understood as the actions of a young transformational leader.

A second area of analysis involves *sexuality and leadership* and addresses the way human sexuality intersects with the responsibilities of leaders. Because leaders operate in virtually all areas of human endeavor, but sexuality is a complex topic, leaders must deal with sexuality issues even when they lack clear understanding or training. There has been a long history of leaders who have made poor decisions with regard to sexual issues. Problems leaders face in this regard include dealing with consensual sexual relationships in the workplace, as well as sexual harassment and sexual violence.

In this component of sexuality and leadership, protection takes two forms. Leaders must work to *protect* employees from unwanted sexual attention. Leaders must also work to protect themselves and the insti-tution they represent from liability associated with unwanted or unsafe sexual practices. Leaders must also act as *exemplars* for how to behave in sexual ways, even if their area of expertise does not directly involve sexual matters. Consider, for example, David Petraeus, the four-star general who had also served as director of the CIA and who was being considered for a presidential nomination. Petraeus was forced to resign because of an affair he was having with his biographer, Paula Broadwell. Another example of how institutional leaders have failed to cope with the influence of sexuality among their representatives is sexual abuse con-ducted by Catholic priests and the subsequent cover-up of such activity. Through their efforts of protection and exemplification, leaders can also act to institute changes to sexual policies.

The Jerry Sandusky–Penn State sexual abuse scandal illustrates how people in leadership positions can misuse their institution-based authority to satisfy their own sexual desires. This scandal illustrates a third way in which leaders must address issues related to sexuality. Leaders must protect innocent third parties from potential mistreatment by members of their organizations. The Penn State scandal demonstrates how people in authority can be complicit in these actions by failing to respond appropriately or sufficiently. Although Joe Paterno, the head coach of the

Penn State football team, followed the necessary protocol after hearing about Jerry Sandusky's behavior, many people argued persuasively that Paterno should have been more proactive in protecting children from Sandusky's abuse. In their analysis of the scandal, Jeremy Fyke, Bree Trisler, and Kristen Lucas describe the scandal as "*the* cautionary tale" (italics in original) regarding the way leadership needs to be appropriately involved with regard to sexuality in the workplace. They frame the scandal in terms of the need for leaders to communicate effectively about sensitive manners and, perhaps even more importantly, to act in a courageous manner with regard to fulfilling their ethical obligations. Leadership failed because the organization failed to protect constituencies as well as to live up to the high standard we might expect from leaders.

In her chapter on teacher–student sexual relations, Charol Shakeshaft also examines reasons why leaders who encounter instances of educator sexual abuse fail to act. She uses data from a variety of sources, such as depositions, training manuals, student records, and health and mental health records, to better understand administrators' failure to act.

Although companies and organizations can establish their own checks and balances to protect workers, as a society we often turn to the government to enact laws to protect citizens. In an examination of the experiences of gay, lesbian, and bisexual employees, Shaun Pichler notes that they are victims of a significant degree of workplace discrimination, and yet there is no comprehensive federal legislation that prohibits discrimination on the basis of sexual orientation. In his chapter, he examines the way that transformational and heroic styles of leadership can contribute to the implementation of polices geared toward establishing greater fairness toward gay, lesbian, and bisexual employees in the workplace. In the absence of legislation, the actions of forward-thinking leaders can contribute toward the development of greater workplace parity.

Sexuality is often seen as problematic for leaders in business and education settings; as a facet of human behavior that can only lead to difficulties such as personnel conflicts or the threat of lawsuits. But it is important to note that leadership processes are also important in businesses where sexuality is front and center. In her chapter on the leadership processes involved in managing a strip club, Maggie Stone examines how leadership styles such as laissez-faire or autocratic are used in different types of strip clubs. She explores the ways in which the central goal of earning money motivates different classes of employees (managers, strippers, bartenders) and leads to the development of different sorts of structural controls. As she illustrates, different categories of strip clubs make use of different leadership styles, with the goal of providing a service to customers but in ways that also ensure the safety of both customers and employees.

The third area of study, the *sexuality of leaders*, refers to the relationship between a leader's own sexuality and his or her role as leader. As previously stated, Henry Kissinger noted that "power is the ultimate aphrodisiac." The power that leaders possess can make them more desirable in the eyes of others. This power can also increase their level of sexual desire. Power and the trappings of power may also undermine a leader's decision-making competency. In a commentary on the luxurious perks associated with being a general in the US military, former Defense Secretary Robert Gates noted, "There is something about a sense of entitlement and of having great power that skews people's judgment" (Chandrasekaran & Jaffe, 2012). In an intriguing analysis of the relationship between leadership and sexuality, Emma Turley examines the power dynamics that exist between participants who engage in sex play involving bondage, discipline, sadism, and masochism (BDSM). She adopts the perspective that such behavior is not pathological and instead reflects a complex relationship between power and control for both the dominant and submissive partners. She challenges the notion that the submissive lacks power and only the dominant partner possesses it. Moreover, the power dynamics that exist between the dominant and submissive players can be seen as reflecting on power and authority processes that exist in the larger world outside of BDSM play. She notes that participants tend to be white, well educated, and middle or upper-middle class. In other words, those who engage in BDSM may in fact be business and community leaders. She also identifies the ways in which BDSM participants take steps to protect themselves from unintended negative consequences.

Leaders can be both victims of processes related to sexuality and also victimizers (knowingly or not). It is possible to view Bill Clinton in several different ways with regard to his leadership and sexuality. First, he can be seen as the victimizer who took advantage of his power as president to unfairly influence Monica Lewinsky into engaging in sexual relations with him. It is also possible to see him as a victim of a concerted Republican effort to impeach him. He can also be seen as a victim of his own foolishness, a man who staked everything on a brief sexual thrill and, in the process, turned his presidency into a punch line. In an analysis of the Bill Clinton–Monica Lewinsky scandal, James Beggan adopts a contrarian position with regard to Bill Clinton's decision-making skills. On the basis of an analysis of the likelihood of getting found out, as well as the possible hedonistic value of the affair, he argues that Bill Clinton's decision should not be automatically viewed as poorly thought out.

THE CHALLENGE OF SEXUALITY FOR LEADERS

Because of taboos associated with sexuality, leaders may be unable or unwilling to deal with issues related to sexual behavior. Advice given to leaders about sexuality often frames it as a negative—something to be defended against, minimized, or even ignored. This strategy can backfire, because the issues do not go away just because people pretend they do not exist. Those same taboos often make it difficult to get clear information about sexual behavior. Sex talk aimed at leadership often has a defensive tone—that is, it might focus on how to avoid sexual harassment or sexual harassment lawsuits. Another problem is that attitudes about sexually related matters can change very rapidly. Attitudes about gay marriage, the rights of transgender people, and the expression of sexuality are changing, and sometimes quickly. How are leaders going to navigate the evolving terrain?

Two forces combine to create a great dilemma for leaders. One force is the acceptance of unrealistic expectations. For example, we have created a culture that valorizes marital fidelity, even though we realize that by objective standards, that goal is difficult to attain. Depending on the source and whether we are talking about men or women, between 20 and 70 percent of individuals have been willing to engage in infidelity. Despite this baseline, research indicates we feel we are better than others at resisting sexual temptation (Garos, Beggan, & Kluck, 2005). We also think we are better sex partners than others (Beggan, Vencill, & Garos, 2013). In other words, we possess unwarranted optimism about our virtue in sexual domains.

The other force that operates is the actor–observer difference (Nisbett, Caputo, Legant, & Marecek, 1973), wherein people tend to explain their own behavior differently than they explain the behavior of others. In certain situations, we have more tolerance for our failures than for the failures of others. We might be inclined to attribute others' extra-marital affairs to their characterological flaws. With ourselves, we would tend to attribute our sexual indiscretions to situational circumstances. We are unfaithful because our spouse does not understand us; they are unfaithful because they are bad people. We are quick to turn on our leaders for sexual indiscretions, even though we might do the same thing given the same circumstances. Our leaders know this, of course, so when they are caught, they are quick to deny it. If and when the truth comes out, we are quick to condemn them for lying, even though our unrealistic expectations have contributed to them lying to us in the first place.

The difficulty that leaders experience negotiating in the sexual domain may be compounded when recommendations to leaders or by leaders represent unrealistic solutions at odds with basic principles about human nature. Policies related to sexuality often have a moralistic tone, which can ultimately be unrealistic and therefore, rather than creating a solution, merely creates more problems. Consider the example of two employees of the same company who have a sexual attraction to each other. The fear of interpersonal conflict, compounded by a fear of potential litigation, leads a company's decision makers to simply devise a policy that forbids workplace romantic relationships. Does a proclamation that employees cannot date colleagues prevent workplace romance? Maybe in some cases that policy will succeed, but a host of basic psychological principles argue against it. What it really does is drive the dating process underground, where people hope and think they can avoid detection. But what happens is that the secrecy is both worrisome and exciting. Paradoxically, the ban can increase the frequency and intensity of the problem (Wegner, 1989).

The difference between what people portray a sexually related situation as and the other practices or processes which may be going on beneath the surface is explored in the chapter on sexuality in relationship to social dancing. James Beggan and Scott Allison examine the phenomenon of social dancing with regard to the way in which a dichotomous definition of sex (as male or female) plays into the assignment of roles (as lead or follow) in social dancing. They also explore the way in which dancers may downplay the role that sexual desire or sexual attraction plays in motivating the desire to social dance.

Throughout the animal kingdom, sexual behaviors are conducted in the service of reproductive goals that will enhance the survival of the species. For modern humans, particularly those dwelling in developed nations, the urgency of the reproductive goal has been minimized. Our entertainment industry provides a vicarious experience of reproductive urgency in the television series *The Walking Dead*. Scott Allison and Olivia Efthimiou focus on the heroic self-sacrifice of bringing children into the post-apocalyptic world of lawlessness, hunger, and brutality. The decision to reproduce illustrates heroism and heroic leadership at two different levels of analysis. First, the choice to have children in the post-apocalyptic world reflects heroic self-sacrifice on the part of the individual decision maker (Allison & Goethals, 2011). A woman who chooses to have a child in a world with no formal healthcare system risks her own physical wellbeing. Second, the choice to repopulate the broken world of *The*

Walking Dead also reflects a system-wide societal drive toward regeneration and restoration. The decision to reproduce thus reflects the heroic embodiment of human society as an organism intent on surviving and even flourishing.

Leaders have to "do sexuality," but sexuality is also "done to them." This occurs at both a personal and an institutional level. As leaders operating with a fiduciary responsibility to their constituents, they have to take a proactive rather than a reactive stance and put institutional mechanisms into place to deal with sexual issues. As individuals who happen to be leaders, they may possess and act on and respond to others' actions as sexual beings. Problems occur when the distinction between these two levels becomes blurred. We hope the chapters in this book will provide guidance and also light the way for further scholarly work on the relationship between sexuality and leadership.

REFERENCES

Agan, A. Y. (2011). Sex offender registries: Fear without function? *The Journal of Law and Economics, 54*(1), 207–39.

Allison, S. T., & Goethals, G. R. (2011). *Heroes: What they do & why we need them.* New York: Oxford University Press.

Baumeister, R. F. (2010). *Is there anything good about men? How cultures flourish by exploiting men.* New York: Oxford University Press.

Beggan, J. K., Vencill, J. A., & Garos, S. (2013). The good-in-bed effect: College students' tendency to see themselves as better than others as a sex partner. *The Journal of Psychology, 147*(5), 415–34.

Buss, D. M. (1995). Evolutionary psychology: A new paradigm for psychological science. *Psychological Inquiry, 6*(1), 1–30.

Buss, D. M. (2015). *Evolutionary psychology: The new science of the mind* (5th ed.). New York: Routledge.

Buss, D. M., & Schmitt, D. P. (1993). Sexual strategies theory: An evolutionary perspective on human mating. *Psychological Review, 100*(2), 204–32.

Chandrasekaran, R., & Jaffe, G. (2012, November 17). Petraeus scandal puts four-star general lifestyle under scrutiny. *The Washington Post.* Retrieved September 18, 2017 from https://www.washingtonpost.com/world/national-security/petraeus-scandal-puts-four-star-general-lifestyle-under-scrutiny/2012/11/17/33a14f48-3043-11e2-a30e-5ca76eeec857_story.html?utm_term=.486fb3c103a9

Cohn, G., Hall, C., & Welkos, R. W. (2003). Women say Schwarzenegger groped, humiliated them. *Los Angeles Times.* Retrieved May 20, 2017 from http://articles.latimes.com/2003/oct/02/local/me-women2.

Cook, K. S., Cheshire, C., Rice, E. R., & Nakagawa, S. (2013). Social exchange theory. In J. DeLamater & A. Ward (Eds.), *Handbook of social psychology* (2nd ed.) (pp. 61–88). New York: Springer.

Dabhoiwala, F. (2012). *The origin of sex: A history of the first sexual revolution*. New York: Penguin Books.

Dixson, A. (2015). Primate sexuality. In P. Whelehan & A. Bolin (Eds.), *The international encyclopedia of human sexuality* (pp. 343–50). New York: Wiley.

Freedman, E. B. (2013). *Redefining rape: Sexual violence in the era of suffrage and segregation*. Cambridge, MA: Harvard University Press.

Gamson, J. (2001). Normal sins: Sex scandal narratives as institutional morality tales. *Social Problems*, *48*(2), 185–205.

Garos, S., Beggan, J. K., & Kluck, A. (2005). Temptation bias: Seeing oneself as better able than others to resist temptation. *Research in the Scientific Study of Religion*, *15*, 235–61.

Hogben, M., & Byrne, D. (1998). Using social learning theory to explain individual differences in human sexuality. *Journal of Sex Research*, *35*(1), 58–71.

Irvine, J. M. (2014). Is sexuality research "dirty work"? Institutionalized stigma in the production of sexual knowledge. *Sexualities*, *17*(5–6), 632–56.

Kennedy, S., & Ruggles, S. (2014). Breaking up is hard to count: The rise of divorce in the United States, 1980–2010. *Demography*, *51*(2), 587–98.

Longmore, M. A. (1998). Symbolic interactionism and the study of sexuality. *Journal of Sex Research*, *35*(1), 44–57.

Masters, W. H., & Johnson, V. E. (1966). *Human sexual response*. Boston, MA: Little, Brown.

MacCannell, J. F. (2000). Politics in the age of sex: Clinton, leadership, love. *Cultural Critique*, *46*(Fall), 241–71.

Nisbett, R. E., Caputo, C., Legant, P., & Marecek, J. (1973). Behavior as seen by the actor and as seen by the observer. *Journal of Personality and Social Psychology*, *27*(2), 154.

Parker, R., Barbosa, R. M., & Aggleton, P. (2000). *Framing the sexual subject: The politics of gender, sexuality, and power*. Berkeley, CA: University of California Press.

PolitiFact New Jersey. (2012, February 20). Steve Sweeney claims two-thirds of marriages end in divorce. *Truth-O-Meter*. Retrieved May 19, 2017 from http://www.politifact.com/new-jersey/statements/2012/feb/20/stephen-sweeney/steve-sweeney-claims-more-two-thirds-marriages-end/

Santelli, J., Ott, M. A., Lyon, M., Rogers, J., Summers, D., & Schleifer, R. (2006). Abstinence and abstinence-only education: A review of US policies and programs. *Journal of Adolescent Health*, *38*(1), 72–81.

Simon, W., & Gagnon, J. H. (2003). Sexual scripts: Origins, influences and changes. *Qualitative Sociology*, *26*(4), 491–97.

Stuppy, A., & Mead, N. L. (2017). Heroic leaders and despotic tyrants: How power and status shape leadership. In S. T. Allison, G. R. Goethals, & R. M. Kramer (Eds.) *Handbook of heroism and heroic leadership* (pp. 476–94). New York: Routledge.

Thompson, A. E., & O'Sullivan, L. F. (2016). Drawing the line: The development of a comprehensive assessment of infidelity judgments. *Journal of Sex Research*, *53*(8), 910–26.

Vugt, M. V., & Ronay, R. (2014). The evolutionary psychology of leadership: Theory, review, and roadmap. *Organizational Psychology Review*, *4*(1), 74–95.

Wegner, D. M. (1989). *White bears and other unwanted thoughts: Suppression, obsession, and the psychology of mental control.* London: Guilford Press.

PART I

Sexual leaders

1. Playboy, icon, leader: Hugh Hefner and postwar American sexual culture

Carrie Pitzulo

In 1965, a Midwestern pastor's wife identified only as "S.J.M." wrote to *Playboy* magazine founder, Hugh Hefner, to praise his magazine (Letter from S.J.M., 1965).* She spoke of her and her husband's belief in sexual education and experimentation. The woman told Hefner that *Playboy* was serving an important function in expanding the American sexual imagination. She implored Hefner,

> I ... sincerely urge you to continue to press forward in your intelligent campaign to break down the ignorance and stupidity of the official attitude toward sex. It will require ... tremendous courage on your part. But ... it can be done. By 1975, an entire generation will have matured under your influence.

To modern eyes, it may seem strange that anyone would have such high expectations for a magazine like *Playboy*. But in the 1960s, Hefner had carved out for his publication a significant place within American sexual culture. After its founding in December, 1953, *Playboy* quickly became more than a monthly girlie magazine. Of course, its centerfold Playmates established for the nation—and much of the world—narrow, often unattainable standards of youthful beauty. But in its pages could also be found the brightest lights of the literary scene, cutting-edge political reporting, and leading fashion and design commentary. Moreover, Hefner's creation rapidly expanded into an international cultural empire, including iconic nightclubs, resorts, publishing, television shows, and myriad bunny logo-embossed paraphernalia. Not merely a publisher, not merely a celebrity playboy, Hugh Hefner was a leader in the formation of a new sexual culture in the post-World War II years.

Hefner modernized midcentury sexual culture in several ways. He articulated flexible, more closely aligned versions of masculinity and femininity; argued for greater tolerance of and protections for homosexuals; and was vociferous in his support for women's rights, especially abortion. All of these positions put him at the forefront of a changing heterosexual culture.

At the center of his empire, Hefner fashioned a lifestyle magazine that was about more than sex. *Playboy* promoted upward economic mobility for men through regular features on dress, gourmet food, jazz, home design, travel, and more. It made a name for itself with important interviews with both domestic and foreign political leaders and cultural creators, such as Martin Luther King, Jr., Fidel Castro, and Joan Baez. *Playboy* wore the mantel of liberal politics, espousing support for the Civil Rights Movement, standing against the Vietnam War, and embracing liberalization of drug laws, among other things.

By the mid-1960s, Hefner's empire had become an institution. For instance, in 1962, a final exam in a Harvard business course focused on the entrepreneurial practices of Hefner, while the *Playboy* Philosophy—a rambling editorial series focused on Hefner's world views—found its way into Sunday morning sermons (Davidson, 1962). One church's weekly service program asked, "What is the contemporary moral incarnation of The *Playboy* Philosophy—and of the Christian gospel?" ("Chimes," 1965). The mainstream media acknowledged the breadth of Hefner's influence. William F. Buckley, Jr., noted that *Playboy* and its hedonistic credo was a "movement" that included "professors and ministers and sociologists." Writing for the *Los Angeles Times* in 1972, Digby Diehl called *Playboy* a "major instrument of social and moral change in the mid-20th century" (p. W20).

Scholars have overlooked much of this postwar legacy. Traditionally, academics have portrayed Hefner as sexist, conservative, or even reactionary. Reflecting conventional feminist critiques, Hefner is seen as the embodiment of patriarchy, an antifeminist crusader whose magazine objectified women and upheld the culture that was challenged by the progressives of the 1960s. Barbara Ehrenreich (1983) helped establish this narrative. Ehrenreich situated *Playboy* within a perceived postwar crisis of masculinity. She argued that *Playboy* helped to liberate masculinity for a new, hedonistic lifestyle. Ehrenreich pointed to *Playboy*'s open hostility toward the traditional pressures that obliged men to marry and become fathers, arguing that *Playboy* "hated wives." According to her, the magazine "presented … a coherent program for the male rebellion" against domestic obligation (pp. 42, 50). This view was reinforced by historian Beth Bailey (1988) when she wrote that Hefner was the "guru of [gender] separateness" and that his magazine promoted male dominance. Joanne Meyerowitz (1996) suggested a more nuanced view of the magazine. Meyerowitz analyzed women's letters to the editor in publications such as *Playboy* and argued that the letters pointed to a complex view of gender and sexuality held by postwar women.

The magazine was viewed as a cultural arbiter that freed men from the constraints of traditional manhood by acting as a "celebration of a masculine universe of consumption and narcissistic display ... while hedonistic fun and sensual indulgence were defining virtues" (Osgerby, 2001, p. 122). Osgerby's work repeated the assertion that the *Playboy* world was one of sexism and masculine self-interest.

In considering the scope of *Playboy*'s influence, scholars have explored popular editorial columns to examine the ways the magazine both challenged and reinforced traditional gender expectations. For instance, the regular culinary features co-opted food preparation from women and transformed it into a sexy bachelor activity for a new middle-class culture of leisure and consumption (Hollows, 2002). Similarly, Beatriz Preciado (2004) explored *Playboy*'s conceptualization of the bachelor pad. She wrote that in "recolonizing" the traditional, private sphere of women, *Playboy*'s design articles created an "antidomestic" interior space for men that was ultimately an attack on the privatization of the suburbs, and, by extension, American women.

Historian James Gilbert (2005) examined the dominant paradigm that saw the postwar period as a time of identity crisis for American men. He argued that the "manhood" of the era cannot be easily categorized as either traditional and declining, or rebellious and threatening. He demonstrated that there were various models of manhood with which one could identify, including that of *Playboy*'s own editorial director, A. C. Spectorsky. He argued that Spectorsky used *Playboy* to exploit anxious manhood and to rail against what he saw as the growing feminization of American culture.

Of course, the centerfold Playmates have warranted much attention. Exploring the ways in which feminists have created, consumed, and exploited pin-up imagery, Maria Elena Buszek (2006) focused on what she saw as "casual misogyny" in the magazine. Within the existing academic literature on *Playboy*, views like Buszek's are common, and often echo the antipornography writings of activists like Catharine MacKinnon (1988), Andrea Dworkin (1981), and others.

In spite of this overwhelming criticism, there is a growing body of literature that refutes these views of *Playboy*. Sociologists have done revisionist work on *Playboy*'s relationship to gender and sexuality and have come to drastically different conclusions than its critics. Joseph E. Scott and Steven J. Cuvelier (1987) published an essay that challenged the claims of antiporn writers such as MacKinnon, who have accused publications like *Playboy* of promoting violence against women. Scott and Cuvelier conducted a study regarding images of violence in *Playboy* and found them almost totally lacking. Anthony F. Bogaert, D. A. Turkovich, and C. L. Hafer (1993) examined Playmate centerfolds from 1953 through 1990 for evidence of sexual objectification, and again found such occurrences to be very low.

Sociologists James K. Beggan, Patricia Gagné, and Scott T. Allison (2000) published a statistical analysis of *Playboy*'s advice column, the "Advisor." They found that the Advisor consistently promoted compassion, tolerance, and equality among men and women, and challenged stereotypes and the double standard. Beggan and Allison (2001, 2005) then examined the text accompanying Playmate centerfolds, which often included descriptions of the types of men the models desired. Beggan and Allison argued that in these descriptions the Playmates, and by extension *Playboy*, celebrated masculinity that included traditionally feminine characteristics, thus expanding definitions of manhood. They demonstrated that *Playboy*'s editorial approach promoted the cultivation of a gentlemanly demeanor that held women's opinion and acceptance in high esteem.

Increasingly, other scholars have acknowledged a more complex view of Hefner and his magazine. Looking at the magazine's treatment of consumerism, work and leisure, and money, Elizabeth Fraterrigo (2009) argues that *Playboy* was central to creating a new vision of the "good life" for American men in the postwar years, and suggests that the magazine took a progressive stance on questions of gender and sexuality. The definitive biography of Hefner, written by Steven Watts (2008), argued that the publisher and icon was not only one of the most significant cultural figures of the twentieth century, but also "a serious shaper of ... modern American values ... [his magazine] a historical force of significant proportions" (p. 3).

Although scholarly consideration of Hugh Hefner has grown more sophisticated, even *Playboy*'s defenders have not acknowledged the extent to which Hefner claimed an audacious mantle of progressive sexual leadership in the prerevolutionary years of the 1950s and early 1960s. It is well established that *Playboy* helped to create a new brand of postwar masculinity centered on hedonistic consumerism. The iconic centerfold nudes of the magazine have received much attention, but have left most observers with the assumption that *Playboy* promoted unfettered male heterosexual privilege. What most scholars have overlooked are the various ways in which Hefner blazed a trail for sexual and gender respect, tolerance, and progressive politics.

Though *Playboy*'s sprawling postwar cultural authority was understood by contemporaries, as in the Sunday sermons and the Harvard course, it may be surprising in the early twenty-first century. There are ways in which even *Playboy*'s assumed forte—representation and discussion of sex itself—was more influential, and more progressive, than many modern commentators acknowledge. Hefner's magazine pushed at the boundaries of acceptable sexual expression amid the socially conservative 1950s, anticipating and helping along the sexual revolution of the coming decade.

At no point could anyone have challenged *Playboy*'s status as "entertainment for men," although its target audience was more narrowly defined as *heterosexual* men. Indeed, Hefner (1963, p. 128) admitted "a strong personal prejudice in favor of the boy-girl variety of sex." He vociferously challenged the postwar status quo by trumpeting casual, straight sex, but he was not just interested in teasing men with titillating photos of women. Hefner was on a crusade against the dark, repressive forces he found responsible for American sexual inhibition, particularly organized religion. That battle actually predated *Playboy*. As a college student and campus journalist, Hefner wrote about the tradition of American sexual repression as he saw it; and in the first issue of *Playboy*, he referenced the important influence of Alfred Kinsey. The culmination of this drive was a highly politicized, progressive magazine that addressed a variety of social and political questions about sexual equality and justice. A team of liberal, even radical, editors contributed to this slant. But nothing appeared in the magazine's pages without Hefner's sanction. From the Playmates, to the fashion, to the politics, *Playboy* was a vision of the world according to Hefner.

Despite his focus on straight masculinity, Hefner staked a claim for sexual openness when he quietly opened a conversation about tolerance in the mid-1950s. At that time, gay men and lesbians were targeted with social, professional, and political persecution. Homosexuality was considered a mental illness (American Psychiatric Association, 1952), discrimination in hiring and housing was legal, and law enforcement professionals often raided gay hangouts. But in 1955, less than two years after bursting onto the publishing scene, Hefner resisted the tide of straight society and offered a public defense of homosexuality. In August, *Playboy* ran a science fiction story by Charles Beaumont called "The Crooked Man." It told the futuristic tale of a world in which heterosexuality was considered abnormal and deviant, and homosexuality was the standard. Heterosexuals were persecuted and subject to surgery to correct their "problem." Apparently *Esquire* originally bought the piece but decided against running it. *Playboy* then "snatched it up," Hefner told Ray Bradbury (Hefner letter, 1955), because "a good story is a good story."

One reader responded to the piece by saying, "Such an absurd hypothetical topsy-turvydom must surely leave one ... to quite incredulous chuckle ... to see such a gifted writer twisted into full-scale warfare with a paper-tiger enemy." The editors replied to this letter: "We saw it as a kind of plea for tolerance—shoe-on-the-other-foot sort of thing. At any rate, it's a story that prompts thought and discussion, and that's why it is important" (Letters to the Editor, 1955). Mainstream American society would slowly begin to re-evaluate its entrenched homophobia by the 1970s. But in the 1950s, that painful process would have seemed a long way off. The country was suffering the political and psychological traumas of McCarthyism, when homosexuals were considered easy prey for communists and purged from government jobs (Cuordileone, 2005). Urban gay and lesbian communities emerged after World War II, but the dominant culture viewed homosexuality with suspicion and often outright hostility. Yet in 1955, a whisper of sympathy found its way into the pages of *Playboy* magazine. Dignity for gay men and lesbians was crucial to Hefner's vision of sexual liberation, because in his view, a society that liberalized enough to accept homosexuals would surely grant full freedom to straight men and women.

Playboy's treatment of homosexuality grew more prominent, along with its political voice, in the 1960s. The magazine became an important and compassionate forum for the discussion of gay and lesbian issues years before the Stonewall riots of 1969. The official position on the issue supported free expression and legal protection; by the start of the gay liberation movement at the end of the decade, *Playboy* was claiming it "consistently defended the civil rights and civil liberties of homosexuals" (Editorial response, 1969). Indeed, editors reported on legal and political developments relevant to gays and lesbians in the "Forum," a popular readers' letter column devoted to contemporary social and political issues which grew out of the response to Hefner's sprawling editorial series known as "The *Playboy* Philosophy," which ran from December 1962 to May 1965.

By the mid-1960s, discussions of homosexuality had increased in *Playboy*, paralleling an expanding cultural discussion. For example, in response to a question (1964) posed to *Playboy*'s advice column, known as the "Advisor," M.M. from California was reassured that he need not fret over his girlfriend's lesbian sexual experimentation in college. Later that year, the Advisor gave support ("Response to R.W.") to a woman who worried about her family's objection to her friendship with a gay man. In April 1964, Hefner expressed support for homosexuality in "The *Playboy* Philosophy": "our belief in a free, rational and humane society demands a tolerance of those whose sexual inclinations are different from our own—so long as their activity is limited to consenting adults in private and does not involve either minors or ... coercion" (p. 128). Hefner argued that pervasive homophobia existed in the United States because "The American male's concern over his masculinity amounts to an obsession" (p. 128). Even as a postwar arbiter of straight masculinity, Hefner was unafraid to question the status of manhood in postwar America, a stance he had embraced since the earliest days of the magazine.

Hefner's consideration of homosexuality was complex, though. In addition to the support offered in his magazine, Hefner believed that there was the possibility that a gay man could "find his way back to a predominantly heterosexual life" if society's repressions did not force him "into a nether world inhabited almost exclusively by homosexuals" (p. 128). Hefner challenged discrimination against, and persecution of, homosexuals, but—like many midcentury Americans—he believed that gay men could be, and possibly should be, rehabilitated into active heterosexuality. Given homosexuality's status as a mental illness at midcentury, clinical treatment was commonly offered as a cure.

The question of whether behavioral therapy should be used to turn gay men straight ignited a controversy in the Forum. In March 1969, Franklin E. Kameny, Ph.D., founder and president of the Mattachine Society and chair of the Eastern Regional Homophile Conference, wrote to the Forum to defend homosexuality as "a preferred orientation or propensity, not different in kind from heterosexuality." He went on to say, "Homosexuality is not intrinsically inferior to heterosexuality; it is not a second-best condition." *Playboy* offered a lengthy response:

> We share your distaste for emotionally charged words such as "sickness" to describe what is more aptly called a "deviance" (the neutral term used ... to denote a departure from behavioral norms) ... [T]he exclusive homosexual is not following a preference at all but, rather, a compulsion based on phobic reactions to heterosexual stimuli ... [H]omosexuality, when compulsive and phobic, is in itself a problem that exists *in addition* to the problems caused by society's attitude. For this reason, homosexuals should not be discouraged from seeking therapy when they want it ... In spite of our disagreement on these issues, we share your belief that the situation of the homosexual in America today would be vastly improved were it not for an intolerant and hostile society that subjects him to enormous stresses. To do away with that kind of social intolerance has been a constant and fundamental purpose of "The *Playboy* Forum." (Editorial response to Kameny, 1969)

In a later comment, *Playboy*'s editors insisted that they took issue only with "the exclusive homosexual," that is, an individual who was capable of sexual response only with members of their own sex, rather than at least occasional arousal with someone of the opposite sex. On the question of the "exclusive heterosexual," *Playboy* acknowledged, somewhat subversively, "heterosexuals often respond positively, occasionally even erotically, to the attractiveness of members of their own sex." In the case of a man who was worried about a homosexual experience he had had as a teenager, the Advisor responded, "Your experience is trivial and important only to the extent of your own concern about it. Psychiatrists point out that such experiences are commonplace and harmless" (Editorial response to L.G., 1970). Similarly, a confused college student wrote that he had never had sex with a girl he "really liked," but had "come close to falling in love with a few of [his] male friends," and had one homosexual experience. The Advisor thought that he was too young to commit himself to either heterosexuality or homosexuality: "At your age, it's not unusual to be fond of your male friends ... you're a young man who responds to a variety of stimuli" (Letter and response to J.P., 1971).

This view of sexuality as a continuum, with most people at some point responding to either sex, was in keeping with the conclusions that Alfred Kinsey had promoted a generation earlier in his groundbreaking studies of sexuality. *Playboy* argued that a range of sexual feelings for and experiences with both sexes—"nonexclusive" sexuality—was healthy and natural. Sexuality, Hefner told his readers, was a fluid, personal construction. Though the magazine celebrated the virtues of heterosexual desire each month, Hefner and his editors did not react to the possibility of gay "stimuli" with macho insecurity, fear, or hysteria. Rather, they told their male readers that it was alright to desire other men, at least occasionally, as long as they left themselves open to women at some point as well. *Playboy*'s approach to the issue was sympathetic, not celebratory. But many gays and lesbians found public sympathy hard to come by in the 1960s, so in spite of the magazine's conditional support, many gay men saw an ally in Hefner.

In 1964, Charles Philips, president of the Janus Society, a Philadelphia gay rights organization, called Hefner's early editorials on homosexuality "the most profound and realistic appraisal of sexuality found in the American press to date ... *Playboy* and Hefner stand almost alone in advancing a sane concept of sexuality" (p. 64). An anonymous reader wrote, "As a homosexual, I have learned not to expect a great deal of tolerance from members of the heterosexual world ... I was very surprised ... to read your statements ... Your attitude is intelligent and open-minded and I only wish it was more common" (Anonymous, 1964). Another said, "As a practicing homosexual myself, I know all too well that many otherwise liberal persons will not speak out for *our* civil liberties, out of sheer fear that somebody might think that *they* are 'faggots' themselves. Your courage is truly admirable" (Anonymous, 1967).

Playboy was known then, as it is now, as a paean to male hetero-sexuality. Nonetheless, some homosexuals found Hefner's philosophy progressive and supportive, and therefore considered his magazine an appropriate place to discuss their roles as men and their position in society.

In particular, police harassment of gay men was a common topic in the Forum. By the late 1960s, numerous letters had been printed by men who claimed to have been arrested or physically attacked by members of vice squads. In the December 1967 issue alone, almost one third of the letters published were about homosexuality,[1] five of which discussed police and governmental harassment and entrapment of gay men. James Wittenberg of San Jose stated in 1967, "although I do not rob or kill or defraud, I am a criminal, because I am a homosexual." Another man who witnessed a police assault in a gay bar asked: "Who or what am I harming merely by my existence?" (Anonymous, 1967). Alternately, a straight man won-dered, "If the laws and mores in America are changed to accept homosexual behavior, who is going to protect me, the average American male, from homosexuals and perverts?" *Playboy* responded, "Legal-ization of homosexual acts in private ... and public acceptance of such behavior does not automatically mean that sexual assault ... will also be accepted ... But we believe you exaggerate the threat to the average American male" (Letter and response, 1968). Though *Playboy* was unapologetically heterosexual, some gay men and lesbians found comfort in Hefner's campaign for sexual freedom.

Hefner's position on homosexuality was entirely logical, given his overall vision of sexual freedom; likewise his philosophy on women's reproductive rights. Despite the traditional feminist critique of Hefner—which decried his magazine as sexist, objectifying, and patriarchal—*Playboy* took a progressive stance on women's rights and was particularly vocal in support of abortion. Evidence of this can be found in the magazine's articles and editorials and the charitable donations of the Playboy Foundation, the philanthropic arm of the magazine, which con-tributed thousands of dollars to abortion rights organizations before *Roe v. Wade* legalized abortion in 1973. In addition, the Foundation provided the American Civil Liberties Union with funds for their work on women's rights, and helped fund daycare centers for working mothers. The Foun-dation was created to enact the social and political philosophy that Hefner had laid out in "The Playboy Philosophy." Like the conversations about homosexuality, the letters and editorial responses included in the *Forum* became an important public dialogue about abortion rights.

Like the larger women's movement, the abortion rights movement had reached a peak by the early 1970s, but had been active in a limited capacity since the early 1960s. In the mid-1960s, abortion was being discussed in the popular American press, though the movement for abortion rights was still in its infant stages. Lawrence Lader, who, with Pat Maginnis, helped to found the National Abortion Rights Action League (NARAL) in 1969, was active in the nascent abortion rights movement in the mid-1960s. He said of national support, "There was almost nobody in the beginning, so it was lonely ... I couldn't even tell whether the incipient Women's Movement was interested in abortion" (Messer and May, 1994, p. 199).

Lader and Maginnis found an ally in *Playboy*. The magazine published its first statement in support of the legalization of abortion in its December 1965 *Forum*, as readers increasingly contributed their thoughts on the issue. Some, such as Janelle Lindsey, opposed legalization. She decried the "pain and confusion" of abortion, and demanded that men take responsibility for contraception before pregnancy: "I ... distrust any man running around trying to get abortion legalized—that's *me* he's tossing around like a political football ... For the female readers of *Playboy* who aren't taking birth-control pills ... your subscriptions should be cancelled immediately!" *Forum* editors responded:

> We can't contradict your contention that the best birth-control method is a contraceptive used at the proper time ... We do feel, however, that the question of abortion is one of alternatives rather than absolutes ... [T]he legalization of abortion would simply increase the alternatives available to [a pregnant woman] ... We're not a woman ... if we were, we would welcome the additional freedom of choice that legalized abortion would provide. (Letter and response, 1965)

In spite of *Playboy*'s status as a men's magazine, many women wrote in to explain why they had sought abortions. In 1966, one anonymous woman wrote:

> in desperation, I decided even possible death could not be worse, so went through with [the abortion]. The experience turned out to be even worse that I had anticipated ... How different this might have been if laws had permitted me to go to a hospital where my own doctor could have attended me. (p. 66)

Another woman described her "horrid" experience in a home for unwed mothers and concluded, "Men make the laws and women suffer the consequences. I'm for letting the girl make her own choice—without legal interference" (Anonymous, 1967).

In May 1967, *Playboy* expanded its coverage of the movement to include practical information for readers. In the *Forum*, editors listed the states considering abortion reform, as well as the names of the respective congressional representatives. *Playboy* called on readers to write to their congressmen and demand abortion reform. Readers responded with a flood of letters. Fully one half of the 24 *Forum* letters published in August 1967 were about abortion; the majority were in favor of reform (pp. 35–7). To one letter from a woman who described her guilt and shame over an abortion she had as a teenager, *Playboy* replied, "It is our hope that a general increase of openness and honesty about sex, more adequate sex education for teenagers ... and a liberalization of abortion laws will spare other girls from experiences such as yours" (p. 37). With letters submitted by activists and average women, as well as progressive legislators and abortion providers, as well as *Playboy*'s own commentary, men and women alike received not only political consciousness-raising in the *Playboy Forum*, but an education as well.

With growing public debate, as evidenced in *Playboy* and throughout the culture, the abortion rights movement became truly national in scope in the late 1960s and particularly by 1970. By then various states, including Colorado and New York, had begun to expand access to abortion (DuBois & Dumenil, 2016, p. 647). By that time, the Playboy Foundation had been working for increased access to contraceptives and abortion for several years. One of the Playboy Foundation's important causes was the legal defense of abortion rights advocate Bill Baird, director of the Hempstead, New York Parents' Aid Society. With "Hef's enthusiastic approval," the Playboy Foundation gave Baird legal assistance when he was prosecuted for distributing birth control and abortion information (Lehrman to Rosenzweig, 1969).

Playboy began reporting on Baird's crusade when Baird himself wrote a long letter to the Forum describing the legal trouble he had run into for distributing contraceptives in New York, New Jersey, Massachusetts, and later Wisconsin. Editors responded with an update on state contraceptive laws, and pledged their moral and financial support (Baird, 1968). Baird and others, such as representatives of Planned Parenthood; the Abortion Counseling, Information and Referral Services of New York; and various other activist organizations, used the *Forum* as a clearinghouse to publicize abortion services, provide practical information on procedures and to tell readers how to contact them (*Forum*, June 1971). The *Forum* became such a prominent proponent of legalization that at least one

organization, the California Committee to Legalize Abortion, claimed it
was "formed in response to an appeal published in [the] *Forum*" (Wright,
1967).

As the debate over abortion reached a cultural peak, the issue claimed
a significant number of pages in *Playboy*. In September 1970, the
magazine ran a piece by Dr. Robert Hall entitled "The Abortion Revolution," described as "a doctor's chronicle of the bitter and continuing
battle to abolish our obsolete laws against terminating pregnancy"
(p. 112). Hall was an outspoken advocate for legalization; calling
abortion laws "absurd," he echoed the typical stance of the "Playboy
Philosophy" when he wrote that the contemporary debate surrounding the
rights of the fetus had no place in a country founded on the principle of
separation of church and state (p. 112).

Reader responses to Hall's article included a letter from Mary S.
Calderone, a leading activist for sex education in the United States, who
thanked *Playboy* for publishing the piece. Similar praise came from
Representative Leland H. Rayson of Illinois, who sponsored state abortion reform bills, and noted psychotherapist Albert Ellis. Like the Hall
article, *Forum* letters reflected the questions surrounding the larger
cultural debate. A woman from Indianapolis described her experience of
obtaining an abortion in 1969: "I did not kill an infant ... What the
abortionist took from my body was an organism ... Far from feeling like
a murderess, I believe I saved two lives—my own and that of the man
who made me pregnant" (Letter, p. 86). Another woman said she was
abandoned by the father of her child, and was unable to travel to get an
abortion in time. She wrote: "It breaks my heart to think what must
happen to women without financial resources when they get into this
predicament" (Letter, 1971, p. 53).

In September 1971, *Playboy* included "A Special 'Playboy Forum'
Report," aimed at aiding women in obtaining abortions. In the report,
the magazine surveyed the changing state abortion laws but ultimately
concluded that recent progress had stalled: "The holy war to protect the
'right to life' of the fetus gets into high gear—and American women are
the victims" (Backlash, 1971). The piece provided contact information
for pro-choice organizations such as NARAL and offered guidance on
how to obtain an abortion, which again included practical information
such as phone numbers for abortion consultation services in various
states and overseas; for states without such hotlines, *Playboy* listed
national organizations such as Planned Parenthood (p. 77).[2] Further,
updates on legal battles surrounding abortion and other contemporary
issues were featured monthly in a portion of the *Forum* called
"Newsfront."

Organizations that appeared in the *Forum* enjoyed increased visibility, and were often able to expand their reach. For instance, Ruth Proskauer Smith (1971), president of the Abortion Rights Association of New York, noted that after her organization was mentioned in a previous issue, it received "several hundred requests from *Playboy* readers" for informational pamphlets on abortion rights. Smith's organization was later able to revise and reprint a pamphlet on abortion providers because the "response from [*Playboy*] readers was so great" (Smith, 1972). Likewise, Roberta Schneiderman (1972) of Zero Population Growth Abortion Referral Service thanked *Playboy* for publishing phone numbers for the service, saying: "we received over 700 calls from persons who said they found us through *Playboy* ... Please keep up the good work. Elective abortion couldn't have a better friend and we are enormously grateful." Attorney Harriet F. Pilpel (1969), board member of Planned Parenthood-World Population and of the American Civil Liberties Union, called reproductive freedom "a necessary and fundamental freedom in a democratic society," and praised the *Forum* "for its significant role in reporting developments and opinions in science, law, morality and sociology as they relate to sex, reproduction, civil liberties and human rights." In 1972, Bill Baird continued his struggle for expanded access to birth control and abortion, and continued to be prosecuted in various states. He appealed to *Playboy*'s readers once again that year, and thanked the foundation for its support. After the Supreme Court ruled in favor of a woman's right to an abortion in the 1973 case *Roe v. Wade*, *Playboy* celebrated the decision and the role it saw itself as having played in changing the social dialogue surrounding the issue (p. 71).

Playboy was known then, as it is now, as a paean to straight male privilege. But as its record of support for sexual difference and women's reproductive rights demonstrates, Hefner used his magazine to claim a position of progressive leadership in postwar sexual culture. When he founded *Playboy* in 1953, America was awash in a conservatism that marked gay men and liberated women as deviant, even mentally ill. To suggest in 1955, as the magazine did, that heterosexuals should sympathize with same-sex orientations, or to advocate for legal abortion in 1965, meant that Hefner and his team were willing to take a risk and a stand for sexual tolerance and freedom. Likely, these positions truly were in line with Hefner's personal progressive values. But should this new sexual system come to pass—should more marginalized Americans gain dignity, equality, and choice—it would mean that men like Hefner would advance to full sexual freedom by default. It would symbolize the defeat of the forces of oppression that Hefner had railed against his whole life.

At the height of *Playboy*'s popularity in early 1970s, Hefner witnessed the changes his magazine had helped to spark in the years preceding the sexual revolution. Ironically, it was that very evolution that soon worked to challenge *Playboy*'s position as an arbiter of American sexual mores. Popular culture became increasingly sexualized, and magazine competitors, such as *Penthouse* and *Hustler*, upped the ante on explicitness in ways that shocked, even disgusted, Hefner. Playboy influenced American sexual culture in the 1950s and 1960s, but in the coming years the magazine's vision would be surpassed by the revolution it helped to create. This irony was not lost on Hefner and his team. In 2015, he was still the head of the organization, but after pressure from lead editor Cory Jones, Hefner made the shocking decision to stop publishing the iconic nude Playmate centerfolds. As the *New York Times* reported, "Its executives admit that *Playboy* has been overtaken by the changes it pioneered. 'That battle has been fought and won,' said Scott Flanders, the company's chief executive. 'You're now one click away from every sex act imaginable for free. And so it's just passé at this juncture'" (Somaiya, 2015, p. A1). While Hefner's role as cultural leader faded over the decades, there can be no doubt that the sexual system that dominated much of the past 50 years bore the salacious stamp of the *Playboy* bunny.

REFERENCES

Scholarly Sources

Bailey, B. (1988). *Front porch to back seat: Courtship in twentieth-century America*. Baltimore, MD: Johns Hopkins University Press.

Beggan, J. K., & Allison, S. T. (2001). What do *Playboy* playmates want? Implications of expressed preferences in the construction of the "unfinished" masculine identity. *The Journal of Men's Studies*, *10*(1), 1–38.

Beggan, J. K., & Allison, S. T. (2005). Tough women in the unlikeliest of places: The unexpected toughness of the *Playboy* playmate. *The Journal of Popular Culture*, *38*(5), 796–818.

Beggan, J. K., Gagné, P., & Allison, S. T. (2000). An analysis of stereotype refutation in *Playboy* by an editorial voice: The advisor hypothesis. *The Journal of Men's Studies*, *9*(1), 1–21.

Bogaert, A. F., Turkovich, D. A., & Hafer, C. L. (1993). A content analysis of *Playboy* centrefolds from 1953 through 1990: Changes in explicitness, objectification, and model's age. *Journal of Sex Research*, *30*(2), 135–9.

Buszek, M. E. (2006). *Pin-up grrrls: Feminism, sexuality, popular culture*. Durham, NC: Duke University Press.

Cuordileone, K. A. (2005). *Manhood and American political culture in the Cold War*. New York: Routledge.

Davidson, B. (1962, April 28). Czar of the bunny empire. *Saturday Evening Post*, *235*(17), 34–8.
Digby, D. (1972, February 27). Q&A Hugh Hefner. *Los Angeles Times*, pp. W20.
DuBois, E. C., & Dumenil, L. (2016). *Through women's eyes: An American history with documents* (4th ed.). New York: Bedford/St. Martin's.
Dworkin, A. (1989). *Pornography: Men possessing women*. New York: Perigree.
Ehrenreich, B. (1983). *The hearts of men: American dreams and the flight from commitment*. Garden City, NY: Anchor Press/Doubleday.
Fraterrigo, E. (2009). *Playboy and the making of the good life in modern America*. New York: Oxford University Press.
Gilbert, J. (2005). *Men in the middle: Searching for masculinity in the 1950s*. Chicago: University of Chicago Press.
Hollows, J. (2002). The bachelor dinner: Masculinity, class and cooking in *Playboy*, 1953–1961. *Continuum: Journal of Media & Cultural Studies*, *16*(2), 143–55.
MacKinnon, C. A. (1988). *Feminism unmodified: Discourses on life and law*. Cambridge, MA: Harvard University Press.
Messer, E., & May, K. E. (1994). *Back rooms: Voices from the illegal abortion era*. Buffalo, NY: Prometheus Books.
Meyerowitz, J. (1996). Women, cheesecake, and borderline material: Responses to girlie pictures in the mid-twentieth-century US. *Journal of Women's History*, *8*(3), 9–35.
Osgerby, B. (2001). *Playboys in paradise: Masculinity, youth and leisure-style in modern America*. Oxford: Berg.
Preciado, B. (2004). Pornotopia. In B. Colomina, A. Brennan, & J. Kim (Eds.), *Cold war hothouses: inventing postwar culture, from cockpit to Playboy* (pp. 216–53). New York, NY: Princeton Architectural Press.
Scott, J. E., & Cuvelier, S. J. (1987). Sexual violence in *Playboy* magazine: A longitudinal content analysis. *The Journal of Sex Research*, *23*(4), 534–9.
Watts, S. (2008). *Mr. Playboy: Hugh Hefner and the American Dream*. New York: John Wiley & Sons.

Archival Sources

American Psychiatric Association. (1952). *Diagnostic and statistical manual of mental disorders* (1st ed.). Arlington, VA: American Psychiatric Publishing.
Letter from Hefner to Ray Bradbury, July 11, 1955. HMH Papers, Box 1, 1954–55, Folder #8.
Letters to the Editor, *Playboy*, November 1955, pp. 5–6.
Hugh M. Hefner, "The *Playboy* philosophy," Part XVI, (collected volume), HMH Publishing, Co., Inc., 1963, 1964, 128
Anonymous, "Forum," *Playboy*, June 1964, 53.
Response to M.M., "The *Playboy* advisor," *Playboy*, July 1964, 25.
Response to R.W., "The *Playboy* advisor," *Playboy*, September 1964, 62.
Charles Philips, "Forum," *Playboy*, October 1964, 64.
"The chimes of the first Methodist Church," February 21, 1965. PRC, carton 2325, folder "Healthy Sex Society."

Letter from S.J.M. to Hefner, HMH Papers, Box 54, 1965 D-Editorial, Folder #5.

Letter from Janelle Lindsey and editorial response, "Forum," *Playboy*, December 1965, 227–8.

"Forum," *Playboy*, November 1966, 66.

Anonymous, "Forum," *Playboy*, February 1967, 38.

James P. Wittenberg, "Forum," *Playboy*, December 1967, 84.

Anonymous, "Forum," *Playboy*, December 1967, 84.

Letter from Pamela Wright, "Forum," *Playboy*, April 1967, 172.

Letter from Anonymous, "Forum," *Playboy*, May 1967, 149.

"Forum," *Playboy*, August 1967, 35–7.

Letter from William R. Baird, "Forum," *Playboy*, February 1968, 48, 174.

Anonymous letter and Editorial response, "Forum," May 1968, 61.

Letter from Harriet F. Pilpel, "Forum," *Playboy*, January 1969, 51.

Editorial response to Kameny, "Forum," *Playboy*, March 1969, 46, 48.

Memo from Nat Lehrman to Dick Rosenzweig, March 27, 1969. HMH Papers, Box 135, 1970 Lehrman – L Misc., Folder #4.

Editorial response, "Forum," *Playboy*, August 1969, 48.

Editorial response to L.G., "Advisor," *Playboy*, August 1970, 38.

"The Abortion Revolution," *Playboy*, September 1970, 112.

Letter from Anonymous, "Forum", *Playboy*, December 1970, 86.

Forum letter, *Playboy*, March 1971, 53.

Letter and editorial response to J.P., "Advisor," *Playboy*, May 1971, 56, 58.

Letter from Ruth Proskauer Smith, "Forum," *Playboy*, May 1971, 73.

"Forum," *Playboy*, June 1971, 185.

"The abortion backlash: A special 'Playboy Forum' report," *Playboy*, September 1971, 77.

Letter from Roberta Schneiderman, "Forum," *Playboy*, April 1972, 195.

Letter from Bill Baird, "Forum," *Playboy*, July 1972, 57.

Letter from Ruth Proskauer Smith, "Forum," *Playboy*, September 1972, 58.

Forum editorial, *Playboy*, May 1973, 71.

Ravi Somaiya, "Nudes are old news at Playboy," *New York Times*, October 12, 2015, p. A1. Retrieved January 6, 2017 from http://www.nytimes.com/2015/10/13/business/media/nudes-are-old-news-at-playboy.html

NOTES

* Portions of this essay originally appeared in Carrie Pitzulo, *Bachelors and Bunnies: The Sexual Politics of Playboy* (Chicago: University of Chicago Press, 2011).

1. Out of 33 letters published, 9 discussed homosexuality.

2. The information provided was for legal services based on state law. A similar guide had been published in *New York* magazine on September 28, 1970.

2. Planned Parenthood: 100 years of leadership and controversy

Sheila Huss and Lucy Dwight

Birth control—even in "natural" forms—has been a socially, morally, and legally constructed issue throughout history and one that has been inextricably tied to formal and informal social control. The target population of various forms of social control relating to birth control has been women (Schneider & Ingram, 1993). Over time, attitudes and policies surrounding birth control crossed multiple boundaries and became politicized. Like so many other "moral" political issues, concerns about information and access to birth control were disconnected from societal unity and focused on creating certain types of individuals whose reproductive decisions fell into the hands of male-dominated institutions, including the state. Denying access to birth control as a political and public health issue constituted an injustice, which became an organized grievance, a legal topic, a human rights concern, and even an issue of demography. Planned Parenthood, its precursors, and related organizations, such as the International Planned Parenthood Federation (IPPF), have assumed a central leadership role in representing women's rights in reproductive health for more than a century. Moreover, these organizations have provided resources, discourse, and the social and political space for social and legal change to occur, both domestically and internationally.

HISTORY

In 1916, Margaret Sanger, her sister, and other advocates opened the first fully operational birth control clinic in the US, in Brooklyn, NY (Alter, 2016).[1] Sanger had coined the term "birth control" the year before (Gordon, 2002). Sanger's clinic was in a poor Jewish and Italian immigrant area of Brooklyn, and it was designed to provide various healthcare services to women. Specifically, this clinic provided birth

37

control information, as well as physical fitting of devices such as early diaphragms and cervical caps. So many women sought help from Sanger's clinic that they were lined up outside the building hoping to get in for services. Despite helping many women and addressing an obvious need in the Brooklyn community, Sanger's clinic was shut down after only nine days (Alter, 2016). Sanger and her coworkers were arrested and subsequently served time in jail for distributing contraceptive materials in violation of the Comstock Act of 1873, which outlawed the distribution of material deemed obscene. These birth control advocates, however, used their trials to publicize the plight of poor women who endured unwanted pregnancies (Gordon, 2002).

Then, five years after the first clinic was opened and closed, Sanger founded the American Birth Control League, which in 1942 was renamed the Planned Parenthood Federation of America (PPFA). This new name reflected an intentional effort to frame birth control in positive and family-friendly terms and provide distance from the radical roots of the birth control movement (Gordon, 2002).

Margaret Sanger served as President of Planned Parenthood until 1962 and also co-founded the IPPF in 1952. The IPPF included representative organizations from the United States and several nations across Asia and Europe (Claeys, 2010). Today, Planned Parenthood's healthcare services in the US reach two and a half million people per year, and their sex education services reach one and a half million (General Health Care, 2016). Other services provided by the clinics include contraception counseling, testing and treatment for sexually transmitted diseases, pregnancy testing and prenatal care, and screens for cervical and breast cancers (General Health Care, 2016).

In the mid-1950s, when birth control discussions started occurring on a national level (Chadwick, Burkman, Tornesi, & Mahadevan, 2012), there was also controversy about the legality of abortion. Planned Parenthood began to mobilize the medical community to discuss and advocate for the revision and repeal of antiabortion laws. The prochoice/legalization of abortion movement coincided with other important progressive movements, such as the women's movement and the civil rights movement. Additionally, other powerful organizations formed during this time, including the National Organization for Women in 1966 and the National Abortion Rights Action League (NARAL) in 1969 (Tersigni, 1998).

In the early 1970s, there was "heightened public concern over the increasing population of the nation and the improved medical ability to control conception" (Brodie, 1971, p. 424). In response to these concerns, Richard Nixon sponsored the Family Planning Services and Population Research Act in 1970. This legislation provided federal funding to organizations such as Planned Parenthood to provide family planning and contraception counseling for low-income women. Furthermore, the legislation established the National Center for Population and Family Planning, which conducted research on factors that impacted population growth and various reproductive issues (for example, sterility, contraception, human reproduction) (Brodie, 1971).

The Planned Parenthood Federation of America is a century-old non-profit organization with approximately 661 affiliate health centers nationwide (Lafer & Richards, 2015). PPFA provides STI/STD testing and treatment, pap tests and breast exams, primary care services, birth control information and services, and health reproductive services. PPFA organizations reached 2.5 million patients in 2015 (Foley, 2016; Lafer & Richards, 2015). They have also expanded internationally through Planned Parenthood Global to partner with medical providers and advocates in other countries to provide access to reproductive healthcare for men and women (Lafer & Richards, 2015).

Throughout its history, Planned Parenthood and its affiliates have faced a number of controversial issues. Disputes have included issues ranging from founder Margaret Sanger's association with eugenics, to the provision of access to and information about birth control and abortion services, to current controversies over alleged fetal tissue sales. The remainder of this chapter describes several of these controversial issues which the organization has faced over the years.

EUGENICS

Margaret Sanger and, by implication, Planned Parenthood have been linked with racial eugenics among anti-birth control activists, as well as the antichoice movement, from early in the birth control movement. Broadly, eugenics refers to support for "selective breeding" of human beings to enhance perceived positive traits within the population and minimize perceived negative traits. It can be differentiated into positive and negative forms: positive eugenicists encouraged individuals with "positive traits" to have more children; negative eugenicists advocated for involuntarily limiting reproduction among people deemed less fit (O'Brien, 2013). The relevant traits, assumed to be genetically inherited, included physical, mental, or developmental fitness; intelligence; class; propensity to be criminal; and racial and ethnic membership. Eugenicists varied over time in how they defined desirable and undesirable traits (Kevles, 2016).

The eugenics movement was embedded within a burgeoning and multifaceted revival of social movements in the late nineteenth and early twentieth centuries. These movements included experimental utopian communities such as Oneida, "free love" societies, and first-wave feminism. Margaret Sanger's activism grew out of several of these movements, including radical socialism and suffragism, although she increasingly moved toward family planning as her primary issue (Gordon, 2002).

Eugenics was not particularly controversial at the turn of the twentieth century, even though it was framed by and utilized differently among individuals and organizations with competing ideological commitments. Sanger advocated for what today may be viewed as extreme negative eugenics, including forced sterilization for some groups, such as the "feeble minded." However, she was not entrenched in the eugenics movement, partly because it was not her main issue, but also because she rejected positive eugenics. Sanger advocated for small family sizes and self-determination for women of all backgrounds and all races, with the exception of those women she viewed as "unfit" to make such decisions for themselves, irrespective of race or class (O'Brien, 2013).

Feminists such as Sanger viewed eugenics through the prism of women's autonomy, but ultimately, an antifeminist form of eugenics won the day. This antifeminist eugenics claimed that because highly educated and empowered women had fewer children than poor ones, society was in danger of "race suicide." According to Gordon (2002), the race suicide movement embodied several themes: (1) birth control was sinful; (2) it reduced family size when the nation needed to grow its population; (3) it limited the population of northern Europeans disproportionately relative to nonwhites and immigrants; (4) it was seen as a rebellious movement of women against their natural place. The intertwining of these themes reinforced one another and resulted in a "situation [that] was culturally and morally fatal" (Gordon, 2002, p. 87). To the degree that this form of eugenics was a critique of women and feminism, it was leveled at wealthy white women, not disadvantaged women or women of color.

Sanger opposed the framework of "race suicide," given its opposition to feminism and, specifically, birth control, though she continued to use a negative eugenics frame throughout her public career (O'Brien, 2013). In retrospect, of course, the rhetoric of both positive and negative eugenics is highly problematic, both due to its association with the horrific practices of Nazi Germany and because of its implicit class, ethnic, and racial disparagements. After World War II, Planned Parenthood's leadership promoted a much more individualistic point of view for family planning, manifested recently as "choice" with respect to abortion rights.

Eugenics in any form was no longer compelling or, after the Holocaust, remotely justifiable. Gordon noted:

[a]s a Planned Parenthood pamphlet put it, parents should build families "commensurate with their abilities to provide for them adequately." When a prospective parent says this to herself, it is common sense; when a birth control organization says it, with an explicit or implied "ought," it is urging different family sizes upon different classes. (2002, p. 246)

Today, a number of organizations under the Planned Parenthood umbrella provide family planning services. These activities, particularly the provision of abortion services, remain controversial. The early association of Planned Parenthood's founder with eugenics is utilized extensively in the antiabortion movement (Enriquez, 2013). Crucial federal and state funding for Planned Parenthood has been threatened because of its association with this controversy and others that followed it. The eugenics controversy overlapped with another dispute which, like eugenics, has declined in magnitude but is historically significant in Planned Parenthood's leadership role in women's reproductive health and rights: that regarding access to and information about birth control. This controversy also reflects the sustainability of Planned Parenthood and IPPF, as long-term survival of advocacy organizations is not the norm.

BIRTH CONTROL ACCESS AND INFORMATION

In the late eighteenth and the nineteenth centuries, birth control and family planning were framed, in part, as techniques of population control. Malthusians believed that population growth was responsible for poverty, but did not support birth control to limit population growth (Gordon, 2002). A radical subgroup of Malthusians, "neo-Malthusians," formed and over time became the dominant perspective. Neo-Malthusians supported the use of contraception, believing that smaller families would diminish poverty. Malthusians held six international conferences between 1881 and 1925, their popularity growing during this time. The sixth conference was held in New York and, significantly, saw the establishment of institutionalized support for birth control with the International Federation of Birth Control Leagues (Claeys, 2010). The intersection between population growth and contraception was problematic and polarizing—demographers focused on population, while others who were concerned about family planning focused on a rights-based framework.

In 1873, the United States Congress passed the Comstock Act, a piece of federal legislation that applied to both Washington D.C. and "any of the Territories of the United States." The legislation was established as part of an anti-pornography movement, resulting from the widespread access to pornography during the Civil War (Abramson & Pinkerton, 2002). The legislation also targeted the dissemination of information about birth control and reproductive health.

In 1930, an International Birth Control conference situated family planning as a fundamental part of public health. Many argued that information about birth control was the best way to fight abortion. Several individuals who attended this conference were integral in later founding the IPPF (Claeys, 2010). Efforts to advocate for birth control access and information essentially stopped during World War II, but picked up again when Elise Ottesen-Jensen, a Swedish woman, became a leader in changing public opinion and creating new legislation on contraceptives. Specifically, she worked with trade unions, political groups, and others to educate the public on reproductive rights issues. She also organized an international conference, during which the seed was planted for a new international organization. Over the following years, there were more conferences with additional discussions about the need for a new international organization. To manage the large number of interests represented (population control, family planning clinics, sex education, and so on), the name "Planned Parenthood" was selected (Claeys, 2010). On November 29, 1952, the IPPF was created, with Margaret Sanger and Lady Rama Rau from India as co-presidents. Simultaneously, in the United States, the Population Council was established; the frame of birth control as a means of population control was alive and well.

The IPPF operated worldwide with regional offices, one of which was in New York. It accommodated a number of different priorities and activities, including the use of contraception to manage the danger of an expanding population with limited natural resources, research on new forms of contraception, and rising rates of abortion. Notably, contraception methods in 1952 had not changed since the 1880s: items used were condoms, cervical caps, spermicides, and pessaries. From its inception, the IPPF focused partly on the medical aspects of birth control. In 1954, Sanger facilitated a grant, funding from which was used for research in the area of oral contraceptives ("the Pill"). The IPPF also created a medical committee to track medical developments in family planning. The function of the medical committee grew over time, and the committee established medical policies for the organization, served in an advisory capacity, and established standards for family planning services (Claeys, 2010). As the committee's responsibilities expanded, the IPPF formed subcommittees to carry out the tasks. The committee is now the

International Medical Advisory Panel, and the IPPF still uses it. The IPPF formed a separate research committee in the late 1950s, an impetus of which was developments in oral contraception. In 1960, the FDA approved the oral contraceptive pill. The IPPF offered the Pill and advocated for it to be inexpensive or free. In spite of the progress that resulted from the scientific and medical developments and the instrumental role of the IPPF in creating an international platform on which these advancements were recognized and provided, the changes set the stage for extensive conflict in political, social, and legal realms.

When the Pill initially was approved, it was not a commodity in the free market; it had to be prescribed by a medical doctor. Hence, medical doctors controlled women's access to birth control pills, and only a small minority of them would prescribe birth control to unmarried women (Bailey, 1997). Sex was as much a moral issue as it was a health issue, a political issue, and a legal issue, and it certainly was not an individual issue outside of the realm of formal or informal social control. In 1965, 26 states had laws against providing birth control pills to unmarried women (Thompson, 2013). That year, the Supreme Court held that these laws were unconstitutional (*Griswold v. Connecticut*). A few years later, Bill Baird was arrested and faced up to ten years in prison for giving a female student at Boston University a condom and contraceptive foam (a felony). The Planned Parenthood League of Massachusetts advocated for Baird, encouraging legislative changes to resolve the problems of criminalizing access to birth control for unmarried women. Five years later, Baird's battle ended with the Supreme Court decision *Eisenstadt v. Baird* (1972), which legalized birth control for all women and set the stage for *Roe v. Wade* (1973), which legalized abortion during the first trimester of pregnancy. Although *Planned Parenthood v. Casey* (1992) referred to abortion rather than birth control, the Supreme Court reiterated the spirit of its *Baird* ruling: "[if] the right of privacy means anything, it is the right of the individual, married or single, to be free from unwarranted governmental intrusion into matters so fundamentally affecting a person as the decision whether to bear or beget a child." Summarily, as the disagreement over women's reproductive rights (specifically birth control) became increasingly intersected with formal social control in the form of legal prohibitions and subsequent appellate challenges, Planned Parenthood maintained the capacity to support women who were disenfranchised by the law.

The "sexual revolution" also was occurring on a local level, and involved social change that was largely disconnected from the legal changes that facilitated it. For example, Bailey (1997) conducted a case study in Lawrence, Kansas to show how local efforts constitute part of larger, national-level change. In Lawrence, she argued that institutional changes that opened the possibility of the Pill becoming accessible to unmarried women included legitimate authorities in the area (doctors, professors, university administrators, and public health officials) speaking out and being recognized. She also argued that national change occurred because people who participate in national professional organizations and other efforts came from different areas throughout the country.

Even and sometimes especially at local levels, Planned Parenthood has been influential in creating change with respect to women's reproductive health. For example, in 1963, Kansas passed a law allowing the distribution of contraceptive material. The law did not provide for funding, nor did it require the distribution of educational material; it simply removed legal sanctions for the distribution of this material. So, in 1966, the Greater Kansas branch of Planned Parenthood found a number of volunteers to comprise an "educational arm" in Lawrence, Kansas. Volunteers were motivated because they had concerns over population growth, but nevertheless, they organized. The local Planned Parenthood chapter also tried to establish a partnership with the Health Department. It offered to provide publicity, education, and counseling, as well as refer women to the Health Department for contraception. The Health Department refused the agreement. Within a few months, Planned Parenthood was operating a biweekly clinic. The clinic involved a number of activities, including staff showing films, a social worker offering counseling, and a doctor providing services for exams and offering a prescription for contraception (Bailey, 1997).

International shifts in attitudes toward and policies surrounding birth control access and education also have been evident over the past several decades. The government demonstrated some support for family planning, and there were discussions of family planning as a human right. Internationally, the United Nations approved a resolution connecting population growth and human rights, stating that parents had a basic human right to freely and responsibly decide how many children they wanted to have and how they wanted to space their children. Furthermore, parents had a right to information and education. Over the course of four UN conferences in the 1990s, many organizations agreed on the need for universal access to reproductive healthcare by 2015. Human rights should include women's right to control and freely decide on issues related to sexuality. In 2000, the Millennium Development Goals were established, the fifth of which was to reduce maternal mortality. This goal (MDG 5b) was supplemented with a need for strong advocacy for universal access to reproductive health. These Millennium Development Goals have not been effectively implemented, in part because of a lack of political will (Claeys, 2010).

Throughout history and in different geographical places, many people and organizations have influenced the construction of birth control information and access. The important role of the IPPF and the Planned Parenthood organization cannot be overemphasized. These organizations have engaged in a number of strategies, including direct service provision, education, networking, legal work, and direct action to organize and mobilize. They have been instrumental in formulating the dialogue surrounding debates over birth control information and access and in facilitating desirable social and legal change. Having such a large structure and worldwide presence focusing on a narrow set of issues facilitates the organizational capacity to define a grievance and assume a leadership role in mobilizing to rectify it. Although abortion services are a relatively small part of Planned Parenthood's activities, the controversy surrounding it arguably best illustrates Planned Parenthood's capability to withstand moral, legal, and political opposition. It is to this issue that we now turn.

ABORTION

Each year, more than one million women in the United States have an abortion (Salganicoff, Sobel, Kurani, & Gomez, 2016). There are two ways to end an unwanted pregnancy through abortion. One is the medical procedure of the fetus or embryo being removed from the woman's body before it can survive outside the uterus. The other is the woman taking medication that will cause her body to remove the fetus and placenta tissue. Generally, the moral debate surrounding abortion focuses on whether women have the right to make decisions about their bodies or whether the fetus and embryo have "a right to life" (Grimes & Stuart, 2010). Many people readily associate Planned Parenthood with abortion, but as noted earlier, among all medical services provided by Planned Parenthood, abortions constitute less than 3 percent of services (Lafer & Richards, 2015). Planned Parenthood began offering abortion as a medical service following the Supreme Court's *Roe v. Wade* (1973) decision.

Between 1967 and 1973, several states modified or eradicated their abortion laws, reflecting a shift in public opinion toward abortion (Gold, 1990). In 1973, a Texas woman who became known as Jane Roe sought to end her pregnancy during the first trimester. Because Texas law of the time did not allow abortions unless a woman was raped, "Roe" and two other women in a similar situation sought legal assistance. Attorneys representing the women brought suit against the state of Texas. The case that ensued, *Roe v. Wade*, was decided in 1973 and became one of the most impactful and controversial cases in history. The Supreme Court supported Roe's argument, struck down the Texas law, and said that the constitutional right to privacy under the 14th Amendment extends to a woman's decision to terminate a pregnancy (Ely, 1973). When *Roe* was decided, most states had statutes preventing abortions except when the mother's life was endangered, when a woman was raped or a victim of incest, or when the fetus had severe abnormalities (Masci & Lupu, 2013). Although statutes varied, they reflected legal consistency in that they prohibited abortions unless an extreme circumstance existed. Even though the justices did not agree on their analysis of abortion, the majority rejected the "fetal rights" argument and agreed that until the point of fetal viability, abortions could not be restricted unless a state could demonstrate a "compelling interest" in the restriction.

Summarily, the Supreme Court gave women the constitutional right, with the highest constitutional protections, to terminate their pregnancy in the first trimester.

Since 1973, abortion has remained legal, but is one of the most emotionally charged and controversial issues in society. Because of the public nature of the contentiousness over the right to have an abortion, Planned Parenthood has come under heavy fire for offering abortions at some of its clinics. Yet, not all Planned Parenthood centers perform abortions—only about half of them do, and only about 3 percent of the organization's medical services include abortions (Lafer & Richards, 2015). The provision of safe, legal abortions is indeed an issue of life and death: in 1965, the mortality rate for abortions was so high that 17 percent of all pregnancy and child-related deaths were from abortions (Gold, 1990). Today, less than 0.5 percent of women who have an abortion experience serious complications (Henshaw, Singh, & Haas, 1999). Moreover, according to Rosenthal (2007), abortion rates are equal in countries with legalized abortions and countries that do not legalize the practice, and death rates are much higher in countries where abortions are not legal.

Following the *Roe v. Wade* decision, the "right to life" movement organized to challenge the prochoice movement that was quickly amassing (Karrer, 2011). The three main objections to abortion use religious, moral, and philosophical arguments, and most antiabortion advocates believe that life begins at conception (Turner & Balch, 2014). The ultimate goal of the right to life movement is to abolish women's access to abortion and return to the government the reproductive decisions women are currently able to make. The movement has made it a priority to reverse *Roe v. Wade* (Enriquez, 2013). Some "right to life" advocates accept abortion in certain cases, such as incest, rape, and when the life of the mother is threatened.

THE HYDE AMENDMENT

Congress passed the Hyde Amendment in 1976, which prohibits the use of federal Medicaid funding for abortion services as part of the comprehensive health care services provided to people on low incomes (Fried, 2007; Palencia, 1980; Rosoff, 1980). It was considered unconstitutional for Medicaid to pay for abortion services (with limited exceptions), but not prenatal care, family planning, and other medical services associated with childbirth (Fried, 2007). Presently, the federal Medicaid program authorizes abortion funding in cases of rape or incest and when a pregnant woman's life is in danger.

Research indicates that the Hyde Amendment has resulted in negative outcomes for some women on Medicaid (Fried, 2007). Because women are unable to use Medicaid monies for abortion services, they are forced to pay for this medical procedure with money they would otherwise use for clothing, food, rent, utilities, and other living necessities (Jones, Upadhyay, & Weitz, 2013). Additionally, not being able to use Medicaid funding for abortion forces women to stay pregnant longer while they acquire money to pay for the abortion, which increases their health risks (Public Funding for Abortion, 2016).

The current Planned Parenthood president, Cecile Richards, repeatedly testifies before Congress to remind politicians that Planned Parenthood is prohibited by the Hyde Amendment from using taxpayer dollars to fund abortions except in cases of rape, incest, or where the life of the mother is at risk. Today, health insurance has greater restrictions on covering abortion services, even though more women are covered by health insurance than in the past. The insurance companies' restrictions have the greatest economic impact on lower-class women, who may be unable to pay for medical services out of pocket (Jones, Upadhyay, & Weitz, 2013).

FETAL TISSUE SALES

As is evidenced by the framing of various aspects of the abortion debate, power among stakeholders is not evenly distributed, and stakeholders define women's reproductive issues such as birth control and abortion quite differently depending on the moral, financial, and political interests at stake. When a well-established group (such as Planned Parenthood) has an institutionalized association with women's reproductive issues, it is not surprising to find it at the forefront of many criticisms and debates. Most recently, the abortion debate has centered on allegations that Planned Parenthood has sold fetal tissue for profit.

For decades, researchers have been using fetal tissue—often, stem cells from the tissue—to study degenerative diseases; many scholars contend that cells from fetal tissue provide a research benefit that other types of cells cannot provide. Federal law prohibits any organization or company from purchasing or profiting from the sale of fetal tissue; however, it does not restrict fees that can be charged for processing. Federal law permits companies to recover costs, but not compensation, for fetal tissue itself (Prohibitions Regarding Human Fetal Tissue, 1993). In spirit, the law was designed to allow fetal tissue to be donated, but to prevent a business from forming around the sale of fetal tissue. State laws on fetal tissue donation differ.

In spite of the longstanding practice of using fetal tissue in research, the battle has shifted from a hypothetical legal one to a largely moral one, albeit one with legal implications. The Center for Medical Progress, an antiabortion group founded in 2013, released videos in 2015 that it alleged provided evidence that Planned Parenthood illegally sold fetal tissue. The videos fueled antiabortionists' proverbial fire and prompted protests, legal investigations, loss of funding for Planned Parenthood organizations, and even government shutdown. In 12 states, political officials ordered investigations into Planned Parenthood activities and compliance with laws related to fetal tissue sales and the proper disposal of fetuses. To date, no legal action has been taken against any Planned Parenthood organization, and in fact a Texas jury indicted two antiabortion activists who were members of Medical Progress (Fernandez, 2016). Nevertheless, some states cut Planned Parenthood funding, at least one of which (Ohio) blocked funding largely as a result of the Center for Medical Progress's videos—though this decision was rejected by a judge (Carmon, 2016).

CONCLUSION: THE NEXT CENTURY

Planned Parenthood and other family planning organizations operating within the United States and internationally continue to be buffeted by controversy. In one of his very first acts as president, for instance, Donald

Trump renewed an Executive Order that prohibits foreign aid not only to organizations that perform abortions, but also to groups that "actively promote abortion" (The Mexico City Policy: An Explainer, 2017). This "gag rule" has been standing policy for Republican administrations in the United States since Reagan. Promoting abortion as safe medical practice includes providing information or referral for abortion services where legal, thus the order's characterization as a "gag rule," since it goes beyond the direct provision of services. Trump's order, however, expands those of his conservative predecessors in that it provides fewer exceptions and covers more sources of foreign aid, such as general public health support (The Mexico City Policy: An Explainer, 2017).

Within the United States, there have been recent and persistent threats to defund state-level support for Planned Parenthood services. For instance, beginning in 2011, the state of Texas initiated several measures to curtail state spending on family planning, particularly targeting Planned Parenthood affiliates. These efforts were associated with a sharp decline in the provision of long-acting reversible contraceptives and a concomitant rise in the rate of childbirth among low-income women in Texas (Stevenson, Flores-Vazquez, Allgeyer, Schenkkan, & Potter, 2016). Interest in and support for Planned Parenthood has increased in the wake of these events, however. For example, Laguens (2013) reported that Planned Parenthood campus chapters doubled nationally in the two years after Texas targeted Planned Parenthood.

Following Donald Trump's election and conservative Republicans' gaining control of both houses of Congress, efforts have already begun to strip funding from Planned Parenthood both nationally and internationally (Rovner, 2017). Given this expectation of federal defunding, in the weeks following the election Planned Parenthood reported a 40 percent spike in donations (Walters, 2016).

Although the substance of debates over women's reproductive rights has varied over time and space, Planned Parenthood has remained at the forefront of these debates. With expertise in advocacy, medicine, law, sexual and reproductive health, and communication, these organizations have led the way in providing access, education, and services related to women's health and safety. In spite of the progress that Planned Parenthood Federation of America and IPPF have made—or perhaps because of it—intersections between the cultural shifts toward making individual behavior a political priority and special interest groups that target women's reproductive rights have led to these organizations becoming ensnared in rhetorical, moral, political, and legal battles. Many of these battles affect Planned Parenthood and IPPF, in terms of the groups' reputations, public perceptions, involvement in the legal system, and resource provision.

Margaret Sanger's activism, along with that of other family planning pioneers, emerged from the turmoil of the twentieth century. Although Sanger's legacy through Planned Parenthood has persisted, history seems to have left open the question of her personal identity. Is she a heroine? A flawed leader? A small part of a larger social movement? The narrative into which contemporary society fits Sanger is important, because it speaks to how we construct people whose advocacy is on behalf of marginalized groups. Allison and Goethals (2011) describe one schema we use to characterize heroes, which includes pursuing the common good rather than personal gain, enduring personal sacrifice, and showing leadership for a cause. Franco, Blau, and Zimbardo (2011) propose that physical or social sacrifice is the main ingredient for heroism. Certainly, Sanger showed strong long-term leadership in the battle for women's rights of self-determination over their bodies, and she endured sacrifice for the cause, including imprisonment as well as financial and social sacrifice—in these ways, she arguably is a heroine. Sanger was not a mythic hero, but a woman who cared about the plights of the poor, refugees, and new immigrants. Because her advocacy was on the part of the marginalized, albeit on an issue that resonated with elites as well, her status as a heroic leader may be compromised. She was flawed, moreover, in embracing the long discredited eugenics movement. Yet she laid the groundwork for future feminist battles by her determination to afford women control over their own bodies.

New social movements, experimental communities, transformational religious movements, and the push for women's political rights all created the forge within which birth control and family planning were championed as legal rights. Ultimately, leadership in promoting women's reproductive rights required autonomy for those women who fought against oppression, but also recognition of the autonomy of all women, manifested in control of their bodies and also blossoming political, economic, and social power over their own destinies. These women realized their own voices in promoting a new vision of womanhood that recognized the power of all women. In this new century, these campaigns have continued, sometimes in altered form, but with claims that resonate with the early battles in the effort to assure women's reproductive rights.

REFERENCES

Abramson, P. R. & Pinkerton, S. D. (2002). *With pleasure: Thoughts on the nature of human sexuality.* New York: Oxford University Press.

Allison, S. T., & Goethals, G. R. (2011). *Heroes: What they do & why we need them.* New York: Oxford University Press.

Alter, C. (2016, October 14). How Planned Parenthood changed everything. *Time.* Retrieved January 15, 2017 from http://time.com/4527330/planned-parenthood-100-history/.

Bailey, B. (1997). Prescribing the pill: Politics, culture, and the sexual revolution in American's heartland. *Journal of Social History, 30*(Summer), 827–56.

Brodie, D. W. (1971). The Family Planning Services and Population Research Act of 1970—Public Law 91-572. *Family Law Quarterly, 5*(4), 424–77.

Carmon, I. (2016, August 12). Judge rules Ohio can't block Planned Parenthood funds. Retrieved January 15, 2017 from http://www.nbcnews.com/news/us-news/judge-rules-ohio-can-t-block-planned-parenthood-funds-n629406.

Chadwick, K. D., Burkman, R. T., Tornesi, B. M., & Mahadevan, B. (2012). Fifty years of "the Pill": Risk reduction and discovery of benefits beyond contraception, reflections, and forecast. *Toxicological Sciences, 125*(1), 2–9.

Claeys, V. (2010). Brave and angry—the creation and development of the International Planned Parenthood Federation (IPPF). *The European Journal of Contraception & Reproductive Health Care,* 15sup2, S67–S76.

Eisenstadt v. Baird, 405 U.S. 438 (1972).

Ely, J. H. (1973). The wages of crying wolf: A comment on *Roe v. Wade. The Yale Law Journal, 82*(5), 920–49.

Enriquez, L. (2013, March 11). 10 eye-opening quotes from Planned Parenthood founder Margaret Sanger. *Lifenews.com.* Retrieved January 15, 2017 from www.lifenews.staging.wpengine.com/2013/03/11/10-eye-opening-quotes-from-planned-parenthood-founder-margaret-sanger/

Fernandez, M. (2016, January 25). 2 abortion foes behind Planned Parenthood videos are indicted. Retrieved January 15, 2017 from https://www.nytimes.com/2016/01/26/us/2-abortion-foes-behind-planned-parenthood-videos-are-indicted.html.

Foley, K. (2016). Standing up for Planned Parenthood. *Journal of the Association of Nurses in AIDS Care, 27*(4), 371.

Franco, Z. E., Blau, K., & Zimbardo, P. G. (2011). Heroism: A conceptual analysis and differentiation between heroic action and altruism. *Review of General Psychology,* advance online publication, doi: 10.1037/a0022672.

Fried, M. (2007). Hyde Amendment: The opening wedge to abolish abortion. *New Politics, 11*(2), 82.

General Health Care. (2016). Retrieved January 15, 2017 from https://www.plannedparenthood.org/learn/general-health-care.

Gold, R. B. (1990). *Abortion and women's health: A turning point for America?* New York: The Alan Guttmacher Institute.

Gordon, L. (2002). *The moral property of women: A history of birth control politics in America.* Urbana, IL: University of Illinois Press.

Grimes, D. A., & Stuart, G. (2010). Abortion jabberwocky: The need for better terminology. *Contraception, 82*(2), 93–6.

Griswold v. Connecticut, 381 U.S. 479 (1965).

Henshaw, S. K., Singh, S., & Haas, T. (1999). The incidence of abortion worldwide. *International Family Planning Perspectives, 25*(January), S30–S38.

Jones, R. K., Upadhyay, U. D., & Weitz, T. A. (2013). At what cost? Payment for abortion care by US women. *Women's Health Issues, 23*(3), 173–78.

Karrer, R. N. (2011). The national right to life committee: Its founding, its history, and the emergence of the pro-life movement prior to *Roe v. Wade*. *The Catholic Historical Review, 97*(3), 527–57.

Kevles, D. J. (2016). The history of eugenics. *Issues in Science and Technology, 32*. Retrieved January 15, 2017 from http://issues.org/32-3/the-history-of-eugenics/.

Lafer, J. & Richards, C. (2015). *Planned Parenthood, 2014–2015 Annual Report*. Planned Parenthood Federation of America. Retrieved January 15, 2017 from https://www.plannedparenthood.org/uploads/filer_public/71/63/71633f42-af81-43e2-90c3-2e5fff989c91/2014-2015_ppfa_annual_report_.pdf.

Laguens, D. (2013). Planned Parenthood and the next generation of feminist activists. *Feminist Studies, 39*(1), 187–91.

Masci, D. & Lupu, I. (2013, January 16). A history of key abortion rulings of the U.S. Supreme Court. *Legal Backgrounder*, Pew Research Center. Retrieved January 15, 2017 from http://www.pewforum.org/2013/01/16/a-history-of-key-abortion-rulings-of-the-us-supreme-court/.

O'Brien, G. V. (2013). Margaret Sanger and the Nazis: How many degrees of separation? *Social Work, 58*(3), 285–7.

Palencia, K. (1980). *Harris v. McRae*: Indigent women must bear the consequences of the Hyde Amendment. *Loyola University of Chicago Law Journal, 12*, 255.

Prohibitions Regarding Human Fetal Tissue, 42 U.S.C. §289g-2 (1993).

Public Funding for Abortion. (2016). Retrieved January 15, 2017 from https://www.aclu.org/other/public-funding-abortion.

Planned Parenthood v. Casey, 505 U.S. 833 (1992).

Roe v. Wade, 410 U.S. 113 (1973).

Rosenthal, E. (2007, October 12). Legal or not, abortion rates compare. *The New York Times*. Retrieved January 15, 2017 from http://www.nytimes.com/2007/10/12/world/12abortion.html.

Rosoff, J. L. (1980). The Hyde Amendment and the future. *Family Planning Perspectives, 12*(4), 172.

Rovner, J. (2017, January 15). That vow to defund Planned Parenthood: Easy to say, hard to do. Retrieved January 15, 2017 from http://www.npr.org/sections/health-shots/2017/01/15/509662288/that-vow-to-defund-planned-parenthood-easy-to-say-hard-to-do.

Salganicoff, A., Sobel, L., Kurani, N., & Gomez, I. (2016, January 20). Coverage for abortion services in Medicaid, marketplace plans and private plans. Retrieved January 15, 2017 from http://kff.org/womens-health-policy/issue-brief/coverage-for-abortion-services-in-medicaid-marketplace-plans-and-private-plans/.

Schneider, A. & Ingram, H. (1993). Social construction of target populations: Implications for politics and policy. *The American Political Science Review*, *87*(2), 334–47.

Stevenson, J., Flores-Vazquez, I. M., Allgeyer, R. L., Schenkkan, P., & Potter, J. E. (2016, March 3). Effect of removal of Planned Parenthood from the Texas Women's Health Program. *New England Journal of Medicine, 374*, 853–86.

Tersigni, J. M. (1998). Putting all our eggs in one basket: Political strategies of Planned Parenthood and the need for multi-dimensional advocacy (unpublished master's thesis). University of Arizona. Retrieved January 15, 2017 from http://arizona.openrepository.com/arizona/handle/10150/278653.

The Mexico City Policy: An Explainer. (2017, January 23). Kaiser Family Foundation. Retrieved January 15, 2017 from http://kff.org/global-health-policy/fact-sheet/mexico-city-policy-explainer/.

Thompson, K. M. J. (2013). A brief history of birth control. *Our Bodies, Ourselves*. Retrieved January 15, 2017 from http://www.ourbodiesourselves.org/health-info/a-brief-history-of-birth-control/.

Turner, O. G., & Balch, M. S. (2014). Defending the pro-life position & framing the issue by the language we use. National Right to Life Committee, Inc. Retrieved January 15, 2017 from http://www.nrlc.org/uploads/WhenTheySay Packet.pdf.

Walters, J. (2016, December 25). Progressive causes see "unprecedented" upswing in donations after US elections. Retrieved January 15, 2017 from https://www.theguardian.com/us-news/2016/dec/25/progressive-donations-us-election-planned-parenthood-aclu.

NOTE

1. Birth control organizations that focused on sharing information with women, including Sanger's pamphlet on methods of birth control, emerged a bit earlier. According to Gordon (2002), Agnes Inglis opened a "de facto" birth control clinic in Ann Arbor, Michigan prior to Sanger's clinic in Brooklyn. However, the latter is generally recognized as the first fully operational clinic.

3. Leadership and the Free the Nipple movement: An autoethnographic case study

James K. Beggan

My first thought in contemplating a chapter about sexual leaders was Alfred Kinsey, an unexpected leader given his rather dry scholarly background, even by the standards of academic disciplines (Bullough, 1998). His initial claim to fame was as an expert on the behavior of gall wasps. He operated out of a place that would not have been anticipated to become a powerhouse of sex research: Indiana University in Bloomington.

As I reflected on the other chapters in the current book, I realized that the individual leaders we identified were already well established, with the formative years of their guiding roles behind them. We had heroic leaders who had gone on epic journeys of transformation in the process of becoming leaders—Hugh Hefner of *Playboy* magazine and Margaret Sanger of Planned Parenthood came to mind. We had leaders who were brought down by their own sexuality—Jerry Sandusky of Penn State and Bill Clinton were representative. Other chapters were less about specific leaders than about the institutions that lead us, such as the matter of clergy who may need training to act as sex counselors, or the issue of the state of the legal system with regard to protecting the rights of certain groups, such as gay men and women.

The sexual leader on whom I finally decided was someone in the early stages of her heroic journey. I also wanted to pick a topic that was more removed from the academic realm. Kinsey's strategy was to collect scientific data about human sexual behavior. His presumed goal was to catalog and understand rather than to enact change, although he ultimately did alter people's views about their and others' sexuality. In contrast, the Free the Nipple movement was not so much geared toward assessing women's experiences regarding how or why their breasts are treated differently than men's as it was about confronting and erasing a double standard related to their treatment. It was an advocacy-based phenomenon. Moreover, as noted by O'Toole (2016, p. 48), "There is a significant gap in research about the 'Free the Nipple' movement."

My experience with Free the Nipple began when I watched the film of the same name. The 2014 movie was directed by Lina Esco, who also cowrote and starred in it. The relationship between the film and the social movement is somewhat confusing. Although at first pass it might be expected that the film is a documentary about the social movement, in reality the movement was started by the director in response to film distributors' unwillingness to screen the movie. The film itself is a work of fiction (Terrill, 2014).

The lead character, a wannabe writer in New York City who goes by the odd name of "With," becomes a key player in a social movement to defend women's right to be topless, even though she herself is very conscious about her body. In the resolution to the story, she becomes liberated enough to participate in the events she is helping to organize. A key element to the plot is the relationship between the women formulating the movement and the New York City police. The police are presented as villains because despite the fact that it is legal for women to be topless in New York, they insist on arresting the women for exercising their legal rights.

My reasons for watching the film were mundane. It was available free on Netflix, and I found its provocative title to be amusing and, no pun intended, titillating. My own opinion was that it was mildly funny, there was a surprising lack of nudity for a film about the importance of going topless, and the script was somewhat clichéd. According to Rotten Tomatoes, the film was poorly received by both critics (2.8/10) and the viewing public (2.5/5). Part of the problem with the film is that it contains several muddled, self-contradicting elements. For example, despite being a film about women's right to go topless, in the opening of the film, when a group of women run topless through New York City, their bare breasts are pixelated, sending a confusing message: if female nudity is OK, then why are these women's breasts being obscured in a movie about women's right to go topless? Another unfortunate plot element is that in the early stages of the main characters' efforts to set up the "Free the Nipple" movement, they rely on assistance from older, male mentors. In a scene where they compile a list of wealthy and/or famous people who might be willing to help them, the list includes Larry Flynt (curiously, spelled incorrectly in the film as Larry Flint) and Hugh Hefner, publishers of *Hustler* and *Playboy*, respectively—both magazines that have been criticized by feminists for literally decades. When they eventually hire a lawyer to help them fight the police, it turns out to be a man. Would no women attorneys in New York be willing and able to take the case? Other elements of the story seem either naïve or examples of poor storytelling. After the main character is fired from her job, she conveniently receives a check in the mail for $5,000—a (rather generous) severance package, which she uses to pay off her back rent and to start funding the Free the Nipple campaign.

THE FREE THE NIPPLE MARCH IN LOUISVILLE

My next connection to the Free the Nipple campaign was at a more local level. Oddly, I cannot recall exactly how I found out that there was going to be a Free the Nipple march organized in Louisville, KY, starting in a park a mere four miles from my house. Was it from a friend? The newspaper? A Facebook link?

The march was set for Saturday September 5, 2015, at 11am. I was curious to attend for several reasons. The first was a voyeuristic desire to see if such an event would actually materialize in the relatively sedate city of Louisville. Was the whole thing a joke? Would women assemble in the park, actually take off their tops, and march through an area of the city called the Highlands? Or would the protest actually be composed of a bunch of men waiting for these women to appear? The Highlands area of the city was probably the best place to stage an event like a Free the Nipple march. Louisville, the largest city in Kentucky, is relatively liberal compared to the rest of the state. In the most recent presidential election, it was an island of blue in a sea of red. The Highlands area of the city is probably a more liberal area than the city as a whole, home to a lot of hipsters who favor coffee shops, microbreweries, consignment shops, and independently owned restaurants.

Another element of the event that made it notable, and a second reason why I was interested, was that it was started by someone unexpected. It was created by an 18-year-old student named Nan, who attended a private high school described on its website as "independent, non-denominational, progressive." Press coverage quoted her saying: "It started out as kind of a joke, with my friends, like, 'Oh, my gosh, we should do this,' and I recently started taking a gender class at my high school and thought I could really do this" (Bowden, 2015).

The third reason why I found the march interesting was that as someone who taught human sexuality, I thought it was an event I should know about, if only so that I could speak knowledgably about it in class. The final reason invoked the trendy abbreviation FOMO, the fear of missing out. If this happened, and I did not attend, would I forever regret not being there—if only so that I could say that I had been there?

When I told my girlfriend about it, she said she was interested in attending as well. I was glad she wanted to go, because I felt that having her with me sent a message that I was not there for the wrong reasons. My instinct was that "the wrong reasons" would involve being perceived to be attending the march only out of the voyeuristic desire to see topless women, as an expression of prurient interest.

PICKING A RESEARCH STRATEGY

Ethnomethodologists challenge assumptions about the meaning of social life (Garfinkel, 1967, 1996) by creating a breach—a trigger event that conflicts with the norms operating in society—and then observing reactions to it. In the case of the Free the Nipple movement, the breaching event is the appearance of a topless woman. In a sense, then, the Free the Nipple movement can be viewed as a sociologically based applied research experiment.

We could look to the effects of the breaching event on observers as well as on the woman who creates the breach. How do the women who take off their tops feel as a result of the experience? Prior to the act, what are their thoughts and feelings about it? During the actual breaching event, what are their reactions? Finally, in the aftermath of the event, how do they feel? Do women who participated in the march feel better, worse, or the same about themselves and about society in general? Another way to focus on the problem was with regard to observers of the march. How do people feel about seeing a large group of women walk topless past them on city streets? Does the march actually lead to a change in attitudes? Are men and women differentially affected? If there are effects, are they lasting or ephemeral (Hill, Lo, Vavreck, & Zaller, 2013)?

One criticism of the Free the Nipple movement is that its influence-method panders to the interests of men. Do the men (or women, even) who observe a Free the Nipple event actually internalize a message about equality, or does the vivid instance of female nudity supplant any possible attitude change?

One limitation that I have as a researcher is that, being male, I cannot fully participate in the movement, because the meaning of my being topless is very different than the meaning associated with a woman baring her breasts. One way around this would be to interview participants more legitimately tied to the movement; that is, women. But there is a pragmatic problem with this strategy: how would I find the women who took part in the march more than a year after it took place? Similarly, how do I obtain a sample of people who were at the event?

Another technique, and the one that I adopted—partly out of necessity—was to use a research strategy known as autoethnography (Ellis & Bochner, 2000). In research using this method, the researcher focuses on his or her own experiences to hopefully shed light on some larger social or psychological process. As a white, middle-aged male, I would not be subject to the same restrictions on my appearance as women. However, in this rare instance, my apparent privilege actually provided me with an outsider status that might allow me to comment on the Free the Nipple movement in ways that women could not. My self-observations were intended to open up conversations and stimulate emotional and intellectual responses in readers—the goal of evocative ethnography.

In summary, then, I decided to integrate two qualitative approaches to research—ethnomethodology and autoethnography—to focus on a problem that, to a large degree, excludes me due to my social status. One irony that needs to be acknowledged is that this approach can be viewed as either novel, resourceful, and perhaps somewhat insightful, or as yet another instance of the operation of hegemonic masculinity, in that I have taken a movement that is geared toward meeting the needs of a group against which I am an outgroup member (a man considering a problem that is situated in being a woman) and made it about myself, a member and beneficiary of hegemonic masculinity. It is possible that by acknowledging this conflict, I have reduced its relevance. It can also be argued that by "hanging a lantern on it," I have created the illusion of resolving it as a problem.

ON THE SCENE

The rendezvous point for the beginning of the march was Willow Park. It is a small triangular piece of land with a gazebo in its center and a playground at one end. I have a personal affinity for this park because during the summer months there is a Sunday evening concert there that I like to attend. The bands play in the gazebo and people sit in lawn chairs on the grass and dance on a concrete area in front of the gazebo. It was odd to think about Willow Park filled with topless women, if it should even happen.

Perhaps because of a fear of missing out, we arrived well before 11am, the posted start time for the event. It was warm and sunny, a perfect day to be topless in Louisville. There were not that many people there. There were a number of young women. It seemed as if one in particular was the busiest. She was wearing a blue sleeveless shirt and gray skirt. I assumed—correctly, as it turned out—she was the organizer, Nan. In addition to clusters of women who seemed occupied with getting ready for the march, there were a number of older men hanging out, many of whom were overweight, and several of whom had expensive-looking cameras. The men tended to be located on the periphery of the park.

Is the demographic for a Free the Nipple rally young women and older men? I realized with some embarrassment and amusement that this is the same demographic an observer might encounter in a strip club.

There were also what appeared to be several legitimate journalists. One man handed Nan a microphone and filmed her talking to the camera. He was notable for the size of his camera as well as the media pass hanging from the strap of his camera bag. Shortly after, Nan was approached by a woman holding a small audio recorder and they also did an interview. Later, Nan was interviewed by a woman who represented the local affiliates of the national television networks.

Several friends of Nan, who also appeared to be about 18 years old, had set up a table labeled "Free the Nipple Social Media Campaign and Info Table." One friend held a sign over her head that read "Come make your free the nipple poster here." The organizers were definitely media-savvy. The signs they were producing were being put to good use. There was a woman with a nose piercing and a tattooed arm, holding a baby in a harness and carrying a sign that read: "I need #freethenipple because my child should be able to eat wherever she is hungry." Another woman held a sign that said "I support #freethenipple because I want a world where my daughters can FEEL FREE to be their beautiful selves without FEAR of being RAPED." I noted that one aspect of the Free the Nipple concept is that it may draw members with very different points of view. As those two posters indicated, people were attending because of issues related to supporting breastfeeding as well as the censure of violence against women.

About ten minutes before the march was set to begin, Nan stepped into the gazebo in the park. Next to her were three women, all holding supportive signs. By now, there were several hundred people in the audience. Nan began her speech, and then came the moment everyone had been waiting for. She began to take off her top. She removed it in a manner that surprised me. Rather than pull it off, she pulled it down and left it wrapped around her waist, like a belt. Topless, she said, "In New York, this is legal. In Kentucky, this is legal," and received a round of cheers and applause. She added:

This is not a protest, this is a promotion ... of the understanding, the acceptance, and the personal acceptance of women's bodies ... We are not here to change laws, we are here to change minds. I want this campaign to be the safest and the most comfortable it can be for women who are here and the supporters who are here.

I was incredibly impressed by her performance. She sounded calm, confident, and articulate. I wondered how much she had rehearsed her speech. Given that I am a professor and have lectured for more than 30 years, I am confident that I could give a speech in front of a few hundred people. I am not sure how I would feel about doing it without my shirt on, even as a male. And I am certain I would not have been able to do it at the age of 18, regardless of how conservatively I was dressed.

By an odd coincidence, a woman in the audience recognized me and told me she had attended one of my courses several years ago. She had become a lawyer and, recently, a mother. She was also in a polyamorous relationship with two men. She introduced me to one of the men with whom she was involved (not the biological father of her child). I introduced her to my girlfriend.

All of us agreed that Nan was very impressive and would go far in whatever profession she chose (I was thinking political activist or attorney). It seemed as if Nan was operating as a transformational leader (Goethals & Allison, 2012), that is, someone who was trying to transform society. Although a transformational leader can be effective, one limitation is that without that leader's presence, the movement may falter. Part of Nan's effectiveness as an influence agent may have been due to her youth making her accomplishments seem all that more impressive.

The march actually began about five minutes early. People showed their support for "Free the Nipple" in varying degrees. Clearly, the most direct method was to be a woman who removed her top. But other women went on the march, either fully clothed or wearing a bra or pasties or tape over their nipples. Men showed their support by marching beside the women, either fully clothed, shirtless, or with tape covering their nipples. One of the more curious forms of protest was that of the women who wore bras but put tape across the nipple area. The taped nipples were most likely a homage to the Free the Nipple movie, as the poster for the movie shows a woman's nude breasts with black tape obscuring the nipples in an "X" pattern.

Women who protested with their shirts on and men who protested with their shirts off represented a curious anomaly in that they conformed to the standards of society, regardless of their presence in the walk. They literally talked the talk but did not walk the walk. Did they support the movement by their very presence, or did they undermine it by their failure to fully commit to the ethnomethodological method of promoting change? But it was not clear how the behavior represented a protest or legitimate sacrifice, given that they exposed nothing private about themselves. The inherent philosophy of broad acceptance would not, of course, allow any of the protesters to publically criticize anyone who chose not to remove their tops.

My girlfriend and I maintained our academic distance. We remained clothed but, at the same time, told ourselves we were in support of the movement and also attending for the intellectual reason of documenting the events.

I had another chance encounter that was noteworthy. I knew a woman from dancing who was quite modest and also quite religious. I saw her sister—whom I also knew from dancing—at the rally. This sister, an artist, was much more liberal and had taken off her top in support of the movement. Was it weird to see someone I knew from the "real world" at this unusual event?

It was weird, but the question was why. One reason was the nature of the topless breach. Although it took place in a discrete place and time, it had implications for the future. When I saw this woman a day, a week, or a month from now, should I acknowledge our mutual presence at Free the Nipple? Another reason was that it had implications not only for the topless woman that I saw but also for other people that we knew, and for my interactions with those people. Should I tell my conservative friend, "Oh, I saw your sister's breasts yesterday"? Or should I keep it a secret? The debate as to whether to tell or not tell drew my attention and made me aware of the odd conventions of our society. In light of the underlying norms of our breast-loving but also breast-fearing culture, I recognize that if I had seen my conservative friend's brother at a beach or even topless in the park, I doubt I would think twice about mentioning it to her. Given this reasoning and the experience of self-consciousness, I could argue that the Free the Nipple methodology was effective as a social movement.

A TOPLESS WOMAN VS. TOPLESS WOMEN

One of the stated goals of the organizers of the Louisville Free the Nipple march was to normalize women's breasts. In an interview about the march, Nan said:

> What we're trying to do is desexualize women's bodies by desensitizing people to the female body, especially the top ... And the point is that hyper-sexualization of women's bodies gives people the excuse to shun

women who are breastfeeding, using breasts for their biological purpose, and
it gives an excuse to slut shame and victim blame. (WDRB, 2015)

This quote identifies a number of lofty positive outcomes expected from
the normalization hoped to result from the march. One is to desexualize
the female breast, another is to legitimize breastfeeding, and a third is to
repudiate negative views of women. Taken together, the act of baring the
breast is thought to have a number of important consequences, such as
promoting equality between men and women; challenging the unrealistic
expectations that both men and women possess about women's bodies,
developed through the representation of women in mass media; and also
repudiating rape culture and other forms of implicit or explicit violence
committed against women, including more opaque processes such as
victim blaming.

Can an event like a Free the Nipple march accomplish all this? From
an ethnomethodological perspective, going topless is a breaching event
that is meant to challenge our assumptions, encourage rethinking of our
world view, and lead to benevolent social change. The influence tactic of
the Free the Nipple movement is a version of immersion therapy. Does a
major dose of female toplessness serve to contradict years of socialization in a society that treats women's and men's bodies very differently?

I thought about the anticipated but amusing awkwardness of telling my
religious friend I had seen her sister's radical breasts. The fact that I
ruminated on it may speak to the possible influence of an act such as a
topless march: even if it seems a little odd at the time, or perhaps even
sexually provocative, can it have a longer-term, more subtle influence on
the way we think about female nudity? In a way, then, is an event like
Free the Nipple an inoculation that might ameliorate the future influence
of sexist thought?

Even without knowing the meaning of the word *ethnomethodology*,
this argument has a certain logic, but it is an open question as to whether
this line of reasoning, which makes intuitive sense, will actually operate
in the manner hypothesized. This is where my background as a
researcher might conflict with the opinions of activists. During the march
and afterward, I was quick to think: "Yes, but, is this the effect that will
occur? How do we prove it?" Even if there is an effect, the next question
has to do with why the effect is occurring.

Who is being affected by the march? It is people who are actually
marching—the topless women—or is it the observers, or is it both? Does
the act of marching topless have an effect on the women who do the
marching? It is a classic idea in social psychology that when people work
hard to achieve a goal, they come to value the goal more (Axsom &

Cooper, 1985). This *effort justification* paradigm can be viewed in terms of a hazing process. The act of taking off one's top is a challenge for the women. Do they value the Free the Nipple campaign more because of this? Do they change as a result of this action? If they do change, how do they change? Does the Free the Nipple march have an effect on the people watching? Does seeing so many topless women cause the observers to rethink the meaning of female nudity? Are men and women affected to the same degree?

An inherent contradiction in the guerrilla technique of going topless *en masse* is that this does not represent the "normal" way in which women's breasts would be displayed in a society more tolerant of women's bodies, or more egalitarian in general. By means of a contrasting thought experiment, imagine the effect of 50 or 100 men walking topless down a busy city street carrying signs. Regardless of what the signs said, the men would draw attention because toplessness—either male or female—is not really considered normative on city streets.

WHAT IS THE ROLE OF MEN IN THE FREE THE NIPPLE CAMPAIGN?

In writing this chapter, I used Facebook as a data source and looked for posts related to the Free the Nipple march. Three posts from two Facebook friends—both women—popped up. On September 4, the day before the event, one of my friends posted, "Well, I know where all the guys will be gathering tomorrow." After the event, she posted: "Haha!! More pervert men showed up than women for the Free the Nipples (sic) March!" A different friend posted, "This was awesome! Over 400 people came out! There were obviously some perverts, but the supporters outnumbered them."

A woman on Facebook with whom I am not friends posted: "All the damn gross creepers lurkin (sic) on the free the nipple protest AFFIRM the reason for the protest in the first place ... I'm specifically referring to those with creepy intentions." A man, also not a friend, commenting on whether it was surprising that creepy men were there, responded: "Cishet men are actual garbage so not really."

My first thought had to do with the hypocrisy of the posts. The posters are quick to judge, but the posts themselves invoke stereotypes and the comment "cishet men are actual garbage" might even cross the line into hate speech. On the other hand, there were many men there with cameras, taking probably hundreds of pictures, so there is perhaps a grain of truth to what the posters argue. But these posts illustrated the dilemma that the Free the Nipple social protest creates for men. If a man supports the movement by showing up, it appears there is a tendency to assume he is motivated by a dark intention (creepy). This derogatory interpretation is intensified by the apparent fact that he is heterosexual as well as comfortable with the idea that his biological sex matches his gender identity. Does being in the company of a woman, which I thought would help my cause, appear to hurt it in the eyes of some?

My second thought is that being a participant in the Free the Nipple march forces me to engage in a great deal of reflexive self-attention. I am supportive of the movement, but more importantly, I recognize that I also need to *appear* supportive of the movement. To gaze overly long (however that amount of time should be operationalized) opens me up to the accusation of being "creepy" or even "actual garbage"—appellations that I would rather avoid—merely because I am heterosexual and I am male. Both of these attributes make me a part of the problem in the eyes of at least some of the women here (and perhaps men, even heterosexual men, as well).

Given the relative rarity of topless women in normal, everyday conversation, the nude female breast is an aspect that draws the eye. I need to resist the urge to look, but, given our societal norm to hide the breast—specifically the nipple—not looking requires a serious bit of attention. Given the novelty of seeing so many topless women, I must practice what Goffman termed *civil inattention* (Hirschauer, 2005), the rule that in a brief encounter people give enough attention to each other to acknowledge their respective presence but not enough to become intrusive. To appear on board with the cause of Free the Nipple, I must work to modulate the amount of attention that I provide, even though in this unique circumstance, I am tempted to look more than I should. In a sense, then, my behavior becomes inauthentic because my motivation to appear sympathetic motivates me to engage in impression management to overrule my natural behavior.

The dilemma in seeking to appear to be supportive of the Free the Nipple cause is further compounded for me by the belief that some of the sentiments expressed by the signs carried by protesters, or their published statements in newspaper articles, do not hold up to rigorous academic scrutiny. If I point out the apparent inconsistency between the sentiment and current research, does that label me as a troublemaker? Am I marked as being antithetical to the cause if I am intellectually honest?

The most prominent example of the conflict between the rhetoric of Free the Nipple and scientific data has to do with the association between women's breasts and sexuality. Statements on placards included "These are not for you" or "Breasts are not a sexual organ." However, there is research indicating that belief is factually incorrect (Møller, Soler, & Thornhill, 1995). Although breasts clearly have the function of providing milk for children, it has been argued that they also serve as a means of sexual attraction. *Sexual selection* refers to the idea that if a potential sex partner prefers a trait, then individuals with this trait will receive preferential treatment with regard to mating opportunities (Buss & Schmitt, 1993). With regard to breasts, then, if men prefer women with larger breasts, then women with larger breasts will have more mating opportunities, and these women will then pass on the trait of possessing larger breasts.

One of the intriguing aspects of human females, as opposed to other primates, is that women accumulate significant amounts of adipose fat in their breasts. One explanation is that the excess fat serves as a cue to reproductive fitness. More fat would indicate greater health and energy reserves, and therefore a better chance of successfully nursing children. To the extent that men use the size of women's breasts as even an unconscious cue to desirability, this indicates that breasts are in fact for them, at least in part.

Similarly, the organizers express the sentiment that the Free the Nipple movement is geared toward ending the sexualization of women's breasts. Other statements or placards refer to "hypersexualization." Using the sexual selection argument as the basis, it seems incorrect to argue that breasts should not be sexualized. I agree, though, that hypersexualization would refer to investing them with a greater level of sexualization than is warranted.

Ideas about breasts as a sexual cue, rather than solely as a source of nourishment, and the distinction between sexualization and hyper-sexualization are not unique to me. I did not invent them, and I know that many women psychologists, sociologists, and historians would be as familiar with them as I am, if not more so. But I am self-consciously aware that if I voice these disagreements, then my criticisms may either be ignored as the protests of a representative of masculine oppression or I may be psychologically disinvited from the positive collective identity created by the mutual act of many women simultaneously taking the social risk of going topless.

CONTINUING THE MOVEMENT

There was press coverage before and after the first Free the Nipple march. Many people joined the Facebook page for the Louisville chapter of the Free the Nipple movement. Shortly after the success of the first march, the organizers created another event in a different part of the city (a kind of top-optional picnic) with grilled food and cornhole (a local game that involves throwing beanbags through a target).

I went to the event but it was lightly attended. The organizers explained the poor showing in terms of bureaucratic red tape. From what I could understand, there were different standards for a permit depending on the way the event was advertised, and the cost of a permit for a well-advertised event was beyond the budget of the organizers. The lower level of advance word yielded a poorer turnout. In all, there were about a dozen people who attended. I attended, with my normalizing girlfriend for company. Neither of us removed our tops, though the organizers did. From an ethnomethodological perspective, the high point of the afternoon was playing cornhole with two topless women.

On February 1, 2016, there was a Q&A at the main branch of the Louisville public library. This event appealed to me because I viewed it as a chance to talk about the ideas that formed the foundation for the Free the Nipple movement. The event was poorly attended and I found that people were unwilling to consider ideas that deviated from the ideological perspective they chose to advance through the Free the Nipple movement. I became unpopular for a time because I was arguing that in advancing the cause of Free the Nipple it was important that advocates not trounce on the feelings of those who felt it was inappropriate for women to bare their breasts in public places. The dominant response to my expressed reservations was that those who were not on board with the Free the Nipple movement should *get over it* and abandon their inhibitions. In other words, feeling they were morally correct gave them liberty to dismiss the protests of those who disagreed.

A second Free the Nipple march in Louisville took place on Sunday August 14, 2016, about a year after the first one. The event started in the same park. The route taken was along the same major road but going in the opposite direction. The biggest notable difference was the much smaller crowd in attendance. The other major difference was the total absence of media. In a group picture that was taken after the walk, there were only about 25 people in the photograph. In contrast, pictures and media reports from the first walk suggest several hundred people attended.

WAS THE FREE THE NIPPLE MARCH A SUCCESS?

Deciding whether the Louisville Free the Nipple march was a success depends, like many things, on how we want to define success. In terms of publicity and numbers in attendance, the first Louisville march was very successful. Using those same criteria, the second march was a minor success. The events that took place between those two marches were failures. The picnic and the planning meeting were poorly attended and did not create traction or buzz for future events. Will there be a third march? I doubt it. Since the success of the first march, Nan had graduated from high school and moved out of state to attend college. When I contacted her about working with me on a paper about her experiences organizing the Louisville Free the Nipple campaign, she declined and stated that while she felt she had learned a lot from her experiences, she was content to leave the Free the Nipple movement in the past.

The absence of media was surprising. There was a police presence and of course many onlookers. Did the organizers drop the ball and forget to alert the media? Or were media outlets uninterested: "we covered it once, why cover it again?"

Charting the varying degrees of success of different aspects of the Free the Nipple movement in Louisville acts as a measure of the difficulty that activists face in actually producing real social change. No one has stepped up to fill the void with regard to leadership. One woman who was somewhat involved with the movement tried without much success to plan marches, but some of her organizational choices seemed ineffective. For example, she tried to have a march in downtown Louisville the same day as the opening ceremonies for the Kentucky Derby. These ceremonies take the form of an airshow and other daytime events and culminate in a giant night-time fireworks display that basically shuts down the city for hours. Needless to say, no one was really willing to attend the march. Despite this woman's good intentions, she did not seem able to organize effectively. The Facebook page for the Kentucky chapter for Free the Nipple has very little activity. There have been one or two posts about marches in other cities or suggestions that have one or two supporters.

One problem that I experienced as a participant-observer during the marches and afterward was that there was not as much critical thinking about the movement as I would have liked. There was little talk about the origins of the double standard for male and female nudity, except perhaps some generic feminist thought related to oppression and patriarchy. In a famous article about how to generate ideas for research, the psychologist William McGuire (1973) said, "The opposite of a great truth is also true" (p. 455). My sense is that questioning the basic tenets of the march would not have gone over well, even if presented as a hypothetical: Are there conditions when a double standard should exist between men and women? Are there reasons why women should not display their breasts? Are there aesthetic or functional differences between men's and women's breasts that should require them to be treated differently?

One limitation of the Free the Nipple movement is that it can be viewed as lacking internal, ideological consistency. During her speech prior to beginning the march, Nan stated: "If we called this an equality campaign or a women's campaign, we would not have gotten press, we would not have gotten people to be here." This statement creates an ideologically dire situation because it acknowledges that women's top-lessness is an influence strategy intentionally adopted to maximize attention from mass media as well as a broader audience. To an extent, then, women are using their breasts as a means of gaining attention. Are they exploiting themselves? Is such a thing possible? In a sense, they are pandering to the desires of the (male) crowd. Underlying this strategy is the belief that by getting everyone's attention they can then enact change. In other words, the ends justify the means.

In the movie *Free the Nipple*, the antagonist was the generalized belief that it is somehow wrong for women to be topless in public. In terms of the goal of creating a tangible villain, the New York City police force represented the power standing in the way of the Free the Nipple movement because they arrested topless women despite nudity (above the waist) being legal for both men and women. In the public demonstration that occurred in Louisville, however, the police transformed—from malevolent law enforcers (ironically, wrongly enforcing a nonexistent law) interfering with free expression, to benevolent protectors. In the Louisville march, not only did the police not arrest topless women but they actually marched along with them (fully clothed, of course), acting as their protectors. By accepting the assistance of the police and displaying gratitude for it, the Free the Nipple members allowed them-selves to be co-opted by the patriarchal characteristics of the mainstream.

Another limitation is that the Free the Nipple constituency who participated in the Louisville marches, although possessing ideological commitment to the basic precepts of the cause, lacked the willingness to fully commit time and effort—perhaps a more valuable coin than simple agreement. Shortly after the march, the organizers created a Free the Nipple Facebook page which quickly attracted members. But after the giddy high of the march's success wore off, these members displayed little interest in the movement.

In an effort to create a chapter based on members' visions, for a period of time the organizers attempted to initiate debate by posting questions on the Facebook page. On December 7, 2015 (about three months after the success of the first march), a posted question asked, "In an effort to create a chapter based on member visions: What are your personal reasons for supporting Free the Nipple?" But there was little, if any, response to the questions and they quickly petered out.

As a case study, the Louisville Free the Nipple march in the summer of 2015 represented a peak event for the movement. It represented an instance in which a strong, transformational leader, assisted by a well-intentioned police force, sympathetic media, and cooperative weather, was able to elicit a surprisingly strong level of support for a social movement. Even with the same leader, the subsequent events were less attended and therefore less influential. The second march, which took place about a year after the first one, was a modest success. Despite the presence of cooperative weather and a well-intentioned police force, the media failed to appear. The crowd was smaller and, though dedicated, failed to have a noticeable influence subsequent to the actual march.

The Louisville Free the Nipple movement illustrates organizers' difficulty in creating longlasting social change. Even with a strong leader, a movement may fail to maintain traction, let alone grow in influence. This might be especially true with a movement along a dimension that has a sexual component. In the case of Free the Nipple, the act of demonstrating ideological commitment did not just unsettle observers, it also unsettled those who did the demonstrating. The Louisville Free the Nipple marches and the attenuated interest that followed after them highlight the work involved in changing people's attitudes, especially about potentially controversial subjects such as human sexuality. The history of the movement as discussed in the present chapter also serves as a means of recognizing the heroic efforts of those who have succeeded in creating permanent changes in our attitudes and behaviors about sexuality.

Attending the marches made me realize the difficulty inherent in attempting to use the methods of logical positivism to study movements geared toward social change (Wilkins, Tufte, & Obregon, 2014). How does a social scientist measure change? Even assuming that the Free the Nipple campaign was effective, the next question involved assessing why change was occurring. There can be many reasons why witnessing topless women might create a change in attitudes or beliefs about women's rights. It is the job of the social activist—in this case, a sexual leader—to work for change. It is the problem of the social scientist to document and understand the effects. But neither has an easy task.

REFERENCES

Axsom, D., & Cooper, J. (1985). Cognitive dissonance and psychotherapy: The role of effort justification in inducing weight loss. *Journal of Experimental Social Psychology*, *21*(2), 149–60.

Bowden, A. (2015, September 4). Free the Nipple walk to be held in Louisville. Retrieved May 29, 2017 from http://www.wlky.com/article/free-the-nipple-walk-to-be-held-in-louisville-1/3760492.

Bullough, V. L. (1998). Alfred Kinsey and the Kinsey Report: Historical overview and lasting contributions. *Journal of Sex Research*, *35*(2), 127–31.

Buss, D. M., & Schmitt, D. P. (1993). Sexual strategies theory: An evolutionary perspective on human mating. *Psychological Review*, *100*(2), 204–32.

Ellis, C., & Bochner, A. (2000). Autoethnography, personal narrative, reflexivity: Researcher as subject. In N. Denzin & Y. Lincoln (Eds.), *The Sage Handbook of Qualitative Research* (2nd ed.) (pp. 733–68). Thousand Oaks, CA: SAGE.

Garfinkel, H. (1967). *Studies in ethnomethodology*. Englewood Cliffs, NJ: Prentice-Hall.

Garfinkel, H. (1996). Ethnomethodology's program. *Social Psychology Quarterly*, *59*(1), 5–21.

Goethals, G. R., & Allison, S. T. (2012). Making heroes: The construction of courage, competence and virtue. *Advances in Experimental Social Psychology*, *46*, 183–235.

Hill, S. J., Lo, J., Vavreck, L., & Zaller, J. (2013). How quickly we forget: The duration of persuasion effects from mass communication. *Political Communication*, *30*(4), 521–47.

Hirschauer, S. (2005). On doing being a stranger: The practical constitution of civil inattention. *Journal for the Theory of Social Behaviour*, *35*(1), 41–67.

McGuire, W. J. (1973). The yin and yang of progress in social psychology: Seven koan. *Journal of Personality and Social Psychology*, *26*(3), 446–56.

Møller, A. P., Soler, M., & Thornhill, R. (1995). Breast asymmetry, sexual selection, and human reproductive success. *Ethology and Sociobiology*, *16*(3), 207–19.

O'Toole, A. M. (2016). Portrayals of gender in the media: A content analysis approach to identifying gender oppression and legitimation of patriarchy in magazine advertisements. *Theses, Dissertations and Capstones*. Paper 1008. Retrieved May 28, 2017 from http://mds.marshall.edu/cgi/viewcontent.cgi?article=2008&context=etd.

Terrill, A. (2014). Meet the women behind the #FreeTheNipple movement. *Elle*. Retrieved May 29, 2017 from http://www.elle.com/culture/career-politics/news/a15444/meet-the-women-behind-freethenipple-movement/

WDRB. (2015, September 6). Hundreds walk through the Highlands as part of "Free the Nipple" campaign. Retrieved May 29, 2017 from http://www.wdrb.com/story/29967618/hundreds-walk-through-the-highlands-as-part-of-free-the-nipple-campaign.

Wilkins, K. G., Tufte, T., & Obregon, R. (2014). *The handbook of development communication and social change*. Chichester: John Wiley & Sons.

PART II

Leadership and sexuality

4. A failure of courageous leadership: Sex, embarrassment, and (not) speaking up in the Penn State sexual abuse scandal

Jeremy Fyke, Bree Trisler, and Kristen Lucas

Late on a Friday night in the small town of State College, Pennsylvania, graduate assistant and former record-setting quarterback Michael McQueary clicked off the television set as the credits to the football movie Rudy *rolled. Unable to leave work behind him on the weekend during off-season, McQueary left his town-house to return to the football facilities on Penn State University's campus. As he approached the locker room door—the one he passed through far too many times to count—he instantly was alerted to the presence of other people by the sounds of running water and rhythmic, skin-on-skin slapping sounds.*

McQueary entered with caution and, using the reflection of the mirrors, looked into the showers. There he saw former defensive coordinator Jerry Sandusky with a boy, perhaps only 10 or 12 years old. Sandusky was directly behind the boy and the boy was up against the wall. Sandusky's arms were wrapped around the boy's midsection. It looked like the encounter was sexual in nature. But could it be? His eyes must have been betraying him. McQueary hastily opened his locker and then looked back again at the showers to make sure he saw what he thought he saw—this time without the mirror's reflection to trick him. Their position hadn't changed and he knew something was wrong. He had seen plenty of guys in a locker room shower before. As an athlete, he had been showering with other boys and men for the better part of his life. In fact, he had been showering in Penn State locker rooms for nearly a decade, first as a player and now as a staff member. But this was different.

He grabbed a pair of shoes from his locker and slammed the door to alert Sandusky of his presence. Sandusky came out of the shower and the two adult men looked at each other, but said nothing. Still frazzled, McQueary left the locker room—leaving the young boy with Sandusky—to retreat to his office and make a phone call to his parents, John and Anne McQueary.

In a quivering voice, McQueary spoke to his father: "I just saw something in the locker room." He took a few more deep breaths and continued, "I saw Coach Sandusky in the shower with a little boy. First, I heard it and I knew that

> *something was going wrong. And I followed—I looked—into the locker room and saw him there with a little boy. Dad, I need some advice."*

In the weeks that followed, the sexual assault that McQueary witnessed was reported to the most powerful men on Penn State's campus: head coach Joe Paterno, athletic director Timothy Curley, senior vice president of business and finance Gary Schultz, and university president Graham Spanier. The top leaders consulted with university legal experts. They contacted campus police—but only insofar as to determine if documentation existed on a 1998 investigation of Sandusky for the sexual assault of another boy. The only penalty they eventually levied on Sandusky was asking him not to invite "guests" into the Penn State football facilities. Sandusky retained his emeritus status at the university, his connections to the football program, his reputation and visibility within the community, and the keys to the locker room.

The incident seemed to be over. But then a decade later, in 2011, Sandusky faced a grand jury investigation and criminal prosecution. He ultimately was convicted of 45 counts of sexual abuse of young boys. Although Sandusky's abuse was widespread—ten victims, nearly 15 years, and multiple sites, including campus, home, and hotels—it was the shower incident witnessed by McQueary that took center stage. It was this incident, the reporting of it up the chain of command, and the ensuing (in)action on the part of organizational leaders that transformed the horrific crimes of an individual into an organizational scandal (Altheide & Johnson, 2012; Moushey & Dvorchak, 2012). Sanctions went to the very top, notably former president Graham Spanier's March 24, 2017 conviction for child endangerment as a result of his failure to stop the abuse (Bidgood & Pérez-Peña, 2017).

Popular and scholarly writing about the Penn State case has been abundant over the past several years. A "football first" culture, the market value of the Penn State program, the public relations implications, the university code of silence, veiled and euphemistic language, and failed leadership are all reasons cited for the decade-long cover-up of sexual abuse (Lucas & Fyke, 2014; Moushey & Dvorchak, 2012; Proffitt & Corrigan, 2012; Wolverton, 2012). In this chapter, we foreground the intersection of sexuality and leadership in the case; the sexual nature of the subject cannot be ignored, but nor can the inability to accurately communicate issues regarding sexuality that ultimately led to concealment and inaction. Indeed, it is well known that leaders went to great lengths to keep news of sexual abuse from reaching the public. To shed further light on the case, we draw from work on courage and courageous communication.

Courage seems an apt connection to the case, especially given the courage and bravery required to lead and compete at a high level on the football field—especially for a team as highly regarded and historically successful as Penn State's. However, when it came to protecting people—or the most vulnerable of them—off the field, leaders displayed a stunning lack of courage. The report of the internal investigation, the "Freeh Report," concluded that Penn State leaders actively chose to conceal the abuse for fear of bad publicity (Freeh, 2012). The decision to conceal was unethical—a popular conclusion in academic and popular circles—but even more so, it was cowardly. We demonstrate how the topic of sexuality—along with its taboos in workplaces generally, but especially within locker rooms, in athletics, and among authority figures—led to watered-down and vague conversations, thereby contributing to a lack of courage.

The Penn State scandal is an illustrative case study of the connection between leadership, sexuality, and courage for two reasons. First, leadership is ultimately about power and influence, and can be used for good or ill. Sandusky used his university access and privilege to lure young boys and ultimately satisfy his sexual desires. Second, because leaders are in such a position of authority, inherent in the job is addressing and responding to various situations in the workplace, including workplace sexual relationships and sexual harassment. Sexuality and sexual acts became front-and-center topics for the top leaders at Penn State, beginning with Joe Paterno, and going up the chain to Curley, Schultz, and Spanier. Leaders are called upon to respond courageously in many situations; in the Penn State case, the situation—and the victims— demanded courageous leadership. As the subject of sexuality is increasingly discussed on college campuses, within gender and sexuality studies courses, in response to sexual assault, and in efforts to promote gender equality, such a view of the case is critical.

We begin by briefly reviewing the literature on courage and courageous communication, and leadership and sexuality. Then, we offer a focal narrative from the case, reconstructed from grand jury testimony and the Freeh Report. This narrative offers the reader a first-hand look at the communication involved in the case. Furthermore, it provides the necessary background and context for analyzing the case. Following the narrative, we unpack the implications on courage, leadership, and sexuality.

COURAGE, COMMUNICATION, AND LEADERSHIP

Courage, also referred to as bravery, heroism, or toughness, is recognized as one of the cardinal virtues, along with prudence, temperance, and justice, and is one of Aristotle's golden means. Early on, influential philosophers such as Plato and Aristotle discussed courage as a virtue. They understood it as masculine and most appropriate in battle (Miller, 2000). In an organizational context, Fredric Jablin (2006), a leading organizational communication scholar, described courage as "a quality of outstanding leadership and followership, [which] appears essential for the vitality and regeneration of groups, organizations and communities, and has many linkages to communication studies" (pp. 99–100). Jablin lamented the lack of research on courage and courageous communication. In this chapter, we explore the cowardly actions contained within the "football first" culture at Penn State that perpetuated the years of sexual abuse endured by countless victims.

In his preliminary work, Jablin (2006) explored the connection between courage, communication, and leadership. This work is pertinent to the Penn State scandal because it relates to leaders taking action (or not) in response to specific situations. Jablin provided an extensive list of concepts that have a connection with courage that are germane but have received limited scholarly attention: motivation (behavior at work, commitment, leader–follower communication, etc.); whistleblowing; organizational socialization and assimilation processes; and emotion at work. Jablin noted the grounding of courage in philosophy (for example, as one of Aristotle's golden means; see also Miller, 2000) and especially in psychology.

In psychology, notions of moral courage are most relevant to our case. Jablin's (2006) original interest in courage arose because he saw it as related to motivation, although he never used the term "moral courage." Moral courage refers to doing what one knows is right in a given situation and having a clear sense of right and wrong, an overall understanding of the value of human beings, and a commitment to the common good (Miller, 2000). The basic idea is that individuals, from an early age, learn what is right and wrong, and to have mutual respect for one another. Hence, these conceptions of right and wrong and mutual respect may lead individuals to act courageously. Moreover, individuals displaying moral courage may be able to help society achieve a better understanding of how to live fruitfully in an ever changing society due to their commitment to the public good and their ability to confront "adaptive challenges" (Daloz et al., 1996, p. 5). In a business setting, adaptive challenges are those that involve a disparity between values and context; where values become the very thing that can be challenged in a given circumstance and, at the same time, the very thing that one must rely on above all else (Heifetz, 1994).

Daloz and colleagues (1996) argue that images from society and our experiences (for example, political and religious rhetoric, media and advertising) shape how we make sense of and act in situations. Thus, this perspective is akin to a social constructionist view whereby our world and thus our behaviors are constructed for us based on what we see and learn. Sheila McNamee (1998) explained that a social constructionist perspective in the context of the workplace foregrounds a relational rather than individual understanding of organizational life. Adding courage into the mix forces us to challenge our traditional understanding of courage as a value that is usually associated with individual acts. For example, we understand Rosa Parks' courageous act of declining to give up her seat on a bus to a white passenger as a profound, independent action that greatly influenced the civil rights movement. Using a term like "courage" connects us to a long tradition of trying to extract individual qualities that create a courageous person. Reinscribing the social construction of courage in the workplace from an individual to a relational notion allows an organization to consider its productivity and value as stemming from relationships within the workplace rather than individual, isolated acts. Therefore, an organization becomes a community that incorporates diverse ideas, goals, and practices (McNamee, 1998). In an organization, workplace culture, leadership, policies and procedures, and the ways in which decisions are made lay the groundwork for the norms of the future.

Elsewhere, in management studies, scholars realize the importance of courage as a trait of effective managers (DePree, 1997). Courage is something that leaders must be aware of in the twenty-first century, not only in terms of their behavior at work but also in their ability to encourage others in the workplace. For instance, prolific leadership scholar Warren Bennis (2003) claimed that courage may be the most important factor in the future of corporate America, to the extent that it might be best understood as the "X" factor, the sine qua non of leadership—like when an athletic program decides to fire a coach for transgressions despite his/her success.

Although courage is an important workplace virtue, the question remains: why might employees *not* display courage? In his seminal book on courage in the workplace, Hornstein (1986) offers many answers. First, he claims employees have learned that their own self-interest is better served when they keep their mouths shut rather than openly speaking out about their beliefs. Furthermore, he argues that many reasons account for employee silence and acquiescence, including threats of: being fired; zero or minimal pay increase; being burdened with assignments; poor performance evaluations; and being ostracized by important in-groups. Moreover, not only can these sanctions be handed down from management, but peers can also find ways of maintaining the status quo through attempts to ruin reputations, and by creating enough of a commotion where their boss thinks them unfit to manage the team.

Ultimately, Jablin (2006) argued that the communicative act of *speaking up* is at the very heart of being courageous. That is, even when a position is unpopular or when a disclosure carries with it uncertainty or risk, courageous organizational members find a way and a will to express ideas counter to the current consensus. Jablin also acknowledged the role of power within organizations; he maintained that leaders hold additional responsibilities for courageous communication by sharing stories and convictions that stimulate followers to act with courage, creating a cultural contagion of courage, and encouraging people to speak up, even in the face of risk.

In summary, courage in organizations is a tricky, but valuable, virtue and practice. Although research has noted various reasons why cowardice might be the norm rather than courage, we place sexuality front and center as a principal site where courage might be elusive. Indeed, while it is easy to encourage people to speak up no matter the potential repercussions, context and content matters; sexuality, for instance, complicates things, adding unique challenges for leaders.

SEXUALITY AND LEADERSHIP

The topic of sexuality in the workplace has occupied academics and practitioners for decades. Consider two factors. First, it is well known that humans spend the majority of their waking lives at work; for most, this amounts to more time spent at work than with family. Second, from a biological and evolutionary perspective, sex and sexuality are inherent to our being—about our innate drives, instincts, and desires—and are necessary for the continuation of society (Florence & Fortson, 2001). As Florence and Fortson note, sex is a particularly "stubborn" issue in the work context. Despite the precept that "you can't legislate morality," organizations have policies and procedures that try to. Indeed, the workplace is typically thought of, and in much academic scholarship—such as industrial/organizational psychology, organizational sociology, management, and industrial relations—talked about, as a rational, ordered place almost devoid of sexuality (Hearn & Parkin, 1995). Although the connection to leadership is often not explicitly addressed, one could argue that if something deals with sexuality in the workplace setting, it is inherently a leadership issue.

Although "nobody talks about sex in the boardroom," Kets de Vries (2015) argued that sexual dynamics and desires constantly hover above us like a cloud, unconsciously impacting our motivations and choices. To lead effectively, senior executives must manage this "sexual cloud." Kets de Vries explained that the best way to confront and manage these issues is to challenge deeply embedded assumptions about gender roles and expectations in the workplace. This research describes sexuality and leadership in organizations as most directly related to establishing and reinforcing gender roles, but this topic has been discussed in other ways as well.

Although the literature is relatively scant, one area of scholarship that has gained momentum in the past decade is workplace romances (WRs). Of central concern to leaders is the fact that motivations drive communication and performance issues in the workplace. Specifically, job-related WR motives are thought to hurt employee performance and negatively affect workplace culture (see Dillard et al., 1994). Simply put, employees' trust in coworkers is damaged when they see peers engaged in WRs, especially superior–subordinate relationships. Consequently, peers tend to be less honest and feel less solidarity with the coworkers they see in WRs. Thus, WRs can be a leadership problem if such relationships are damaging the organization at the cultural level—not to mention the potential legal ramifications. Indeed, Cowan and Horan (2014) urge managers to be aware of and monitor WRs for their impact on workplace culture.

Another popular stream of research, one with classic and contemporary examples, concerns analyses of gender and power (for reviews see Fyke, 2017a, 2017b). Relevant here is work from a social constructionist perspective that highlights how sexual harassment is context dependent, constituted through communication via specific relationships, workplace cultures, politics, and policies (Clair, 1993). Here, sexuality in the workplace is thus a dynamic interplay of "control, pleasure, resistance, and violence" (Ashcraft, Kuhn, & Cooren, 2009, p. 33). This social constructionist, communication-centered approach is important because it fully considers the social dynamics involved, recognizing that the way policies are written and framed, and the way things get talked about in official and everyday discourse, shapes how we react to sexuality and therefore to sexual harassment. In other words, we take cues from our environment as scripts for behavior and communication. Recall our earlier review of courage in organizations: we noted that we learn to act courageously (or not) in a similarly socially constructed way. Thus, if one works in an organization where sexual harassment (whether overt or more subtle) is normalized via everyday talk, then that becomes the standard for responding to such instances. Thus, *where* things take place matters, for locations carry their own cultural scripts and speech codes for communicating and responding. For instance, in a locker room, there are various rules for "not looking" and potentially "not talking."

Finally, leadership and sexuality has become a common topic lately in educational institutions, and for sports programs in particular. For instance, Title IX of the Educational Amendments of 1972, originally designed to prevent discrimination on the basis of sex, has been extended to include protections for men and women against sexual harassment, stalking, and sexual violence. Universities have paid particular attention to these issues of late, creating critical leadership positions to oversee enforcement of the policies; for instance, Title IX coordinators that serve in assistant dean roles. Recent, high-profile cases of rape and sexual assault at universities around the country have demanded increased attention. One highly publicized example has been named by the media "the Stanford rape case." In January 2015, a 23-year-old female, who was not a student at Stanford, visited the campus and attended a fraternity party with her sister. The assailant, 19-year-old freshman Brock Turner, was caught by witnesses attacking the unidentified victim, who was unconscious, behind a dumpster. The witnesses stopped Turner and called police. The especially brutal and callous assault gained a significant amount of attention after a judge sentenced Turner to a mere six months in jail for the assault. Many have argued that Turner was awarded a light sentence because he was a young, white male who was also a star swimmer for Stanford and a contender for the 2016 Olympics (Stack, 2016). Instances such as individuals lamenting Turner's loss of his swimming scholarship and his chances of swimming in the Olympics because of the assault, and Turner's father's complaint that his son's life was destroyed for "20 minutes of action" (Stack, 2016), invigorated conversations about the pervasiveness of campus rape culture (Beard, 2016; Powell, 2016).

As we have shown, courage, sexuality, leadership, and organizations go hand in hand. Indeed, in many ways the Penn State case became arguably *the* cautionary tale that put leadership and sexuality in the foreground of public consciousness. In the Jerry Sandusky/Penn State case, sexuality was front and center in the two ways reviewed at the outset: in Sandusky using his leadership power and access to lure young boys; and in the allegations leading to a leadership responsibility to respond. Furthermore, courage has many foundations, and has been talked about in management and business circles, albeit on a somewhat limited basis. However, despite the fact that courage may be the sine qua non of leadership, as Bennis (2003) claimed, it can be difficult to picture what its presence or absence might actually "look like" in practice. It has been recognized that courage is the "missing ingredient" in workplace behavior, especially in relation to ethics (Comer & Vega, 2011); here, however, we have taken a closer look at some of the dynamics that might lead to its absence.

We now pick up where we began in the introduction to this chapter, and offer a focal narrative as a case study to demonstrate what the communication sounded like in the Penn State case. Specifically, the focal narrative offers the reader a first-hand look at how sexuality, leadership, and courage intersected as the communication unfolded at Penn State. Overall, in line with the technique used in Bisel and Zanin (2016), the focal narrative invites the reader to "participate emotionally" with the various actors in the case. In order to create the narrative, we carefully read all the publicly available documents and built time-ordered display matrices that tracked all references to internal communication (for example, involving McQueary, Paterno, and Penn State leaders) about the shower assault (see Lucas & Fyke, 2014; Miles, Huberman, & Saldaña, 2014). From these matrices, we constructed a script of multi-day, multi-party conversation that includes McQueary, Paterno, Curley, Schultz, and Spanier. To the greatest extent possible, we included the words that were used by Penn State's leaders and altered only as much as was necessary to sustain context (for example, changing verb tense or substituting names/pronouns). When information about context was available, based on testimony, we filled that in (for example, information on McQueary's emotional state). We break the narrative down into a series of exchanges to help tell the story more coherently.

FOCAL NARRATIVE

EXCHANGE 1—MCQUEARY SPEAKS TO PATERNO

Saturday, February 10, 2001 (the morning after the shower assault)

Early the next morning [following the shower assault], *McQueary picked up his phone, took a deep breath, and dialed Coach Joe Paterno's number. After a couple rings, McQueary heard the familiar voice saying hello. He got straight to the point: "Coach, this Mike McQueary. I need to come to your house and talk to you about something." Paterno didn't want to interrupt his Saturday morning with some kid asking for a coaching job. So he gruffly replied, "I don't have a job for you. And if that's what it's about, don't bother coming over!"*

McQueary steeled himself and tried again. "Coach, it's about something much more serious. I need to come over and see you." There was something strange and urgent in McQueary's voice. Perhaps it really was serious. So Paterno relented. "Okay," he said, "Well, you better come over then."

McQueary wasted no time in getting to Paterno's house. He was invited in and the two men sat at the kitchen table. McQueary was visibly embarrassed and nervous. He had a hard time catching his breath. Paterno was growing anxious, too, wondering what was going to be revealed. "Mike, calm down. Just tell me what's going on."

McQueary started, "I went to the locker room last night. And when I got there, I saw Jerry with a young boy in the shower and it was way over the lines."

"In the shower? What do you mean?"

"Last night I saw Jerry with a young boy in the shower and it was really inappropriate. At first, I could hear them. But then I saw them. They were in the shower." McQueary was uncomfortable going into detail and using specific words in front of Joe Paterno, the man he had idolized his whole life. McQueary continued, "Coach, it was all just so upsetting. I was alerted and embarrassed, to be frank, when I heard them in there. And then when I saw them, I, I, I … It's just that you don't expect to see anything like that ever." Shocked and saddened by this revelation, Paterno slumped over at the table.

Paterno did not need the lurid details to understand what McQueary was telling him. "You don't have to tell me anything else. I understand," he said. "And I am just sorry you had to see that. It's terrible." He could see that McQueary was still upset and assured him again. "Mike, you did what was right. You told me." Paterno continued, "I need to think and tell some people about what you saw and I'll let you know what we'll do next."

EXCHANGE 2—PATERNO CONTACTS ATHLETIC DIRECTOR TIM CURLEY

Sunday, February 11, 2001

Paterno paced the floors. He was worried about how to handle the situation because Sandusky was no longer officially employed by Penn State and, therefore, he wasn't his boss anymore. What authority did he have? What responsibility did he have? What liability did he have? Paterno looked through Penn State's guidelines to see what he was supposed to do. The guidelines said he was supposed to call the Athletic Director, Tim Curley. So that is what he did.

Curley: Hello, Joe. What's the occasion for this Sunday morning phone call?
Paterno: We got a problem.
Curley: What's going on?
Paterno: Someone observed some behavior in the football locker room that was disturbing. One of our graduate assistants, Mike McQueary, went into the locker room on Friday evening. He heard and saw, I guess, two people in the shower—Jerry Sandusky and a boy—in the shower area. They were horsing around. I thought you should know.

EXCHANGE 3—CURLEY AND SCHULTZ HOLD "HEADS UP" MEETING WITH PRESIDENT GRAHAM SPANIER

Monday, February 12, 2001

Schultz:	Graham, thanks for meeting with us. There's something that happened in the football locker room that you should know about.
Curley:	We've received a report that a member of the athletic department staff had reported something to Joe Paterno. Joe passed that report on to us yesterday.
Spanier:	Go on.
Curley:	The report was that Jerry Sandusky was seen in an athletic locker room facility showering with one of his Second Mile kids, after a workout, and that they were "horsing around."
Spanier:	Horsing around?
Schultz:	Now, the graduate assistant didn't get a really good look at the scenario. He was around a corner and indirect. But he claims he heard them. And he also said he may have seen them kind of wrestling.
Spanier:	Are you sure that is how it was described to you, as horsing around?
Curley/Schultz:	Yes.
Spanier:	Are you sure that that is all that was reported?
Curley/Schultz:	Yes.
Spanier:	Good, good. But, guys, I'm just really uncomfortable with this situation.
Curley:	I agree. It's totally inappropriate.
Schultz:	Absolutely. I feel the same way, too. We have to make sure that this doesn't happen again.
Spanier:	In terms of moving forward, here's what we need to do. Tim, I need you to meet with Sandusky to tell him that he must never again bring his guests into the showers.
Curley:	Got it. I'll take care of that right away.
Spanier:	We should also inform the Second Mile president that we are directing Jerry accordingly. He should know that we do not wish Second Mile youth to be in our showers anymore.
Curley:	I'll take care of that detail, too.
Spanier:	Well, okay then. Thanks for the heads up. And keep me posted.

IMPLICATIONS: SEX, COURAGE, AND COWARDICE AT PENN STATE

From reading the narrative, it is apparent how sexuality became connected with leadership very quickly in the case. Sexuality and sexual acts became the content that demanded communication from all levels at Penn State, beginning with McQueary, since he was the first witness. Smith and Berg (1987) discuss the paradoxical nature of courage as a subset of the paradox of speaking, of having voice, in a group. Furthermore, Jablin (2006) has discussed courage as essentially a fight or flight response— speaking up or remaining silent. It takes courage to be engaged with a group; it takes courage to trust people enough to disclose in order to become close to the members of a group. Smith and Berg (1987) assert that it also takes courage to find one's own voice in a group, and especially to speak with personal authority in the face of organizational authority. However, finding one's voice can be especially difficult if organizations stifle courageous communication, leading to silence. We find, in fact, that when sexuality is the topic at hand, courage becomes especially tricky.

Although McQueary had institutional experience with Penn State, and would presumably feel comfortable speaking up, the sexual nature of the content of which he spoke stifled truly courageous communication. More importantly, it prevented courageous *action*. McQueary indicated that he took action to protect the child involved in the incident he witnessed by making his presence known so that the action would stop. He also spoke up to the head coach, Paterno, assuming action would be taken. However, McQueary did not move to physically and immediately protect the child by removing him from the situation. Furthermore, what McQueary reported to Paterno was stripped of "lurid" details because McQueary was uncomfortable, and Paterno could tell as much. Research has established that sexual topics are taboo (Lucas & Fyke, 2014; Trinch, 2001), and this case demonstrates that the taboo is intensified when communicating to someone of authority. In fact, Paterno stopped McQueary from giving the full details, which essentially functioned as a disguised retort to McQueary, giving the appearance of action (Lucas & Fyke, 2014): "you don't have to tell me anything else ... I need to think and tell some people about what you saw." Paterno even apologized, saying "I'm just so sorry you had to see that." Paterno essentially decreased his responsibility by refusing to learn the full, horrific details of the situation. As we will see later, this action also allowed Paterno to use language that did not capture the nature or extent of the incident (for example, "horsing around"), which had dire consequences for the way the situation was handled. Thus, as noted earlier, taboo is at play in a variety of instances of which leaders must be aware, from the way people talk about WRs (Cowan & Horan, 2014) to the devastating and silencing impact taboo can have in issues of sexual violence.

Here, we consider power dynamics in a speech situation, especially one of a sexual nature. As noted in the narrative, McQueary had idolized Paterno his whole life, so the speech situation was complicated by that fact alone. On top of that, Paterno was clearly a man of great power: he had coached at Penn State for 46 years and won more games than any other "major-college" football coach (Goldstein, 2012). So, the sexual nature of what would be communicated made the discussion especially difficult. In other words, McQueary likely struggled with how to talk about child rape with someone in great authority whom he looked up to and ultimately wanted to emulate. Thus, although it is recognized that it can be difficult to speak up to someone of higher authority, leaders must be extra cautious and seek clarity if the topic to be discussed is sexual in nature. Leaders must also be conscious that the dissenter is likely uncomfortable, and work to assure her/him that she/he is safe and will be encouraged to speak freely.

Although most courage work speaks to the dissenter or whistleblower as the one who acts/speaks courageously (Kohn, 2011), it might be the recipient of the news—the leader—who has the utmost responsibility. In fact, the very difference between dissenters and whistleblowers is instructive and significant (see Matt & Shahinpoor, 2011): dissenters are individuals who wish to remain inside an organization and hope to resolve matters internally; whistleblowers tend to go outside the organization to expose wrongdoing. Thus, leaders have the responsibility to act courageously to handle wrongdoing effectively and ethically when all eyes are on him/her. In short, courage is a two-way street that can lead to systems of detection and correction to prevent whistleblowing from happening in the first place.

However, despite McQueary's initial attempt to communicate (somewhat courageously) to Paterno, it is at this point that the fight seems to have changed to flight. In an interview, Coach Paterno explained his actions this way: "I didn't know exactly how to handle it, and I was afraid to do something that might jeopardize what the university procedure was, so I backed away and turned it over to some other people, people I thought would have a little more expertise than I did. It didn't work out that way" (Jenkins, 2012, para. 5). Here we see evidence of a flight response such as Jablin described. The coach was not silent, but he effectively hid behind the procedures of the organization, allowing him to take the necessary action of passing it up the chain of command while also avoiding the blame. Thus, while many reasons have been cited for cowardice, our analysis illustrates that leaders might hide behind procedure; the act got reported, but leaders failed to act courageously in seeking clarity and full details of what exactly they were reporting. In effect, then, what happened is similar to Darley and Latane's (1968) classic research on diffusion of responsibility wherein a sense of personal responsibility is lowered in the presence of bystanders (in this case, the "bystanders" were those further up the chain of command). In this action we see evidence of the organization taking priority over the individual: the safety and well-being of children was not as important as the reputation of the university and its football program, and the continuation of the Second Mile program (this can be seen, for example, in the request that Second Mile guests not be brought into the facilities). Trusting procedure to give action to courage only contributes to a system that silences through a lack of action. Therefore, organizations must be mindful of how procedure can be a structural impediment to courage.

Thus, it is important to consider the individual–organizational relationship pertaining to courage. In Jablin's (2006) definition of courageous leadership, leaders are not the only members of an organization with influence. The lack of action, the obstruction of action, and the perseverance of silence are all evidence of cowardice that influences the future actions of members of the organization. Likewise, the action of speaking up—of uncovering a wrong that needs to be corrected, and, in the case of Penn State, of protecting the well-being of young boys—can have great influence on fellow members. This is true of a follower as well as a leader. McQueary did act courageously in his initial reporting. He held back from giving full details, as noted above, but saying something right away was a courageous act. Many years after the graduate assistant spoke up to the head coach, thereby exposing the disturbing and harmful actions of his boss, the influence of this action was still felt at every level of the organization. The board of trustees, upon reading the attorney general's report, made the decision to clean house of leadership that hid behind policy and procedure as excuses for lack of action. The actions of the board of trustees should be seen as appropriate and necessary. The courts will always decide if child abuse took place, but it is up to an institution's leaders to deal with the abuses of its members. Here, a strong reaction was necessary (Lutgen-Sandvik & McDermott, 2008) to make changes in a broken organization. An unequivocal message needed to be communicated that no one within the organization, not its president or even its highly popular football coach, should be allowed to abuse power through a cover-up.

Finally, this case highlights the need for organizational training on how to speak/listen courageously. Lucas and Fyke (2014) note the importance of developing a vocabulary for how to talk about sexually charged content. Building on that, the work of Mary Gentile (2011) might be instructive. In discussing her program of work, "Giving Voice to Values," she notes that moral competence is key to courage, and that preparation and practice are key. That is, employees need the space to practice *what* and *how* to speak and listen with courage. Building on that idea, we note that this is especially true with topics of a sexual nature. Given that such topics are taboo and thereby lend themselves to euphemisms and inaccurate reporting (e.g., "horseplay"; Lucas & Fyke, 2014), no matter how uncomfortable, organizational members must learn what to *say* and how to respond in situations like the one in the Penn State locker room.

CONCLUSION

To quote an old saying, "Courage is not the absence of fear, but rather the judgement that something else is more important than fear." Difficult situations, especially those involving sexuality, face members of society, and especially leaders, every day: in the boardroom, the locker room, the classroom, and the living room. It is vital, in turn, that we continue to dig deep into cases, learn the relevant lessons, and ultimately learn to communicate and act courageously in such situations.

As the events at Penn State unfolded, university leaders silenced concerns, discouraged those of lower ranks from communicating courageously, and fostered a cultural contagion of fear that permeated the university. The Freeh Report identified a "culture of reverence of the football program" and a "president who discouraged discussion and dissent" as barriers to acting in the best interest of the young boys who were abused. Rather than encouraging courageous communication—for example, graduate assistant Mike McQueary speaking up to head football coach Joe Paterno about the "incident" in the shower—the report details a pattern of silencing: the university police department's decision not to file a crime log entry following the first reported sexual abuse case; a janitor's decision not to report a witnessed rape for fear that the university would fire the entire janitorial staff in an effort to protect the football program; and Athletic Director Tim Curley and President Graham Spanier's email exchange determining not to involve outside authorities, but instead to handle the situation internally.

People care desperately about courage. And that is another reason why the Sandusky abuse case and the silence surrounding it is so upsetting. The public wanted to believe that the courage displayed by players and coaches on the field also characterized the team's and the team leaders' actions off the field. People wanted to believe those who are smaller and weaker would be protected by the strong and powerful. In short, the public felt deeply betrayed by the seemingly brave Nittany Lions acting in so very cowardly a fashion. They wanted—and, indeed, those young boys brutally victimized by Jerry Sandusky *needed*—Penn State's leaders to stand up and roar like lions.

REFERENCES

Altheide, D. L., & Johnson, J. M. (2012). Normal crimes at Penn State. *Cultural Studies—Critical Methodologies, 12*, 306–8. doi:10.1177/1532708612446428.

Ashcraft, K. L., Kuhn, T. R., & Cooren, F. (2009). Constitutional amendments: "Materializing" organizational communication. *The Academy of Management Annals, 3*(1), 1–64. doi:10.1080/19416520903047186

Beard, David. (2016). Fathers, sons and the culture of violence. *Duluth Budgeteer.* Retrieved March 30, 2017 from http://hdl.handle.net/11299/184707.

Bennis, W. (2003). *On becoming a leader.* Cambridge, MA: Perseus.

Bidgood, J., & Pérez-Peña, R. (2017, March 24). Former Penn State President found guilty in Sandusky abuse case. *New York Times.* Retrieved March 30, 2017 from https://www.nytimes.com/2017/03/24/us/graham-panier-jerry-sandusky-penn-state.html?_r=0.

Bisel, R. S., & Zanin, A. C. (2016). Moral dissent in health care organizations. In T. R. Harrison & E. A. Williams (Eds.), *Organizations, communication, and health* (pp. 119–33). New York: Routledge.

Clair, R. P. (1993). The use of framing devices to sequester organizational narratives: Hegemony and harassment. *Communication Monographs, 60*, 113–36. doi:10.1080/03637759309376304

Comer, D. R., & Vega, G. (2011). Introduction: Why moral courage matters in organizations. In D. R. Comer & G. Vega (Eds.), *Moral courage in organizations: Doing the right thing at work* (pp. xv–xxii). Armonk, NY: M.E. Sharpe.

Cowan, R. L., & Horan, S. M. (2014). Why are you dating him? Contemporary motives for workplace motives. *Qualitative Research Reports in Communication, 15*(1), 9–16. doi:10.1080/17459435.2014.955587

Daloz, L. A., Keen, C. H., Keen, J. P., & Parks, S. (1996). *Common fire: Lives of commitment in a complex world.* Boston, MA: Beacon Press.

Darley, J. M., & Latane, B. (1968). Bystander intervention in emergencies: Diffusion of responsibility. *Journal of Personality and Social Psychology, 8*(4), 377–83.

DePree, M. (1997). Attributes of leaders. *Executive Excellence, 14*, 8.

Dillard, J. P., Hale, J. L., & Segrin, C. (1994). Close relationships in task environments: Perceptions of relational types, illicitness, and power. *Management Communication Quarterly, 7*, 227–55. doi:10.1177/0893318994007003001.

Florence, M., & Fortson, E. (2001). *Sex at work: Attraction, orientation, harassment, flirtation, and discrimination.* Los Angeles: Silver Lake Publishing.

Freeh Sporkin & Sullivan, LLP. (2012, July 12). Report of the special investigative counsel regarding the actions of the Pennsylvania State University related to the child sexual abuse committed by Gerald A. Sandusky. Retrieved from https://www.documentcloud.org/documents/396512-report-final-071212.html.

Fyke, J. P. (2017a) Gender-specific language. In Allen, M. (Ed.), *The SAGE encyclopedia of communication research methods* (Vols. 1–4; pp. 616–18). Thousand Oaks: Sage.

Fyke, J. P. (2017b) Power in language. In Allen, M. (Ed.), The SAGE *encyclopedia of communication research methods* (Vols. 1-4; pp. 1315-1317). Thousand Oaks: Sage.

Gentile, M. C. (2011). Giving voice to values: Building moral competence. In D. R. Comer & G. Vega (Eds.), *Moral courage in organizations: Doing the right thing at work* (pp. 117–29). Armonk, NY: M.E. Sharpe.

Goldstein, R. (2012, January 22). Joe Paterno, longtime Penn State coach, dies at 83. *New York Times.* Retrieved March 3, 2012 from http://www.nytimes.com/2012/01/23/sports/ncaafootball/joe-paterno-longtime-penn-state-coach-dies-at-85.html.

Heifetz, R. A. (1994). *Leadership without easy answers.* Cambridge, MA: Harvard University Press.

Hearn, J., & Parkin, W. (1995). *The power and paradox of organisational sexuality.* New York: St. Martin's Press.

Hornstein, H.A. (1986). *Managerial courage: Revitalizing your company without sacrificing your job.* Hoboken, NJ: John Wiley & Sons.

Jablin, F. M. (2006). Courage and courageous communication among leaders and followers in groups, organizations, and communities. *Management Communication Quarterly, 20,* 94–110.

Jenkins, S. (2012, January 12). Joe Paterno's first interview since the Penn State–Sandusky scandal. *The Washington Post.* Retrieved March 25, 2012 from https://www.washingtonpost.com/sports/colleges/joe-paternos-first-interview-since-the-penn-state-sandusky-scandal/2012/01/13/gIQA08e4yP_story.html?utm_term=.7a6e0c7c6a8f.

Kets de Vries, M. F. R. (2015). The sexual "cloud" in the executive suite. *Journal of Research in Gender Studies, 5*(2), 191–204.

Kohn, S. M. (2011). For the greater good: The moral courage of whistleblowers. In D. R. Comer & G. Vega (Eds.), *Moral courage in organizations: Doing the right thing at work* (pp. 60–74). Armonk, NY: M.E. Sharpe.

Lucas, K., & Fyke, J. P. (2014). Euphemisms and ethics: A language-centered analysis of Penn State's sexual abuse scandal. *Journal of Business Ethics, 122,* 551–69.

Lutgen-Sandvik, P., & McDermott, V. (2008). The constitution of employee-abusive organizations: A communication flows theory. *Communication Theory, 18*(2), 304–33. doi: 10.1111/j.1468-2885.2008.00324.x.

Matt, B. F., & Shahinpoor, N. (2011). Speaking truth to power: The courageous organizational dissenter. In D. R. Comer & G. Vega (Eds.), *Moral courage in organizations: Doing the right thing at work* (pp. 157–70). Armonk, NY: M.E. Sharpe.

McNamee, S. (1998). Reinscribing organizational wisdom and courage: The relationally engaged organization. In S. Srivastva & D. L. Cooperrider (Eds.), *Organizational wisdom and executive courage.* Lanham, MD: Lexington Books.

Miles, M. B., Huberman, A. M., & Saldaña, J. (2014). *Qualitative data analysis: A methods sourcebook* (3rd ed.). Thousand Oaks, CA: Sage.

Miller, W. I. (2000). *The mystery of courage.* Cambridge, MA: Harvard University Press.

Moushey, B., & Dvorchak, B. (2012). *Game over: Jerry Sandusky, Penn State, and the culture of silence.* New York, NY: William Morrow.

Powell, A. (2016, June 7). Unpacking "rape culture" after Stanford and beyond. *Social Justice Blog.* Retrieved March 30, 2017 from http://www.social justicejournal.org/unpacking-rape-culture-after-stanford-and-beyond/.

Proffitt, J.M., & Corrigan, T.F. (2012). Penn State's "success with honor": How institutional structure and brand logic disincentivized disclosure. *Cultural Studies &Critical Methodologies, 12,* 322–5.

Smith, K. K., & Berg, D. N. (1987). *Paradoxes of group life: Understanding conflict, paralysis, and movement in group dynamics.* San Francisco, CA: Jossey-Bass.

Stack, L. (2016, June 6). Light sentence for Brock Turner in Stanford rape case draws outrage. *The New York Times.* Retrieved January 25, 2017 from https://www.nytimes.com/2016/06/07/us/outrage-in-stanford-rape-case-over-dueling-statements-of-victim-and-attackers-father.html?r=0.

Trinch, S. L. (2001). Managing euphemism and transcending taboos: Negotiating the meaning of sexual assault in Latinas' narratives of domestic violence. *Text, 21,* 567–610. doi:10.1515/text.2001.012.

Wolverton, B. (2012, July 1). Records suggest Penn State officials knew sexual nature of Sandusky encounter. *The Chronicle of Higher Education.* Retrieved August 23, 2012 from http://chronicle.com/article/Records-Raise-More-Questions/132725/.

5. Because they can: Adult to student sexual abuse in preK-12 schools

Charol Shakeshaft

This is a book about the relationship between sexuality and leaders. I study school employees who sexually abuse students. The relationship between my research and the purpose of this book relates to my focus on how educator sexual misconduct has been allowed to continue.[1] When asked why school employees sexually abuse children, I respond, "because they can." By that I mean that little is done to stop this abuse.

Sexual abuse of students by school employees is an ongoing problem. The most recent data available teaches us that 7 percent of students report having been the target of physical sexual misconduct by a school employee, most often a teacher or coach (Shakeshaft, 2004). When multiple forms of assault are combined—for example, verbal sexual misconduct (talk about a teacher or student's sex life or sexual stories) and visual sexual misconduct (print or media pornography, masturbating in front of students without touching)—10 percent of students report being victims nationally. Thus, at least 4.5 million students in the United States have experienced abuse by employees in schools.[2]

The lack of practical and empirically grounded attention to the safety of 10 percent of school students is shocking. Prevention is the job of school leaders, who are administrators, school board members, teacher union/association organizers and managers, parent group officials, schools of education, and state and federal legislators. Given the broad group of stakeholders in leadership roles, why has so little been done to prevent students from being sexually abused by adults at school?

One explanation is that very little is known about the etiology of sexual abuse of students by staff members. Newspaper articles summarize and often sensationalize the crime, but do not describe how or why it was allowed to happen within educational organizations. There are some stories from victims that are helpful for understanding the effects on the student as well as her or his experiences with the abuser and school personnel, but these do not tell us how the abuse was discovered, how school officials responded, what policies were in place, and what worked or did not work. Because of this, administrators argue that effective prevention strategies are unknown and, therefore, cannot be taught. Others argue that these abusers hide in plain sight and there is nothing that indicates who might be dangerous and who is not.

A second explanation is that the needs of adults come before the needs of children. Predators put their needs ahead of children's. It is all about what the adult wants, not what is good for the child. At the same time, adults who do not abuse also put their needs above the safety of children. While teacher and administrator bystanders claim to put children first, when it comes to calling a colleague on his or her interactions with children, the comfort of the adults trumps the needs of the child. While I understand that this seems a harsh assessment of otherwise good people, I am struck by how often I hear bystanders make excuses for inaction: "I thought something seemed 'off', but I didn't feel that I should say anything," or "It [the behavior of the abuser] is not something I would ever do, but it's not really my business [concern, job] to lecture others."

A third explanation for why sexual abuse of students still exists in the school system is that many administrators and school employees code this abuse as sex, particularly for post-pubescent students. The language used to describe the sexual abuse that is occurring defines it as a relationship or dating. Normalizing abuse shifts it from a safety-related or criminal act to a sexual problem.

RESEARCH METHODS

Sexual abuse of students in schools is difficult to study. If we could (or would) do postmortem examinations each time a student is sexually abused by an adult in a school, we might be able to identify the trigger points where policies, training, supervision, and reporting increase prevention. These are sensitive issues for school administrators and communities, and most of the time the stakeholders just want to put the ugly incident behind them—a response which does little to prevent future abuse.

An additional barrier to postmortems is securing entry into a critical mass of school districts. However valuable direct inquiry might be, it turns out not to be feasible to get permission to interview students, teachers, administrators, victims, parents of victims, and predators. Very few, if any, sites would allow such scrutiny.

In thinking about how it would be possible to achieve the same end—a 360-degree inquiry of a case of sexual abuse of a student by a staff member in a school—I realized that the documentation from civil cases where a parent or child files a suit against a school district for not preventing the child's abuse by an employee would provide *detailed and vetted* information for a study from the perspectives of the school district, the victim, the predator, and bystanders.

This chapter relies on data—where data are called for—from evidence presented in civil cases where a student has been sexually abused by an employee. Among the data points included in civil case documentation that I have used are school district policies, training materials and requirements, hiring policies and practices, personnel files, student files, medical/mental health files, environmental scans of the school buildings, police files from the criminal prosecution, and pictures of classrooms. In addition, depositions, as sworn testimony, are as close to that person's "truth" as is likely to be available. People being deposed swear an oath to tell the truth and the penalties of perjury apply, just as they would in trial testimony. In the cases I have analyzed, there are depositions from the victim, family members, the abuser, members of the abuser's family, classmates of the victim, and school personnel—teachers, coaches, custodians, school lunch monitors, teacher aides, building administrators, district administrators, and school board members. This is a broad and inclusive group of people who are "telling their stories" in each of the civil cases/settings/contexts of sexual abuse.

I have documents from more than 50 civil cases in which I have been an expert witness. I have received permission to use materials from all of these cases to study sexual abuse in schools under the following conditions: (1) pseudonyms for school districts, people involved, case names, and attorneys would be used; (2) there would be no way to identify any individuals in the research report. My role in these cases was to provide expert testimony about the presence or absence of policies and procedures that are related to abuse prevention. I was not an expert for either the plaintiff or the defendant. My role was to examine evidence to determine the conditions surrounding the abuse. Nothing that I produced in these cases was used in this research.

Sampling multiple cases allowed me to look at a variety of similar and contrasting cases (Creswell, 2013; Yin, 2014). Stake (2005) titles these "multiple" or "collective" case studies (p. 445) and considers them to be an extension of the instrumental case study. Demonstrating that a finding shows up in more than one place will strengthen the validity, stability, and reliability of the conclusions I draw from the findings (Miles et al., 2014; Yin, 2014).

I applied six parameters for selection of the school districts included in a multi-site case study from which I am using data for this chapter: (1) a student has been sexually abused by an employee of the school district; (2) the employee has admitted the sexual abuse and been found guilty in criminal court; (3) the school is a preK-12 public school; (4) sufficient documents are available to describe patterns of abuse, school district conditions, and responses of those involved; (5) consent for use of documents has been given by the plaintiff attorneys; and (6) both the criminal and civil cases are closed. The cases listed are varied: they are from 33 states; they represent both state and federal complaints; they include elementary and secondary student plaintiffs, from urban, rural, and suburban school districts that contain both high- and low-income school districts, that serve predominantly white, predominantly black or Latina/o, or mixed race students. The victims in these cases include both males and females and the predators include both males and females. Thus, the sample replicates the socio-demographic properties of school districts and plaintiffs from the country as a whole.

SEXUAL PREDATORS ARE HARD TO IDENTIFY

In movies, on TV, and in the public imagination, a person who sexually abuses children is usually an odd looking and even odder acting male social misfit, a male who is a stranger to the victim and/or who appears sinister. There are such men, and some of them sexually abuse children. But not very often. The majority of children in schools are sexually abused by people who look unremarkable. Offenders, unfortunately, come in many varieties, most of which do not seem the least bit threatening.

The right question to ask is: what kind of person sexually exploits a student? Are they females? Popular teachers? Good teachers? Bad teachers? Coaches? Beginning teachers? Veteran teachers? Young teachers? White teachers? Black teachers? Latina/o teachers? Counselors? Administrators? Bus drivers? Band directors? Drama club sponsors? People with children? People who are married? Single? Heterosexual? Homosexual? Churchgoers? Atheists? The answer to all these is: yes.

The value of isolating the characteristics of a sexual abuser is obvious. If we were able to identify the characteristics of educators who might sexually abuse students, we could screen them out before they entered the profession or, once in, we might identify them and stop their behavior. Researchers, mental health workers, and criminal justice personnel have spent decades trying to isolate a singular description of the child sexual offender. While we are learning more about who offends and why, the most important identifying characteristics are how the person behaves, not his or her background or appearance.

OFFENDER CONTINUUM

Adults who sexually victimize students can be placed on a continuum from situational to preferential sex offenders. Because diagnostic labels are not perfectly correlated with action, Finkelhor and Araji (1986) note that descriptions such as "pedophile" are not very helpful; instead, they suggest that offender sexual orientation be labeled on a scale from "exclusive sexual interest in children" to "exclusive sexual interest in adults." The offenders in my study fall roughly into two groups: *preferential* and *situational offenders*.

Preferential Offenders

Preferential offenders are those who receive their sexual gratification or arousal from children. Preferential molesters are sometimes called fixated abusers or pedophiles, with the latter term used to name all people who are sexually attracted to children.[3] Preferential abusers who target pre-pubescent children are almost always male.

Educator preferential molesters who are sexually attracted to children have chosen to work in schools so that they can be close to children. Preferential molesters are methodical in identifying and pursuing students. These targeted students are vulnerable in some way (although all children are vulnerable when faced with an adult who will do harm). Typical of vulnerable children who are targeted are those who are black or Latina/o, lagging students, part of dysfunctional families, angry, or self-harming. Their vulnerability might not be apparent, but all are children who want and need attention and affection. Preferential abusers report conscious strategies to find child sexual partners, and note that they particularly try to choose children who are looking for adult interactions, understanding, and positive attention.

Since preferential abusers know that what they do is both illegal and considered wrong by most of society, they work very hard to find children who will be "safe" targets. These predators understand that vulnerable children need attention and care and will often sacrifice a lot for what seems like love. They also know that these victims are often not believed by authorities. A preferential abuser in a school counts on the strength of his or her reputation and standing in the community as a shield. She or he knows that even if a child reports the sexual abuse, the abuser is likely to dodge suspicion, both because the abuser is believed to be an outstanding teacher and because the child is branded an unstable source.

Nevertheless, fixated abusers are careful and usually enter into relationships slowly, building trust with the victim at the same time as working to make the victim feel complicit. Fixated abusers report that they test prospective victims to see if they can be trusted to keep secrets. By putting the children through a series of "tests" that lets the adult predator know which kids are likely to talk about the experience and which are not, these abusers are able to eliminate children who might report the sexual abuse. A fixated abuser might say to a child, "I have a secret to tell you, but you can't tell anyone." Then the abuser tells the child that she or he really hates green beans and won't ever eat them. The abuser checks to make sure that the child hasn't told anyone, and then offers a confidence that is more intimate. Going through a series of revelations, the fixated abuser makes the child feel special and leads her or him to real and harmful secrets.

Often the abuser then tries to connect with the child and have her or him relate to the abuser's secret. For instance, a common pattern of adult males targeting male students is for the adult to "confess" that sometimes he likes to touch his penis and make himself feel good. He then asks a boy target if he has ever felt that way. When the boy says yes, the pedophile uses that connection as a foundation for moving to a next step of sexual intimacy and exploitation. The abuser reassures the male student that his feelings are normal and appropriate and then suggests that they both sit on the couch and touch themselves to feel good. Once that has happened, a future meeting might move to touching each other. Alcohol is often part of the mix, with underage children being given beer early on so that it becomes part of the pattern. This kind of escalation leads to sexual abuse of the child, while making the child believe consent occurred.

Fixated abusers court their victims, slowly introducing physical touch or pornography in ways that entrap victims and make them feel responsible. These adults make their victims feel special. They give them attention, gifts, confidences, friendship, and guidance. These offers are especially appealing to children who don't feel loved, wanted, or important to anyone. But even the most loved of us enjoy attention and nurturing, a human condition that makes all children vulnerable and endangered by people who sexually exploit children.

As explained by a New York City teacher who is a member, the NAMBLA group claims that it is a constitutional right to have sexual relations with children and that by making it illegal to have sex with minors, society is depriving minors of their rights. Although old, a NAMBLA newsletter of 1993 describes the patterns I have observed in my research of male to male sexual abuse in schools. The patterns described below are nearly textbook for many educator preferential molesters.

My first suggestion is to restrict your sexual involvement and overtures to boys who need you, boys who value you and your friendship. They might be fatherless or they might feel misunderstood, unappreciated, or neglected by whatever family they currently have ... Before risking any direct sexual overture, you can tell a lot about a boy with a few well-placed sexual jokes or comments. This works best in one-on-one situations, with just you and your friend ... If he blushes, becomes exceedingly embarrassed, or refuses to comment at all, forget about going any farther. The boy who isn't comfortable talking with you about sex sure as hell won't be happy doing it with you. The reaction you are looking for is relaxed acceptance ... Every kid is different and requires sensitivity and pursuit at his own pace. (I invested two years courting one particularly good-looking boy before he invited me into his pants) ... Anyway, I recommend progressing in stages, increasing the level of contact one step at a time, with careful study of his reaction between every move ... Eventually you want to joke about masturbation. You want to admit to each other that you masturbate ... The time between each advance is critical. You have to develop patience and a sense of attentive timing. I am talking about anywhere from five minutes to a year! ... Invite one of [your] friends over—again by himself. Leave a pornographic magazine someplace where he is sure to find it, but where the discovery can still be considered accidental ... If you think you might like working with disadvantaged kids, you won't need much help ... Take good care of them and trust that some will take good care of you ... You'll do yourself a world of good by performing oral sex on your boys. It's an acquired taste, but once you get used to it you'll find you can suck for hours. The advantage it gives you is that it will bring the boy almost certain pleasure. This is what you want. I have yet to meet a boy who disliked being blown. By giving him pleasure, you increase the chance he will keep your secret to himself in our homophobic and pedophobic culture. You also give him an excellent reason to come back for more.

Fixated abusers often go undetected for years, resulting in multiple victims. A study of pedophiles in Oregon found the average number of children that convicted pedophiles admit to abusing is nine, but most professionals think that estimate is conservative. Fixated abusers who are arrested often report hundreds of incidents throughout their lives.

POPULAR, WELL-LIKED, OUTSTANDING TEACHERS

The preferential sexual abuser in schools is most likely male, works in an elementary school, and is popular among students, staff, and parents. These employees disprove the stereotype of an abuser as a character that most people would be able to recognize as someone to avoid. In schools, the abuser is often one of the people that students most like and parents most trust. Those who sexually abuse are often considered among the best teachers in a district, and they are often very popular among students and parents. It is this popularity and trust that confounds district officials and community members and that often leads professionals to ignore allegations against a teacher on the grounds that such an "upstanding" teacher would never sexually abuse.

Those who sexually abuse elementary and middle school children are often high achievers in the profession and, compared to their nonabusing counterparts, hold a disproportionate number of awards and teaching recognitions. They are more often recognized in the community, the state, and sometimes the nation as distinguished and dedicated educators. It is common to find that educators who have been sexually abusing children are also the same educators who display on their walls teaching awards and commendations. Many an "Outstanding Teacher of the Year" has sexually abused.

These teachers receive their acclaim because they spend a lot of time with children, they often try to reach children who are needy, they are usually engaging and personable, and they put their students at the center of their lives, therefore giving time and emotional energy beyond what most teachers are able or willing to offer. If that was all they did, they would deserve those teaching awards. But what they do in addition to all their good works is betray the trust of the children they teach by abusing some among them.

Being an outstanding teacher is not the "mark" of a child abuser. Most distinguished teachers are not sexual predators. However, those who are preferential predators in elementary schools work at being recognized as good teachers or coaches or custodians in order to be able to sexually abuse children. Being a good teacher is the way they get to children, especially in the case of those who abuse elementary and middle school students. Therefore, these educators should not be given a "pass" if there is a complaint.

Teachers who sexually abuse are often those who have the most access to students in unsupervised or unobserved settings. For instance, victims are likely to report they were abused by someone who worked with them as a tutor, in an afterschool program, or in other activities where one-to-one contact was embedded in the activity.

Preferential abusers frequently work to gain the trust of the victim's parents. Many of the students targeted for abuse are students who are having problems in school or conflicts with their families. Parents are often pleased when a teacher begins to take an interest and help their child, particularly if it leads to fewer conflicts at home and improved grades or increased school performance and involvement. It is hard for these parents to believe that someone who is helping their child could also be hurting them.

Situational Abusers

These are people who sexually abuse children and teenagers but who would not be classified as fixated abusers. They are mostly found in upper middle and high school. In these cases, the sexual abusers do not have a particular obsession with sex with children. These are abusers who take advantage of a situation such as female student who wants to stay after class and talk to the teacher.

These abusers describe the molestation as an "affair" or "relationship." They code the student as a willing sexual partner, to be treated like any other. These abusers are unwilling or unable to understand the power relationship in their role or the ethical conduct required of a professional who works with adolescents. They justify these abuses by believing that students enter into the situation "of their own free will" and that since there is nothing coercive in the relationship, it is acceptable. They fail to acknowledge the power relationship involved in a teaching or staff role, and they prefer not to reflect on their ethical and professional responsibilities. Many of these educators maintain that they were unaware their actions were illegal, believing that consensual sex with a student is acceptable.

Many opportunistic abusers I have studied hadn't thought about the consequences of their actions before they entered into what they called a sexual or romantic relationship. They had not bothered to weigh the possible harm to students, and thought of little beyond what they, the adult, wanted or needed. These were often self-absorbed, self-focused, unreflective people who were themselves very close to an adolescent emotional level.

An example of the truncated professional, ethical, and emotional development that is common among situational educator abusers is the response of a bus driver and teacher aide in a daycare center who also directed afterschool youth programs. He sexually violated 22 male children in ten years: "I didn't visualize myself as a thirty-four-year-old guy having sex with kids. It was just two guys having sex. I didn't think there was any harm in what I was doing. I'd do it when I was frustrated. I'd do it when I was in a good mood."

Situational abusers who target females often begin by commenting on the student's attractiveness and making comments about the way she dresses. To begin with, in grooming the student, these abusers use words such as "hot" and "sexy," usually in a playful way, to describe the student. Opportunistic abusers try to lead targeted students into conversations about sex, sometimes talking about the problems they are having with a spouse or their sexual experience when they were in high school. They also try to provide a shoulder to cry on and a person who will listen. "I know parents are really hard on kids. You should have seen what mine did. I'm always here for you." Or, "I'm worried about you. I've heard that you and Tommy are getting pretty close. If you need someone to talk to about it, I'm here if you need me. I've been there and I can give you a male perspective."

One student reports how she was vulnerable to her sexual abuser, who was also her school counselor: "I got no attention at home. I was lonely and at that awkward age. What he gave me ... I thought was love. I didn't know any better."

Situational abusers often try a romantic approach. A high school history teacher whose sexual relationship with one of his students began when she was 15 is typical of the male romantic abuser. The teacher sent the student love letters and told her she was a "beautiful flower about to bloom." The student says: "[He] would do anything I needed. Our relationship became more as time progressed. He started hugging me and touching me. In time, we started to have a sexual relationship. We would have sex twice a week."

Another student reports that her teacher made her feel special and that she was flattered by his attention. For two years, her teacher

> touched and entered my vagina with his fingers, masturbated me, performed oral sex, took Polaroid pictures of me naked and in various poses, and had me touch and fondle his penis. He attempted to have intercourse with me a couple of times, but I was so frightened, I panicked and I would not allow him to do so.

Most of the time, this abuse occurred in school, during school hours, in empty classrooms, storage closets, or offices. This student thought she was in love. She thought her teacher was in love.

I was a virgin and this was my first sexual experience. I thought that he truly loved and cared about me, and so I swore that I would never tell the "secret." [The teacher] used my inexperience, my innocence, my sense of guilt, and my need to be listened to and loved to satisfy his sick, sexual and emotional needs.

Unlike preferential molesters, situational abusers run the gamut of ability. Some are considered excellent teachers, but most are thought mediocre or poor and described by their colleagues as having boundary problems, judgment problems, or emotional problems. Women who sexually abuse students often flirt with the student, touching them, wearing skirts that are too short and tops that are too low. They often believe they are in love and treat their abuse as a consensual, boyfriend–girlfriend relationship, in some way reenacting a high school experience.

Much of the grooming of students for sexual activity occurs during the ordinary day of school—talking in lunch rooms, walking to class, helping with a project. However, many abusers take advantage of time alone with a student or time after school, where interactions are less formal and less likely to be scrutinized. For instance, a disproportionate number of coaches, drama, art, music, and gym teachers are found among those who sexually abuse. Male coaches of female teams are highly represented in abuse categories.

In these cases of abuse by trusted coaches, acquiescence usually occurs not through threats but through offering children attention, affection, and warmth. These educators understand what children need and often take a great deal of time to court their victims, making them feel wanted, important, and special. Within schools, coaches hold a special status. They are more visible to the public than most other teachers. The coach of a winning football team is accorded star quality. Some coaches target those they coach. Others use their celebrated status to attract and target a student for sex.

PREVENTION BEHAVIOR

Most school personnel have been alerted to their responsibilities as mandated reporters. This is usually done in a short session when the employee arrives, usually within an orientation. After this, the majority of school employees in my studies might get an annual reminder when teacher handbooks are distributed: "Don't forget to read your handbook and your responsibilities as a mandated reporter." Unfortunately, mandated reporter training is not effective for preventing educator sexual misconduct. Most don't realize that they are mandated to report suspected abuse by adults in the school.

The teachers in my study defined mandated reporting as looking for harm that came from the home. They have learned to look at the behavior or appearance of the child as an indicator that abuse or maltreatment might be occurring. A much better indicator is to look at the behaviors of the adults as they interact with students. Training in the types of behaviors that might be red flags of boundary crossing and sexual abuse teaches bystanders—those who don't abuse but see the everyday grooming and interactions of those who do—what and when to report. This training, however, is rarely undertaken.

Schools Meet the Needs of Adults before They Meet the Needs of Students

Sexual abuse of a student is all about meeting the needs of the adult. Abusers are focused on themselves and what they want, not what the child needs. While they might rationalize their actions as good for the child, abusers are putting themselves first. But they aren't the only ones. For instance, when training employees on boundaries with students, it is not uncommon for someone to become belligerent and complain that "if I have to worry all the time about crossing boundaries, then I'm just not going to interact with the students." This too is all about the adult. Refusing to understand and learn good boundaries is just another way of saying, "I don't care about the children. This is too hard for me."

When administrators I studied do attempt to address boundaries, they often introduce the work as something they are doing "to protect you from false accusations." Rarely is the training introduced by saying, "This training is to help you understand appropriate boundaries between you and students, to honor those boundaries, and, when you see others who aren't, to intervene." An all too common approach in the cases I have studied is illustrated by an elementary principal who had complaints from parents about a male teacher's inappropriate touching of female third graders. The principal said to him, "I'm concerned that you are going to be falsely accused by one of your students and it would ruin your career. Be careful how you interact." This principal did not investigate the complaints of the parents, but rather warned the teacher that he might be blamed for something he had not done.

Another adult comfort technique occurs when someone says, "I don't want to hear about it." Or "I don't listen to rumors." Or "That kind of talk upsets me." Or when they describe sexual abuse as a relationship.

A final example of privileging adults over children can be seen in the responses I received when I asked bystanders why they didn't report a colleague's behavior that they found troubling. The response is almost always some form of, "I couldn't do that. If I was wrong, I would have ruined the career of a good teacher." In the cases I studied, there were no bystander concerns that by not reporting, they might ruin the life of a child.

Wrong Paradigm

The way we talk about abuse inhibits prevention in a number of ways, particularly by refusing to use precise language, setting the abuse within the context of adults' consensual activity, and failing to distinguish between a teacher's behavior that is acceptable in a school and a teacher's behavior that is criminal.

Imprecise Language

Administrators and teachers in my study described sexual misconduct using words such as *inappropriate, molestation, fondling*. While there is nothing wrong with those words, they do not convey the actions that occurred. For instance, instead of saying the teacher was rubbing his erect penis, which was still in his pants, on the student's back, the language might be "inappropriate touching." Words such as penis, vagina, and breasts are seldom used. Behavior needs to be described so that all know what is not acceptable. It is not enough to tell teachers not to cross boundaries or not to be sexually inappropriate. Specific examples are necessary.

Normalizing Abuse

The language used to describe adult to student sexual misconduct is often set in a normalizing context. For instance, instead of announcing that a student was raped by a teacher, an administrator might say that the teacher had a relationship with the student. Because minors cannot legally consent to sex with an adult, any sexual act is nonconsensual. States have different definitions of these crimes, and rape is one of the definitions. By using the language of consensual sex, educators normalize adult to student sexual content, particularly with high school students.

"Unacceptable" or "Criminal"

In the cases I studied, administrators often remarked that they didn't try to terminate an employee because what the employee did was not a criminal offense. For instance, constant sexual jokes in a classroom or sexual comments to students about how they look are often seen as something that has to be tolerated.

But they are not. It is important for schools to determine what professional behavior is and to enforce those expectations. If a teacher continues to be alone after school with a student, even if no one admits to sexual contact, this is still unacceptable behavior. Employees who continue to violate professional boundaries don't have to be prosecuted in order to be terminated. Setting up expectations and consequences in policies and procedures provides a way to enforce safe behavior.

SUMMARY

Educator sexual misconduct is not about sex, even though sexual behaviors may occur. Sexual misconduct is harming a child. It is a safety issue and a professional behavior issue, not a sexual one. Working with leaders to prevent sexual abuse of students by employees requires training for those who might abuse, but also, more importantly, for those who are bystanders. It requires prodding leaders to rethink how they talk about the abuse of children and ways in which the culture takes care of adults at the expense of children. This will not happen without leadership.

REFERENCES

Creswell, J. W. (2013). *Qualitative inquiry and research design: Choosing among five approaches.* Thousand Oaks, CA: Sage Publications.

Finkelhor, D. & Araji, S. (1986). Explanations of pedophilia: A four factor model. *Journal of Sex Research, 22*(2), 145–61.

Miles, M. B., Huberman, A. M., & Saldana, J. (2014). *Qualitative data analysis: A methods sourcebook* (3rd ed.). Thousand Oaks, CA: Sage Publications.

NAMBLA Bulletin. (1993). January–February.

Shakeshaft, C. (2004). *Educator sexual misconduct: A synthesis of existing literature.* Washington, DC: Policy and Program Studies Services, US Department of Education.

Stake, R. E. (2005). Qualitative case studies. In N. K. Denzin & Y. S. Lincoln (Eds.), *Handbook of qualitative research* (3rd ed.) (pp. 443–66). Thousand Oaks, CA: Sage Publications.

Yin, R. K. (2014). *Case study research: Design and methods* (5th ed.). Thousand Oaks, CA: Sage Publications.

NOTES

1. In this chapter, I am using the following terms interchangeably: educator sexual abuse or misconduct; trusted other sexual abuse or misconduct; sexual abuse of students by school employees. All will refer to a sexual offender in a school district who is employed or a volunteer who has sexually abused a student.
2. This study most probably underestimates the scope of the problem, since these numbers were generated using nationwide survey results that asked students if they had experienced a number of actions which were *unwanted*.
3. That term is clinically incorrect, since abusers are identified by the age of the children they target. There is an evolving set of definitions that make distinctions among fixated abusers. Infantophilia is the label for those most attracted to children younger than six; pedophiles prefer prepubescent children (ages 6–11); hebephiles target those on the cusp of puberty (11–14); ephebophiles are attracted to post-pubescent children (15–16); and teleiophiles target those aged 17 and older. These are diagnostic labels and not very useful for identifying abusers in school, except to point out that preferential child sexual abusers span a range of ages in their targets.

6. Heterosexism in organizations: The importance of transformational and heroic leadership

Shaun Pichler

Society today presents a mixed picture in terms of political and social landscapes for lesbian, gay, and bisexual (LGB)[1] individuals, otherwise known as sexual minorities (Pichler, 2007). On the one hand, recent US Supreme Court decisions have led to the legalization of same sex marriages (*United States v. Windsor*, June 26, 2013; *Hollingsworth v. Perry*, June 26, 2013), and public opinion is increasingly favorable regarding homosexuality (Gallup, 2014). On the other hand, sexual minorities face pervasive discrimination and harassment in society and in the workplace (e.g., Pichler, 2012; Pichler, Varma, & Bruce, 2010; Ragins & Cornwell, 2001). There is currently no comprehensive federal antidiscrimination legislation in the United States protecting workers from discrimination based on their sexual orientation. Although such legislation has been proposed in Congress in every year but one since 1994, passage has yet to be successful (see Hunt, 2011). Moreover, members of Congress are reportedly considering reintroducing the First Amendment Defense Act (FADA), which is likely to succeed, given support from President Trump (Ohara, 2016). This Act would make it illegal for the federal government to take action against businesses or persons that discriminate based on sexual orientation.

This is why LGB-supportive policies, such as antidiscrimination policies, domestic partner benefits, and inclusive diversity training (Ragins & Cornwell, 2001) are so important. Although there is research on the moral and business case for such policies (King & Cortina, 2010; Pichler & Ruggs, in press), there is very little research in the management and organization literature on how leaders are involved in the development or implementation of these policies, or on how leadership might be related to heterosexism. This is surprising since one might argue that industry has led the way in support for LGB workers relative to the federal government, as is explained below. The purpose of the current chapter, therefore, is (1) to review the literatures on heterosexism and LGB-supportive policies, and (2) to integrate these literatures with theory and research on leadership and (3) offer a conceptual model that proposes relationships between transformational and heroic leadership, the adoption and implementation of LGB-supportive policies, and heterosexism (Figure 6.1).

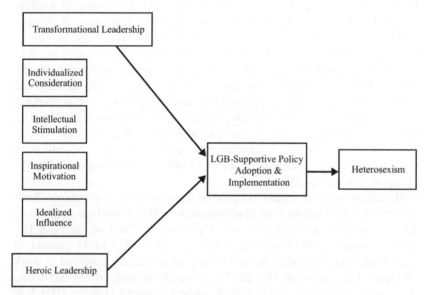

*Figure 6.1   Model of transformational and heroic leadership,
            LGB-supportive policy implementation and heterosexism*

SEXUAL MINORITIES AND HETEROSEXISM

Sexual orientation is multidimensional and represents emotional, romantic, sexual and affectionate attraction (Pichler, 2007). Some dimensions may not be in accordance with another dimension within the same individual; an individual's sexual identity may be inconsistent with their sexual attractions and behavior. In other words, engaging in sex acts with persons of the same sex does not necessarily mean an individual will identify as a homosexual or sexual minority. Homosexuality refers to persons who have sex primarily with persons of the same sex. Although the term "gay" can be applied to both men and women, the terms "lesbian" and "gay" are used in the scholarly literature to refer to women and men, respectively, who are homosexual. Bisexuality refers to persons who have sex with persons of both sexes. Lesbian women, gay men, and bisexual people are referred to as sexual minorities (Pichler, 2007).

Estimates of the proportion of the workforce that is gay, lesbian, or bisexual vary for multiple reasons, including because of different definitions or measures of sexual orientation (for example, behavioral vs. identity-based), but estimates generally indicate that this is a relatively large minority group. Some estimates suggest that 1 in every 50 workers in the US is gay or lesbian (Michael, Gagnon, Laumann, & Kolata, 1995), or that between 4 and 17 percent of the workforce is gay or lesbian (Gonsiorek & Weinrich, 1991). Heterosexism is a term used to describe prejudice and discrimination against sexual minorities (Sears, 1997). Herek (2004) defines heterosexism as "the cultural ideology that perpetuates sexual stigma by denying and denigrating any nonheterosexual form of behavior, identity, relationship, or community" (p. 16). Sexual orientation harassment, on the other hand, is defined as "verbal, physical, and symbolic behaviors that convey hostile and offensive attitudes about one's actual or perceived lesbian, gay or bisexual identity" (King & Cortina, p. 315).

Heterosexism and sexual orientation harassment are pervasive. Self-reports of sexual orientation discrimination in the workplace range from 15 to 66 percent depending on the sample (see Badett, Lau, Sears, & Ho, 2007; Croteau, 1996; Ragins & Cornwell, 2001). Up to 41 percent of sexual minorities reported being verbally or physically harassed at work (Badgett, Lau, Sears, & Ho, 2007). Research on hate crimes has found that sexual minorities are most likely to be victims of violence (Herek & Sims, 2008), such as verbal harassment and assault, and that gay men and lesbians are more likely to be victimized than other stigmatized groups (Nelson & Krieger, 1997). Moreover, sexual orientation harassment has been documented even among more progressive employers (Colgan et al., 2007). Pichler (2012) differentiates formal sexual orientation discrimination, that is, institutional discrimination tied to employment decisions or outcomes, from informal or interpersonal discrimination. He therefore argues that quid pro quo same sex sexual harassment is formal discrimination, whereas hostile work environment and sexual orientation harassment are types of informal discrimination.

Although gay men and lesbians are relatively understudied in the management and organization literature in general (Ragins, 2004; Pichler, 2007), there is an increasingly large and sophisticated literature on sexual orientation discrimination. Similar to self-report and other hate crime statistics, scholarly research suggests that sexual orientation discrimination is pervasive (see for example Brewer & Lyons, 2016). The literature has consistently shown that gay men and lesbians are discriminated against in selection decisions (Hebl, Foster, Mannix, Dovidio, 2002; Pichler, Varma, & Bruce, 2010) and receive lower performance evaluations (Horvath & Ryan, 2003), and that there are wage differences between persons based on sexual orientation (for example, Antecol, Jong, & Steinberger, 2008). Explanations for discrimination vary, and include the stigma of sexual orientation itself (Hebl et al., 2002; Pichler et al., 2010), perceived job misfit by decision makers based on the gendered nature of jobs (Pichler et al., 2010), and occupational sorting among gay men and lesbians (Antecol et al., 2008; Tilcsik, Anteby, & Knight, 2015). Moreover, gay men and lesbians face interpersonal discrimination in addition to formal discrimination, in the form of, for example, less interpersonal interaction, less eye contact (Barron & Hebl, 2013; Hebl et al., 2002), and ultimately perhaps social exclusion (Dovidio, Kawakami, & Beach, 2001). This may be why sexual minorities are sometimes trapped in "gay ghettos" or low-paying classes of work (Ragins & Cornwell, 2001) and are practically invisible in the upper echelons of organizations (Gedro, 2010), with some notable exceptions, such as Apple CEO Tim Cook, who came out publicly in 2014 (Cook, 2014).

Discrimination and harassment are tied to predominant attitudes about gay men and lesbians as well as other individual differences, such as religiosity and social dominance orientation (see for example, Pichler, Varma, & Bruce, 2010). Links between social dominance orientation, political–economic conservatism, and attitudes about homosexuality have been documented in meta-analyses (Whitley & Lee, 2000). Individuals with more traditional attitudes about gender roles, who have less contact with sexual minorities, are sexist, reside in localities with more common antigay attitudes, or have strong conservative religious ideologies are more likely to have antigay attitudes (Masser & Abrams, 1999). Public opinion and attitudes have changed over time, however. Public opinion about sexual minorities has historically been negative (Kite & Whitley, 1996). Whereas a 1965 survey found that 70 percent of respondents indicated a belief that homosexuality was harmful to American life (Herek, 2002), more recently this percentage had fallen: 40 percent of Americans expressed a belief that homosexuality is wrong (Bowman, Rugg, & Marsico, 2013). More and more Americans are supportive of protections for sexual minorities, including hate crime laws and employment protections (Gallup, 2014).

In terms of outcomes of heterosexism, research has shown that perceived heterosexism is related to psychological stress and strain among sexual minorities (Mays & Cochran, 2001; Meyer, 2003; Ragins & Cornwell, 2001). Perceptions of heterosexism are also related to negative job attitudes and lower organizational self-esteem (see for example Button, 2001; Driscoll, Kelley, & Fassinger, 1996; Griffith & Hebl, 2002; Ragins & Cornwell, 2001; Waldo, 1999), increased job anxiety (Button, 2001), and psychological symptoms such as depression and anxiety (Ragins et al., 2007). These findings are consistent with the minority stress model, which has shown that the stress tied to feeling like a target of prejudice and discrimination in society is so great that it can lead to serious psychological consequences (Waldo, 1999). Perceptions of heterosexism are also negatively related to disclosure or coming out in the workplace (Ragins & Cornwell, 2001). There is little if any research in the management and organization literature tying leadership to hetero-sexism. The sections that follow go some way to rectifying this.

LGB-SUPPORTIVE POLICIES

As mentioned above, there is no comprehensive federal antidiscrimin-ation legislation prohibiting discrimination on the basis of sexual orien-tation. In other words, it is not illegal to use sexual orientation in employment decisions. This is despite extensive evidence showing that sexual orientation discrimination is pervasive. Only 21 states and the District of Columbia prohibit sexual orientation discrimination (Human Rights Campaign, 2014). Some municipalities also adopt antidiscrimina-tion policies (Ragins & Cornwell, 2001), but most Americans live in areas without protections.

Political leaders have questioned whether comprehensive federal anti-discrimination measures are effective in terms of reducing discriminatory behavior (Barron & Hebl, 2013), and empirical research suggests they are. For instance, when employees are protected by local ordinances, they perceive less sexual orientation discrimination (Ragins & Cornwell, 2001). When confederates of the experimenters acting as job applicants in Texas applied for jobs in person wearing baseball caps that read either "Gay and Proud" or "Texan and Proud," the ostensibly gay applicants were treated more negatively in terms of interpersonal discrimination in areas without employment protections (Hebl et al., 2002). In a fictitious hiring scenario involving human resource managers as decision makers, gay applicants were rated as less hirable than heterosexual applicants, but only in areas without antidiscrimination legislation (Barron, 2009). Similarly, Tilcsik (2011) found that gay applicants received more call-backs in an audit study in areas with antidiscrimination legislation than in areas without. In sum, the empirical evidence to date suggests that federal antidiscrimination policies could be effective. It seems that federal antidiscrimination policies are warranted, yet there is a lack of leadership at the federal level to enact them.

Recent literature reviews indicate there is increased interest in institutional support for LGB issues, including among business organizations (Maher et al., 2009). More and more corporations are coming out in support of sexual minority workers by adopting supportive policies, which include nondiscrimination policies, domestic partner benefits, inclusive diversity training, employee resource groups, and public commitment to the LGBT community (see for example Human Rights Campaign, 2016; Ragins & Cornwell, 2001). One might argue that business organizations, as opposed to the federal government, have led the way when it comes to adopting policies that support sexual minority workers. These trends are consistent with and probably responsive to changes in societal attitudes. According to the Human Rights Campaign (2013), in 2002, 61 percent of Fortune 500 companies had non-discrimination policies; in 2013, this figure had risen to 88 percent. That said, Fortune 500 firms do not necessarily represent the typical American firm. A recent study of a nationally representative set of firms estimated that 4.26 percent of firms had nondiscrimination policies and domestic partner benefits in place in 1996, whereas 20.58 percent did in 2009 (Pichler, Cook et al., in press). These estimates varied across states and regions. As will be explained in more detail below, given that adoption of LGB-supportive policies is not mandated nor widespread, a key proposition of this chapter is that leadership—transformational and heroic—is useful, if not necessary, to the adoption and effectiveness of these policies.

There is limited research on why organizations choose to adopt these policies (see for example Chuang, Church, & Ophir, 2011) and the consequences of policy adoption (see for example Pichler, Cook, Blazovich, Huston, & Strawser, in press). There is little information in the academic literature as to the role of leaders in organizations when it comes to adoption of LGB-supportive policies. It is important to note that policy adoption can have negative outcomes for firms, including boycott of a firm's products or services (Chuang, Church, & Hu, forthcoming; Creed, Scully, & Austin, 2002; Kaplan, 2006), which is surely something that interests business leaders. The potential negative outcomes of adopting LGB-supportive policies and practices are another key reason why leadership is important to the success of these policies, and perhaps especially more heroic forms of leadership. That said, among Fortune 500 firms, even those with what might be considered more negative reputations when it comes to worker protections, such as Walmart, have adopted LGB-supportive policies (see for example Wahba, 2015). There are two sets of rationales in the literature as to why organizations do—or should—adopt LGB-supportive policies and practices: a moral case and a business case.

In terms of a moral case, scholars have called on organizations to adopt LGB-supportive policies and to develop supportive climates for persons of diverse sexual orientations (Bell, Özbilgin, Beauregard, & Surgevil, 2011; Huffman, Watrous-Rodriguez, & King, 2008; King & Cortina, 2010). The rationale here is, in part, that without such protections, employees who are sexual minorities are more likely to be victims of discrimination, harassment, and violence, and thus experience negative psychological outcomes. King and Cortina (2010) therefore argue that employers have a moral imperative to adopt LGB-supportive policies so as to keep their workplaces safe and their employees healthy. Advocacy groups, such as the Human Rights Campaign, have also called for the adoption of LGB-supportive policies based on a moral framework. Research suggests that the number of firms adopting supportive policies increases each year (Lewis & Pitts, 2011)—although there is little research as to the antecedents or effectiveness of policy adoption, including the role of leadership.

Relatively speaking, there is more research on the business case for the adoption of LGB-supportive policies. Gay and lesbian consumers are more likely to have higher disposable incomes; the purchasing power of this "pink market" is thought to be more than $800 million (Paul et al., 2011). Policies that support sexual minorities may be attractive to this market. Moreover, supportive policies are theorized to allow firms to attract better talent (Day & Greene, 2008), including better qualified heterosexual workers who respond favorably to more progressive employers (Badgett & Gates, 2006; Pichler, Cook et al., in press). Based on perceived organizational support theory (Eisenberger et al., 1986), Pichler, Ruggs, and Trau (2017) developed a model of outcomes of LGB-supportive policies, wherein they argued that all individuals, regardless of their sexual orientation, should feel better supported by employers with LGB-supportive policies because of the signal that the employer truly cares about employee well-being. For these and other reasons, business leaders themselves have argued that there is a "business case" for adopting LGB-supportive policies, including maintaining positive relationships with customers, complying with local or state laws and regulations, and potential financial benefits (Metcalf & Rolfe, 2011).

Recent studies that have tested different aspects of the business case for LGB-supportive policies have generally found positive results. For instance, Johnston and Malina (2008), Li and Nagar (2013), and Wang and Schwarz (2010) used stock market reactions to measure financial benefits of the adoption of LGB-supportive policies, and results generally suggest that the stock market reacts positively to announcements of adoption of these policies. These authors have called upon other researchers to test the mechanisms as to why LGB-supportive policies might be related to firm financial performance outcomes. Pichler, Cook, et al. (in press) developed perhaps the most sophisticated test of the business case for LGB-supportive policies to date in a longitudinal study of a nationally representative sample of firms. They found that, across time, adoption of LGB-supportive policies is related to higher firm value, productivity, and profitability, and that these benefits are higher for firms with heavier emphasis in research and development—a proxy for demand for highly skilled labor.

In addition to positive outcomes at the firm level, research suggests that LGB-supportive policies are related to more positive job attitudes among sexual minority workers (Law, Martinez, Ruggs, Hebl, & Akers, 2013; Ragins & Cornwell, 2001; Trau, 2015). Perceptions of discrimination are also lower (see for example Button, 2001; Griffith & Hebl, 2002; Ragins & Cornwell, 2001; Ruggs, Martinez, Hebl, & Law, 2015). Badgett, Durso, Kastanis, and Mallory (2013) qualitatively reviewed the existing literature on employee outcomes of LGB-supportive policies. They found that these policies are related to higher rates of sexual orientation disclosure, lower rates of discrimination, and more positive health outcomes for sexual minority workers. In terms of diversity training, research has shown that integrating goal setting into inclusive diversity training can improve heterosexuals' attitudes toward gay men and lesbians. These results support both the moral and business rationales for policy adoption (Huffman, Watrous-Rodriguez, & King, 2008; King & Cortina, 2010).

Pichler, Ruggs, and Trau (2017) posited that a key reason why LGB-supportive policies are related to positive outcomes at the individual level, such as job attitudes, is that they improve the sexual diversity climate. This is defined as "formal and informal aspects of an institutional environment" regarding support for sexual orientation and gender identity diversity (Liddle, Luzzo, Hauenstein, & Schuck, 2004, p. 33). Pichler et al. (2017) further argued that all employees should have positive job attitudes because diversity climates signal goodwill toward employees (McKay & Avery, 2015). This is consistent with research on diversity climates, which has shown that diversity policies are related to positive diversity climates and, hence, to positive job attitudes on the part of all employees (McKay & Avery, 2015). The available research supports this proposition. In a study of the Safe Schools Program for Gay and Lesbian Students (SSP), Szalcha (2003) found that LGB-supportive policies were positively related to the sexual diversity climate (among both gay and heterosexual respondents), and separately, Velez and Moradi (2012) found that the sexual diversity climate was related to more positive job attitudes. The question, therefore, becomes: what sort of leadership is needed to effectively implement LGB-supportive policies and thereby reduce heterosexism in organizations?

LGB-SUPPORTIVE POLICIES: TRANSFORMATIONAL AND HEROIC LEADERSHIP

As reviewed above, heterosexism, including sexual orientation discrimination, sexual orientation harassment, and hate crimes based on sexual orientation, is pervasive in society and in organizations. Heterosexism results in a whole host of negative attitudinal and psychological outcomes for sexual minority employees. Moreover, the ambient model of harassment would suggest that heterosexism could affect heterosexuals negatively as well. In this connection, research on the business case for LGB-supportive policies would suggest that heterosexist environments, or organizations with unsupportive sexual diversity climates, risk negative outcomes in terms of talent management and profitability (Pichler, Ruggs, & Trau, 2017; Pichler, Cook et al., in press). With all of that said, it seems imperative from moral and business perspectives that organizational leaders advocate for the adoption of LGB-supportive policies, as well as the effective implementation of these policies. Yet, LGB-supportive policies and practices are not yet prevalent among most firms (Pichler et al., in press).

There is limited research on the role of organizational leaders when it comes to adopting or advocating for LGB-supportive policies. Based on propositions from institutional theory (Scott, 2001), Trau, Chuang, Pichler, Lim, Wang, and Halvorsen (2018) argue that local communities shape the views and decisions of business leaders regarding LGB-supportive policies. For instance, social norms in local communities are related to LGB-supportive policies in organizations embedded in these communities, in part because leaders want to avoid backlash from antigay activists and consumer groups. At the same time, LGB activists leverage resources such as political ties, donations, and alliances to affect social norms in local and broader communities as related to sexual orientation. Thus, Trau et al. (2018) argue that business leaders' interactions with individuals and groups in the local communities within which their organizations operate may have a strong influence on their decisions regarding support for LGB workers. This proposition has yet to be tested, and is an important area for future research. That said, there are examples that support this proposition. For instance, King County, Washington has a history of integrating business owners who are sexual minorities into its community, and the county executive recently announced it is to track the number of contracts awarded to small businesses owned by sexual minorities. Members of the chamber of commerce say this has a positive impact on the local economy (Constantine, 2016). Of course, outcomes of interactions between business leaders and communities can be reciprocal, and recent research suggests that business leaders may influence the passage of protective legislation, for instance by establishing LGB-supportive policies as normative (Martinez, Ruggs, Sabat, Hebl, & Binggeli, 2013).

Although there is scant research on organizational leaders' attitudes about or influence over adopting LGB-supportive policies, research suggests that support from top management is key to the successful implementation of these policies (Ng, 2008; Ng & Wyrick, 2011). Top management support refers to executive leaders making a public commitment to LGB-supportive policies and truly "walking the walk," so to speak, when it comes to supporting sexual minority workers (Morrison, 1992). Given that frontline managers are generally responsible for utilizing many LGB-supportive policies, such as nondiscrimination policies, it is important that leaders not only make public their commitment, but also hold managers accountable for their appropriate use of these policies. That said, there is a lack of research on managerial use or implementation of LGB-supportive policies, or the influence of leaders in this connection. Research has shown that when top management support for broader diversity policies is high, minority representation in organizations increases (Hu, Dinev, Hart, & Cooke, 2012). This suggests that top management for LGB-supportive policies could be related to the attraction and retention of sexual minority workers. In fact, Pichler et al. (2017) argue that top management support is key to employee perceptions of LGB-supportive policies, and that when top management support is high, all workers should react more positively to these policies, heterosexual workers included.

Transformational leadership theory (Bass & Riggio, 2006) and heroic leadership theory (Allison & Goethals, 2013) support the proposition that certain forms of leadership, such as making a public commitment to LGB-supportive policies and behaving in ways that demonstrate this commitment, should be related to positive reactions to these policies, as well as their successful implementation within organizations. The basic proposition of transformational leadership theory is that more active forms of leader behaviors can not only affect follower behavior, but also shape and change the sources of motivation within followers (Bass, 1997; Bass & Steidlmeier, 1999). A key proposition of heroic leadership theory is that heroic leaders cause emotional reactions among followers, called "elevation" (Haidt, 2003), which can move followers to engage in prosocial behavior (Allison, Goethals, & Kraemer, 2017). These propositions are closely related, and suggest that transformational and heroic leadership could lead to the adoption (and the effectiveness) of LGB-supportive policies and practices. In fact, transformational and heroic leadership may be *necessary* to the successful implementation of LGB-supportive policies and other policies that are controversial and diffusely adopted, and which may lead to negative reactions from consumers, interest groups, and other stakeholders.

Transformational leadership theory posits that there are four forms of transformational leadership. They are presented here in order from less to more active forms of leadership, with more active forms being more effective (Bass, 1999). *Individualized consideration* consists of leaders getting to know followers on an individual basis and providing tailored guidance and feedback. *Intellectual stimulation* involves leaders promoting rationality, and providing logic, reason, and analysis around problem solving. *Inspirational motivation* involves communicating high expectations in a concise manner while providing support to reach those expectations. Finally, *idealized influences* involves developing and communicating a clear vision and demonstrating behaviors that support that vision. Although vision in the context of business organizations should ultimately be tied to firm strategy, exceptional leaders develop their own visions which influence the direction of organizations—and even of society, such as Bill Gates' vision in the early 1980s that, in the future, there would be a personal computer in every home.

To shape and transform the way organizational members view LGB-supportive policies, and how managers implement them, all forms of transformational leadership seem relevant, especially the more active forms. For instance, when talking about LGB-supportive policies with business unit or line managers, it is important to tailor messages to these followers' unique backgrounds, their values, and the types of employees they manage. Inspirational motivation could be useful in combination by communicating expectations of managers in terms of how they should implement LGB-supportive policies, and by providing feedback as to their performance. Intellectual stimulation could be useful when communicating with individual managers or groups, and leaders could provide rationality by communicating both the moral and business cases for LGB-supportive policies as a way to make their organizations healthier and more effective. Perhaps the most important way in which organization leaders can motivate others is by either communicating a vision as to how LGB-supportive policies should be implemented, and/or tying the rationale for these policies to the vision of the firm.

Of course, demonstrating commitment to this vision through supportive behavior, such as sponsoring and attending LGB employee resource groups, should also be particularly useful (see Ragins & Cornwell, 2001). This is where heroic leadership theory becomes an excellent complement to transformational leadership theory. Heroic leaders have themselves gone through personal experiences that have transformed them; their attention is refocused from the self to others (Campbell, 1988). Moreover, they are autonomous in the sense that they are willing to deviate from and challenge prevailing social norms (Allison & Goethals, 2017). By sharing their transformative experiences with others, and by demonstrating conviction to goals through "walking the walk" (Allison & Goethals, 2013), they make an emotional connection to followers, thus influencing their feelings and behaviors (Goethals & Allison, 2014). This is highly similar to the proposition that unconventional and emotion-inducing behaviors, which characterize idealized influence, should be particularly motivating to others (see for example Bass, 1999). Heroic leaders are those that would be willing to make public commitments to controversial policies, such as LGB-supportive policies, and would demonstrate their moral conviction not only through public statements but also through more personal interactions and support, such as attending LGB employee resources groups and inviting LGB employees' families to company events.

Since transformation and heroic leadership are more active and thus more effective than transactional leadership (Bass, 1999), which involves more contractual types of exchanges between leaders and followers, transformational and heroic leadership should be related to the more effective implementation of LGB-supportive policies so that followers should more fully understand the policies and the rationale for the policies, and should be more motivated to talk about and support them. This being the case, transformational and heroic leadership should ultimately be related to reduced heterosexism (see Figure 6.1). First, transformational and heroic leadership should directly reduce heterosexism, because employees should be demotivated to discriminate or harass on the basis of sexual orientation when leaders are publicly supportive of and committed to sexual minority workers. This seems especially true when leaders demonstrate a moral conviction to LGB-supportive policies and are willing to take risks, even self-sacrificial risks, to ensure the success of these policies, which is what heroic leaders do (Allison, 2018). Second, there should be an indirect relationship between transformational and heroic leadership through the adoption and more effective implementation of LGB-supportive policies. In other words, leadership may just be the key to the success of LGB-supportive policies, as well as reduced heterosexism.

This is important because research shows that just having LGB-supportive policies on paper does not necessarily reduce heterosexism (see for example Ragins & Cornwell, 2001). Moreover, public support for LGB-supportive policies, for LGB workers, and for LGB individuals in general has not been at the forefront of business leaders' agendas, at least perhaps until very recently. This is despite the fact that public support is a key type of LGB-supportive practice that can reduce perceptions of heterosexism (Ragins & Cornwell, 2001). An example of a business leader publicly supporting sexual minorities, and perhaps a surprising one at that, is that of the chairman and CEO of Goldman Sachs, Lloyd Blankfein. He has given public support not only to LGB policies but also to the cause of same sex marriage, having acted as a national spokesperson for the Human Rights Campaign, which calls on politicians to support same sex marriage (Huffington Post, 2012). He has been called courageous for "taking on" social conservatives in the relatively conservative business space of Wall Street (Rosenthal, 2012).

Idealized influence, the most active form of transformational leadership and the most effective, is all about walking the walk, which includes engaging in emotion-inducing or self-sacrificial behaviors—highly similar to heroic leadership. Lloyd Blankfein has walked the walk in terms of his being not only a supporter of but also a spokesperson for gay rights, as well as actively trying to influence gay rights legislation. Although he may not be a quintessential example of a transformational or heroic leader, he has faced backlash from clients regarding his support, and part of the Occupy Los Angeles movement that supported gay marriage has said they don't want Blankfein's name associated with same sex marriage (Du, 2012). Nevertheless, Blankfein continues to support LGB policies at Goldman Sachs, such as a nondiscrimination policy based on sexual orientation, and is an advocate for sexual minorities, however disliked he may be.

DISCUSSION

Sexual minorities are an understudied group in the management and organization literature, yet they are a relatively large minority group, and they face pervasive discrimination and harassment. Public attitudes regarding sexual minorities have become more positive in recent years, including support for employment protections. That said, there is currently no comprehensive federal legislation that would protect sexual minorities from discrimination in employment settings. To varying degrees across industries and regions, organizations have taken it upon themselves to protect and support sexual minority workers. There is very little research on the reasons why organizations adopt LGB-supportive policies, especially perhaps when it comes to the role leaders might play. The purpose of the current chapter, therefore, was to review the literature on heterosexism and LGB-supportive policies and integrate this literature with theory and research on transformational and heroic leadership so as to develop a model of relationships between leadership, LGB-supportive policies, and heterosexism.

The model developed in this chapter suggests that transformational and heroic leaders may be the key to not only the adoption but also the successful implementation of LGB-supportive policies. Line managers generally bear responsibility for implementing and using LGB-supportive policies, such as nondiscrimination policies, and their response to these policies likely depends on their attitudes toward gay men and lesbians, among a number of other individual difference variables (Pichler et al., 2010; Pichler & Ruggs, in press). Thus, it is important that executive leaders transform managers' sense of motivation about these policies, help them see the importance of these policies, and inspire them to use them effectively in their business units and departments. Leaders' vision and engagement can also positively influence employees' perceptions of LGB-supportive policies and sexual minorities, perhaps especially when they demonstrate a moral conviction behind these policies and not just a business case—that is, when they behave like heroic leaders. In total, this would suggest that when leaders engage in emotion-inducing, unconventional, and even self-sacrificial behaviors regarding LGB-supportive policies, firms should be more likely to adopt these policies, they should be implemented more effectively, and thus heterosexism should be reduced. This could improve the well-being of all workers (Pichler et al., 2017) and improve firm financial performance (Pichler et al., in press).

REFERENCES

Allison, S. T. (2018). Heroic leadership. In A. Farazmand (Ed.), *Global encyclopedia of public administration and public policy*. New York: Springer.

Allison, S. T., & Goethals, G. R. (2013). *Heroic leadership: An influence taxonomy of 100 exceptional individuals*. New York: Routledge.

Allison, S. T., & Goethals, G. R. (2017). The hero's transformation. In S. T. Allison, G. R. Goethals, & R. M. Kramer (Eds.), *Handbook of heroism and heroic leadership* (pp. 379–80). New York: Routledge.

Allison, S. T., Goethals, G. R., & Kraemer, R. M. (2017). Setting the scene: The rise and coalescence of heroism science. In S. T. Allison, G. R. Goethals, & R. M. Kraemer (Eds.), *Handbook of heroism and heroic leadership* (pp. 1–16). New York: Routledge.

Antecol, H., Jong, A., & Steinberger, M. (2008). The sexual orientation wage gap: The role of occupational sorting and human capital. *ILR Review*, *61*(4), 518–43.

Badgett, M. V., Durso, L. E., Kastanis, A. & Mallory, C. (2013). The business impact of LGBT-supportive workplace policies. The Williams Institute. Retrieved September 29, 2017 from https://williamsinstitute.law.ucla.edu/wp-content/uploads/Business-Impact-of-LGBT-Policies-May-2013.pdf.

Badgett, M. V., & Gates, G. J. (2006). The effect of marriage equality and domestic partnership on business and the economy. The Williams Institute. Retrieved September 29, 2017 from https://williamsinstitute.law.ucla.edu/research/economic-impact-reports/the-effect-of-marriage-equality-and-domestic-partnership-on-business-and-the-economy/.

Badgett, M. V., Lau, H., Sears, B., & Ho, D. (2007). *Bias in the workplace: Consistent evidence of sexual orientation and gender identity discrimination.* Los Angeles: The Williams Institute, UCLA School of Law.

Barron, L. G. (2009). Promoting the underlying principle of acceptance: The effectiveness of sexual orientation employment antidiscrimination legislation. *Journal of Workplace Rights*, *14*, 251–68.

Barron, L. G., & Hebl, M. (2013). The force of law: The effects of sexual orientation antidiscrimination legislation on interpersonal discrimination in employment. *Psychology, Public Policy, and Law*, *19*(2), 191.

Bass, B. M. (1997). Does the transactional–transformational leadership paradigm transcend organizational and national boundaries? *American Psychologist*, *52*(2), 130.

Bass, B. M. (1999). Two decades of research and development in transformational leadership. *European Journal of Work and Organizational Psychology*, *8*(1), 9–32.

Bass, B. M., & Riggio, R. E. (2006). *Transformational leadership*. Mahwah, NJ: Psychology Press.

Bass, B. M., & Steidlmeier, P. (1999). Ethics, character, and authentic transformational leadership behavior. *The Leadership Quarterly*, *10*(2), 181–217.

Bell, M. P., Özbilgin, M., Beauregard, T. A., & Surgevil, O. (2011). Voice, silence, and diversity in 21st century organizations: Strategies for inclusion of gay, lesbian, bisexual and transgender employees. *Human Resource Management*, *50*, 131–46.

Bowman, K., Rugg, A., & Marsico, J. (2013). Polls on attitudes on homosexuality and gay marriage. *AEI Public Opinion Studies*. Washington, DC: American Enterprise Institute.

Brewer, G., & Lyons, M. (2016). Discrimination of sexual orientation: Accuracy and confidence. *Personality and Individual Differences*, *90*, 260–64.

Button, S. B. (2001). Organizational efforts to affirm sexual diversity: A cross-level examination. *Journal of Applied Psychology, 86,* 17–28.

Campbell, J. (1988). *The power of myth.* New York: Anchor Books.

Chuang, Y., Church, R., & Hu, C. (forthcoming). Effects of movement and opportunities on the adoption of same-sex partner health benefits by corporations. *Journal of Management.*

Chuang, Y., Church, R., & Ophir, R. (2011). Taking sides: The interactive influences of institutional mechanisms on the adoption of same-sex partner health benefits by Fortune 500 corporations, 1990–2003. *Organization Science, 22,* 190–209.

Colgan, F., Creegan, C, McKearney, A. and Wright, T. (2007). Equality and diversity policies and practices at work: Lesbian, gay and bisexual workers. *Equal Opportunities International, 26*(6), 590–609.

Constantine, D. (2016, July 8). Executive's plan to support LGBT entrepreneurs praised by business leaders as a national model. Retrieved September 29, 2017 from http://www.kingcounty.gov/elected/executive/constantine/news/release/2016/July/8-lgbt-small-businesses.aspx.

Cook, T. (2014). Tim Cook speaks up. *Bloomberg.* Retrieved January 19, 2017 from https://www.bloomberg.com/news/articles/2014-10-30/tim-cook-speaks-up.

Croteau, J. M. (1996). Research on the work experiences of lesbian, gay, and bisexual people: An integrative review of methodology and findings. *Journal of Vocational Behavior, 48*(2), 195–209.

Creed, W. E. D., Scully, M. A., & Austin, J. R. (2002). Clothes make the person? The tailoring of legitimizing accounts and the social construction of identity. *Organization Science, 13*(5), 475–96.

Day, N. E., & Greene, P. G. (2008). A case for sexual orientation diversity management in small and large organizations. *Human Resource Management, 47*(3), 637–54.

Dovidio, J. F., Kawakami, K., & Beach, K. R. (2001). Implicit and explicit attitudes: Examination of the relationship between measures of intergroup bias. In R. Brown & S. L. Gaertner (Eds.), *Blackwell handbook of social psychology: Intergroup processes* (pp. 175–97). Malden, MA: Blackwell.

Driscoll, J. M., Kelley, F. A., & Fassinger, R. E. (1996). Lesbian identity and disclosure in the workplace: Relation to occupational stress and satisfaction. *Journal of Vocational Behavior, 48*(2), 229–42.

Du, L. (2012). The LGBT faction of Occupy Los Angeles protested Lloyd Blankfein's support of gay marriage this weekend. Retrieved September 29, 2017 from http://www.businessinsider.com/the-lgbt-faction-of-occupy-los-angeles-protested-lloyd-blankfeins-support-of-gay-marriage-this-weekend-2012-3?IR=T.

Eisenberger, R., Hungtinton, R., Hutchison, S., & Sowa, D. (1986). Perceived organizational support. *Journal of Applied Psychology, 71,* 500–7.

Gedro, J. (2010). The lavender ceiling atop the global closet: Human resource development and lesbian expatriates. *Human Resource Development Review, 9*(4), 385–404.

Goethals, G. R., & Allison, S. T. (2014). Kings and charisma, Lincoln and leadership: An evolutionary perspective. In G. R. Goethals, S. T. Allison,

R. M. Kramer, & D. M. Messnick (Eds.), *Conceptions of leadership* (pp. 111–24). New York: Palgrave Macmillan.

Gonsiorek, J. C., & Weinrich, J. D. (1991). The definition and scope of sexual orientation. In J. C. Gonsiorek & J. D. Weinrich (Eds.), *Homosexuality: research implications for public policy* (pp. 1–12). Thousand Oaks, CA: SAGE.

Griffith, K. H., & Hebl, M. R. (2002). The disclosure dilemma for gay men and lesbians: "Coming out" at work. *Journal of Applied Psychology, 87*(6), 1191–9.

Haidt, J. (2003). Elevation and the positive psychology of morality. *Flourishing: Positive Psychology and the Life Well-Lived, 275,* 289.

Hebl, M. R., Foster, J. B., Mannix, L. M., & Dovidio, J. F. (2002). Formal and informal interpersonal discrimination: A field study of bias toward homosexual applicants. *Personality and Social Psychology Bulletin, 28*(6), 815–25.

Herek, G. M. (2002). Heterosexuals' attitudes toward bisexual men and women in the United States. *Journal of Sex Research, 39*(4), 264–74.

Herek, G. M. (2004). Beyond "homophobia": Thinking about sexual prejudice and stigma in the twenty-first century. *Sexuality Research & Social Policy, 1*(2), 6–24.

Herek, G. M., & Sims, C. (2008). Sexual orientation and violent victimization: Hate crimes and intimate partner violence among gay and bisexual males in the United States. In R. J. Wolitski, R. Stall, & R. O. Valdiserri (Eds.), *Unequal opportunity: Health disparities among gay and bisexual men in the United States* (pp. 35–71). New York: Oxford University Press.

Horvath, M., & Ryan, A. M. (2003). Antecedents and potential moderators of the relationship between attitudes and hiring discrimination on the basis of sexual orientation. *Sex Roles, 48*(3–4), 115–30.

Hu, Q., Dinev, T., Hart, P., & Cooke, D. (2012). Managing employee compliance with information security policies: The critical role of top management and organizational culture. *Decision Sciences, 43,* 615–59.

Huffington Post. (2012). Lloyd Blankfein, Goldman Sachs CEO, supports same-sex marriage. Retrieved September 29, 2017 from http://www.huffingtonpost. com/2012/02/06/goldman-sachs-lloyd-blankfein-same-sex-marriage-_n_12571 00.html

Huffman, A. H., Watrous-Rodriguez, K. M., & King, E. B. (2008). Supporting a diverse workforce: What type of support is most meaningful for lesbian and gay employees? *Human Resource Management, 47*(2), 237–53.

Human Rights Campaign (2013). Corporate equality index. Retrieved August 18, 2014, from http://www.hrc.org/campaigns/corporate-equality-index.

Human Rights Campaign. (2014). Workplace discrimination laws and policies. Retrieved September 29, 2017 from http://www.hrc.org/resources/entry/ workplace-discrimination-policies-laws-and-legislation.

Human Rights Campaign. (2016). *Corporate equality index 2016: Rating American workplaces on lesbian, gay, bisexual and transgender equality.* Retrieved from http://hrc-assets.s3-website-us-east-1.amazonaws.com//files/ assets/resources/CEI-2016-FullReport.pdf.

Hunt, J. (2011). A history of the employment non-discrimination act. *Center for American Progress.* Retrieved January 27, 2017 from https://www.american

progress.org/issues/lgbt/news/2011/07/19/10006/a-history-of-the-employment-non-discrimination-act/.

Hollingsworth v. Perry, 133 S. Ct. 2652 (2013).

Gallup. (2014). Gay and lesbian rights. Retrieved from http://www.gallup.com/poll/1651/gay-lesbian-rights.aspx.

Johnston, D., & Malina, M. A. (2008). Managing sexual orientation diversity: The impact on firm value. *Group & Organization Management*, *33*(5), 602–25.

Kaplan, D. M. (2006). Can diversity training discriminate? Backlash to lesbian, gay, & bisexual diversity initiatives. *Employee Responsibilities and Rights Journal*, *18*, 61–72.

King, E. B., & Cortina, J. (2010). The social and economic imperative of LGBT-supportive organizational policies. *Industrial and Organizational Psychology: Perspectives on Science and Practice*, *3*, 69–78.

Kite, M. E., & Whitley, B. E. (1996). Sex differences in attitudes toward homosexual persons, behaviors, and civil rights: A meta-analysis. *Personality and Social Psychology Bulletin*, *22*(4), 336–53.

Law, C. L., Martinez, L. R., Ruggs, E. N., Hebl, M. R., & Akers, E. (2013). Trans-parency in the workplace: How the experiences of transsexual employees can be improved. *Journal of Vocational Behavior*, *79*, 710–23.

Lewis, G. B., & Pitts, D. W. (2011). Representation of lesbians and gay men in federal, state, and local bureaucracies. *Journal of Public Administration Research and Theory*, *21*(1), 159–80.

Li, F., & Nagar, V. (2013). Diversity and performance. *Management Science*, *59*(3), 529–44.

Liddle, B. J., Luzzo, D. A., Hauenstein, A. L., & Schuck, K. (2004). Construction and validation of the lesbian, gay, bisexual, and transgendered climate inventory. *Journal of Career Assessment*, *12*(1), 33–50.

Maher, M. J., Landini, K., Emano, D. M., Knight, A. M., Lantz, G. D., Parrie, M., Pichler, S., & Sever, L. M. (2009). Hirschfeld to Hooker to high schools: A study of the history and development of GLBT empirical research, institutional policies, and the relationship between the two. *Journal of Homosexuality*, *56*(7), 921–58.

Martinez, L. R., Ruggs, E. N., Sabat, I. E., Hebl, M. R., & Binggeli, S. (2013). The role of organizational leaders in sexual orientation equality at organizational and federal levels. *Journal of Business and Psychology*, *28*(4), 455–66.

Masser, B., & Abrams, D. (1999). Contemporary sexism: The relationships among hostility, benevolence, and neosexism. *Psychology of Women Quarterly*, *23*, 503–17.

Mays, V. M., & Cochran, S. D. (2001). Mental health correlates of perceived discrimination among lesbian, gay, and bisexual adults in the United States. *American Journal of Public Health*, *91*(11), 1869–76.

Meyer, I. H. (2003). Prejudice, social stress, and mental health in lesbian, gay, and bisexual populations: Conceptual issues and research evidence. *Psychological Bulletin*, *129*(5), 674.

Mckay, P., & Avery, D. (2015). Diversity climate in organizations: Current wisdom and domains of uncertainty. *Research in Personnel and Human Resource Management*, *33*, 191–233.

Metcalf, H., & Rolfe, H. (2011). *Barriers to employers in developing lesbian, gay, bisexual and transgender-friendly workplaces*. National Institute of Economic and Social Research. Retrieved October 1, 2017 from http://citeseerx. ist.psu.edu/viewdoc/download?doi=10.1.1.231.3633&rep=rep1&type=pdf.

Michael, R. T., Gagnon, J. H., Laumann, E. O., & Kolata, G. (1995). *Sex in America: A definitive survey*. New York: Warner Books.

Morrison, A. M. (1992). *The new leaders: Guidelines on leadership diversity in America*. San Francisco: Jossey-Bass.

Nelson, E. S., & Krieger, S. L. (1997). Changes in attitudes toward homosexuality in college students: Implementation of a gay men and lesbian peer panel. *Journal of Homosexuality*, *33*(2), 63–81.

Ng, E. S. (2008). Why organizations choose to manage diversity? Toward a leadership-based theoretical framework. *Human Resource Development Review*, *7*(1), 58–78.

Ng, E. S., & Wyrick, C. R. (2011). Motivational bases for managing diversity: A model of leadership commitment. *Human Resource Management Review*, *21*(4), 368–76.

Ohara, E. (2016). First amendment defense act would be "devastating" for LGBTQ Americans. Retrieved January 19, 2017 from http://www.nbcnews. com/feature/nbc-out/first-amendment-defense-act-would-be-devastating-lgbtq-americans-n698416.

Paul, A. K., McElroy, T., & Leatherberry, T. (2011). Diversity as an engine of innovation. *Deloitte Review*. Retrieved September 29, 2017 from http:// www.deloitte.com/view/en_co/co/fda8881dc918d210VgnVCM2000001b56f00 aRCRD.htm#.

Pichler, S. (2007). Heterosexism in the workplace. In P. Raskin & M. Pitt-Catsouphes (Eds.), *Work and family encyclopedia* (pp. 135–48). Chestnut Hill, MA: Sloan Work and Family Research Network.

Pichler, S. (2012). Sexual orientation harassment: An integrative review with directions for future research. In S. Fox & T. Lituchy (Eds.) *Gender and the dysfunctional organization* (pp. 135–48). Cheltenham, UK and Northampton, MA: Edward Elgar.

Pichler, S., Cook, K., Blazovich, J., Huston, J. M., & Strawser, W. R. (in press). Do gay-friendly corporate policies enhance firm performance? *Human Resource Management*.

Pichler, S., & Ruggs, E. (in press). LGBT workers. In A. Collela & E. King (Eds.), *Oxford handbook of workplace discrimination*.

Pichler, S., Ruggs, E., & Trau, R. (2017). Worker outcomes of LGBT-supportive policies: A cross-level model. *Equality, Diversity & Inclusion: An International Journal*, *36*, 17–32.

Pichler, S., Varma, A., & Bruce, T. (2010). Heterosexism in employment decisions: The role of job misfit. *Journal of Applied Social Psychology*, *40*(10), 2527–55. doi:10.1111/j.1559-1816.2010.00669.x

Ragins, B. R. (2004). Sexual orientation in the workplace: The unique work and career experiences of gay, lesbian, and bisexual workers. *Research in Personnel and Human Resources Management*, *23*, 35–120.

Ragins, B. R., & Cornwell, J. M. (2001). Pink triangles: Antecedents and consequences of perceived workplace discrimination against gay and lesbian employees. *Journal of Applied Psychology*, *86*, 1244–61. doi:10.1037/0021-9010.86.6.1244.

Ragins, B. R., Singh, R., & Cornwell, J. M. (2007). Making the invisible visible: Fear and disclosure of sexual orientation at work. *Journal of Applied Psychology*, *92*(4), 1103–18. doi:10.1037/0021-9010.92.4.1103.

Rosenthal, A. (2012, February 6). Congratulations, Lloyd Blankfein. Retrieved Sepember 29, 2017 from https://takingnote.blogs.nytimes.com/2012/02/06/congratulations-lloyd-blankfein/.

Ruggs, E. N., Martinez, L. R., Hebl, M. R., & Law, C. L. (2015). Workplace "trans"-actions: How organizations, coworkers, and individual openness influence perceived gender identity discrimination. *Psychology of Sexual Orientation and Gender Diversity*, *2*, 404–12.

Scott, W. R. (2001). *Institutions and organizations* (4th ed.). Thousand Oaks, CA: Sage Publications.

Sears, J. T. (1997). Thinking critically/intervening effectively about homophobia and heterosexism. In J. T. Sears & W. L. Williams (Eds.), *Overcoming heterosexism and homophobia: Strategies that work* (pp. 13–48). New York: Columbia University Press.

Tilcsik, A. (2011). Pride and prejudice: Employment discrimination against openly gay men in the United States. *American Journal of Sociology*, *117*(2), 586–626. doi:10.1086/661653.

Tilcsik, A., Anteby, M., & Knight, C. R. (2015). Concealable stigma and occupational segregation: Toward a theory of gay and lesbian occupations. *Administrative Science Quarterly*, *60*(3), 446–81.

Trau, R. N. C. (2015). The impact of discriminatory climate perceptions on the composition of interorganizational developmental networks, psychosocial support, and job and career attitudes of employees with an invisible stigma. *Human Resource Management*, *54*, 345–66. doi:10.1002/hrm.21630.

Trau, R. N., Chuang, Y. T., Pichler, S., Lim, A., Wang, Y., & Halvorsen, B. (2018). The dynamic recursive process of community influences, LGBT-support policies and practices, and perceived discrimination at work. In S. Bruce Thomson and G. Grandy (Eds.), *Stigmas, Work and Organizations* (pp. 71–98). New York: Palgrave Macmillan.

United States v. Windsor, 133 S. Ct. 2675 (2013).

Velez, B. L., & Moradi, B. (2012). Workplace support, discrimination, and person–organization fit: Tests of the theory of work adjustment with LGB individuals. *Journal of Counseling Psychology*, *59*(3), 399.

Wahba, P. (2015, June 26). From Walmart to J. C. Penney, retail reflect shifting views on gay rights. Retrieved September 29, 2017 from http://fortune.com/2015/06/26/retailers-gay-rights-supreme-court/

Waldo, C. R. (1999). Working in a majority context: A structural model of heterosexism as minority stress in the workplace. *Journal of Counseling Psychology*, *46*, 218–32.

Wang, P., & Schwarz, J. L. (2010). Stock price reactions to LGBT non-discrimination policies. *Human Resource Management, 49*(2), 195–216.

Whitley, B. E., & Lee, S. E. (2000). The relationship of authoritarianism and related constructs to attitudes toward homosexuality. *Journal of Applied Social Psychology, 30*(1), 144–70.

NOTE

1. The term "LGBT" is often used in the literature, but the workplace experiences of transgender individuals are different from those of other sexual minorities. Since this chapter focuses on experiences of lesbian, gay, and bisexual workers specifically, the term "LGB" will be used throughout.

7. Leadership in strip clubs

Maggie B. Stone

REVIEW OF THE LITERATURE

Gender and Patriarchy

The effect of gender in the workplace, specifically in service industries that are prone to sexualization, is a topic that has been studied through many lenses over the years (Frank, 2007; Gutek, 1985; Kelly, 1991; LaPointe, 1992; Lerum, 2000; Loe, 1996; MacKinnon, 1980; Philaretou & Young, 2007; Williams, Giuffre, & Dellinger, 1999). Occupations in the hierarchy of strip clubs are gendered and patriarchal, with males holding authority positions and controlling the workplace activity of female employees (Price, 2008; Price, 2010). Dancers enact established gender roles and sexual scripts in their interactions with other employees and patrons. Female employees outnumber male employees in lower status positions—most often as dancers and occasionally as bartenders—in which their labor involves providing service to men (Lewis, 2006). In this way, strip club organization is dictated by the performance and commodification of gender (Egan & Frank, 2005). Within this structure, clubs are classed as well (Trautner, 2005). Murphy (2003) describes patriarchal managerial staff as "Big Brother" figures controlling the work of dancers through surveillance and intimidation.

Gendered power in strip clubs is often dichotomized as being either exploitative or empowering to female employees. Women working in strip clubs largely function in subordinate positions that highlight and perpetuate inequality at the institutional level (Brents & Sanders, 2010; Deshotels & Forsyth, 2006; Frank, 2007; MacKinnon, 1980; Wood, 2000). There is evidence of discriminatory practices taking place in gendered work environments such as strip clubs (Sweet & Tewksbury, 2000). On the other hand, many individual accounts are of financial, physical, and emotional empowerment (Ronai & Ellis, 1989). This is certainly the position promoted during hiring initiatives (Stone, 2014). It has been argued that the industry simultaneously exploits females as a whole while empowering some women personally (Barton, 2006; Lerum, 2000; Lewis, 2000).

LEADERSHIP QUALITIES AND STYLES

Leaders are expected to embody a number of qualities that promote the efforts of those who work for them. These include, but are not limited to, integrity, communication skills, task delegation skills, motivational skills, and the ability to discipline. Five general models of leadership styles may be described: *laissez-faire, autocratic, democratic* (that is, participative), *transactional,* and *transformational.* A laissez-faire manager provides little direction or guidance to employees, whereas autocratic leaders are strict in their enforcement of rules, which are set independent of outside input. Democratic leaders consider employee feedback. The transactional leadership style relies on performance results as a means of incentivizing workers via positive and negative sanctions. Transformational leaders value communication with staff and delegation of tasks in order to motivate success through the achievement of productivity goals. Of these styles, autocratic and laissez-faire are the two most evidently practiced in strip clubs, but elements of the other styles may be present. For instance, many clubs employ a characteristic of transformational leadership by offering bonus incentives for drink, dance, and/or champagne room sales, but their overall management style is not consistent with this model.

STRIP CLUB TYPOLOGIES

Two broad typologies have been developed with respect to strip club styles. Bradley-Engen and Ulmer (2009) have classified three types of strip clubs: social, hustle, and show. DeMichele and Tewksbury (2004) define strip clubs by class, as dive or upscale. Social clubs are distinguished by their blue-collar, bar-down-the-street atmosphere and focus on selling a dancer's time more by drinks than by dances, a feature that is reflected in the physical layout of the club, with fewer stages and more common areas such as pool tables. By contrast, a show club is comparable to an upscale gentlemen's club. It caters to business professionals, exudes opulence, and is more likely to book feature performers. Dancers rely on stage performances and lap dances to earn income rather than socializing with patrons or hustling. The industry of hustle clubs emphasizes competition among dancers, scheduling flexibility, manipulation of customers via sexual innuendo and promises in order to increase sales, and a reliance on selling lap dances and champagne room hours. Dive establishments are differentiated by mass presence of working-class patrons, physical contact between dancers and patrons, locations that are lower on the socioeconomic scale, and lower incomes. Upscale establishments, on the other hand, provide a variety of amenities and cater to a higher class of patron (DeMichele & Tewksbury, 2004). It is possible to combine the two typologies such that each strip club is defined according to its class type and club type (for example, social dive, upscale show). That is the model applied throughout this chapter.

Leadership within strip clubs varies according to type. For instance, management in social clubs, by nature of controlling and collecting fees for drinks and dances, have much more direct contact with dancers and allow for less autonomy. In hustle clubs, however, that sort of direct money management and monitoring is eschewed, with the expectation that dancers will provide a tip at the end of their work period that accurately reflects their overall monetary intake. Thus, in this way, management takes on a more laissez-faire style of leadership, but an autocratic style is still at work in other aspects of club supervision.

HIERARCHICAL STRUCTURE

Previous research has established the hierarchical nature of strip club employment roles (Barton, 2006; Bott, 2006; DeMichele & Tewksbury, 2004; Forsyth & Deshotels, 1997; Lerum, 2000; Lewis, 2006; Mestemacher & Roberti, 2004; Price, 2008; Price, 2010, Stone, 2014). Owners and others in management positions, primarily male, control the strip club through initiating and terminating employment, administering disciplinary action, assigning shifts and tasks, and establishing expectations for behavior and appearance (Trautner, 2005; Price, 2010; Stone, 2014). DJs and bouncers—also nearly always male—have less authority than owners and managers but still exercise control over dancers, with both overseeing the behavior of dancers while in the club. In some cases, bouncers also supervise dancers' behavior in the parking lot. Bartenders loosely fall within the same realm of power as DJs and bouncers. In smaller venues they may function as middle management when owners and managers are away from the facility, regulating dancers' conduct to ensure obedience to the rules (Price, 2008). Unlike DJs and bouncers, bartenders may be female, depending on the size and type of club, location, and shift. Hostesses, waitresses, and dancers are typically female, with the exception of the rare male strip club (Dressel & Petersen, 1982; Tewksbury, 1994).

Communication Style

In a study of the strip club interview process, conducted by this author in 2011 at 25 strip clubs in three Midwestern cities, evidence of a hierarchical structure included lower level employees knocking on management doors before opening, waiting for an indication of management's consent before initiating a conversation, and undertaking work-exclusive conversations with instructional content rather than casual banter. This style was more commonly observed among upscale clubs in the sample. Social clubs exhibited two distinct types: those in which personnel were friendly and chatty with each other and those in which the interaction between all employees was minimal.

Rule Enforcement and Flexibility

Regardless of management style, basic rules existed in all clubs and were explained during the job interview. Some standards vary predictably according to club style. The price of drinks, lap dances, and champagne rooms are set by management in social clubs, whereas hustle club dancers determine dance prices themselves and are not compensated for social drinking with a patron. Club guidelines regarding degree of nudity and limits on physical interactions with patrons are dictated by city ordinances (Stone, 2014). DeMichele and Tewksbury (2004), however, note the flexible nature of the procedures established by those in hierarchical power. For instance, a dancer may break the rules of contact on the club floor with bouncer approval; this usually involves a monetary tip. Top income earners who dance for the club may not be held to the same standards or as accountable to the house rules as others, a decision dictated by management. Stone (2014) observed several dynamics related to accountability. Some clubs expressed awareness that dancers occasionally violated codes of conduct, such as showing body parts that were restricted by city ordinance or using illegal substances, but denied approval of such practices, placing all accountability on the dancer herself. In some such clubs, dancers engage in visibly impermissible acts in plain view of management, negating the latter's claims that employees of the club strictly abide by city ordinances. Other strip clubs in cities with more restrictive regulations seemed to unify through rebellion against the agency enforcing ordinances. In these cases, management offer positive reinforcement to dancers that circumvent the law.

Appearance Standards

Yet another expectation communicated by management is that of physical appearance (Deshotels, Tinney, & Forsyth, 2012; Stone, 2014). Criteria for appropriate footwear and garments were discussed as early as the initial interview (Stone, 2014). Deshotels, Tinney, and Forsyth (2012) make the argument that appearance regulations constitute a form of management over the product (that is, the dancer herself), resulting in a predictable, controlled sexual presentation of dancers as a unit. Dancers are expected to wear facial and sometimes body makeup and to remove visible body hair (Deshotels, Tinney, & Forsyth, 2012). The majority of clubs favor platform heels because they are consistent with strip club branding images and enhance the female silhouette. During interviews, managers—more often female than male—who took on a mentoring role would give advice regarding the shoe styles best suited for safety and comfort, as well as the use of moleskin to prevent blisters (Stone, 2014). The communication of dress expectations varies according to nudity ordinances. In cities with complex requirements, the explanation and enforcement of these rules can be rigorous. In general, dancers are expected to don lingerie, evening gowns, or dancewear in accordance with club type. They are coached to dress in layers to enhance the process of clothing removal.

Bodily Safety

The ability of clubs' male staff to ensure the safety of the club's dancers is frequently noted with pride by management (Stone, 2014). Bodily safety includes protection from physical and sexual harm by patrons. A protective environment may be demonstrated through the presence of video cameras, signage, and bouncers whose role is made known through accessories such as a nightstick, security badge, and uniform sometimes imprinted with the word "security." The gendered nature of bodily safety is linguistically evident in assertions made by males in leadership positions, such as "I take care of my girls"—in stark contrast to females who describe club safety as something that is handled by "them" (that is, male club staff) (Stone, p. 736).

Alcohol and Drug Use

Those in leadership positions at strip clubs must routinely manage the use of alcohol and illicit drugs, which are frequently an element of the environment and its culture. In fact, consuming alcohol is an expected function of many dancers, especially those in social clubs that rely on generating money through the sale of drinks with the dancers. According to Lavin (2013), the social norms regarding drug use are largely independent of management unless such use creates a workplace disturbance. Managers' control over drugs may be enacted passively through the allowance of drug dealing and using in private areas; some first engage in an elementary analysis of the risks and benefits that such transactions present to the club (Lavin, 2014). In many cases, managers encourage the use of alcohol over drugs for legal reasons, but they may still monitor dancers' alcohol intake and, in extreme cases, will revoke drinking privileges if this is considered necessary. Upscale club managers are more likely to regulate and punish the use of illicit substances (Stone, 2014). When a club is compelled to actively address complaints or concerns about drug use, management sometimes respond by modifying the physical space (for example, removing bathroom stall doors) or increasing video surveillance (Egan, 2006).

Fees and Tipping

With the exception of some social clubs which earn the majority of their income from beverage sales, most strip clubs rely on dancers to generate profits for the club and its employees. Thus, dancers must charge patrons enough to compensate for the amount of money they will pay to others working in the club, and even owners of the club. Therefore, while dancers are at the bottom of the management hierarchy, it is their labor that sustains the entire club. Mount (2016) examined management's framing of strip club labor as teamwork so that everyone can "share the wealth" (p. 22).

In midsized cities, fees to the house (such as stage fee, base rental, door fee, music fee) may range from $9 to upwards of $40 depending on the shift, the day of the week, and the status of the club. Fees in destination cities that cater to travelers and the tourism industry, such as Las Vegas, can be double or triple the amount. The day shift tends to be less expensive than the night shift. Similarly, Sunday and weekday fees are lower than those charged during prime weekend hours (Friday and Saturday evenings). While patrons pay slightly above average drink prices for their own beverages, drinks purchased for dancers in social clubs include not only the drink but also a fixed amount of time that the dancer spends socializing with the patron while consuming it, and therefore cost significantly more. A "small" drink typically costs $20 to $35 for the beverage and 10 minutes of time. Prices increase according to the amount of time and size of beverage purchased. Social clubs are more likely to keep all proceeds from the first small drink bought for a dancer and a percentage (usually 50 percent) of all drinks thereafter, rather than charging each dancer an outright stage/house fee. Hustle and show clubs typically charge a fee that the dancer pays upfront to the manager on duty. The nicer the club, the more the dancer is expected to pay. It is not uncommon for a club to waive the stage/house fee for a new dancer's first shift. Some clubs offer incentive programs that decrease house fees proportionate to champagne room sales. Dancers are generally expected to tip DJs, bouncers, bartenders, and/or managers. Some clubs make tipping mandatory and even set a minimum amount for the tip, while others leave it to each dancer's discretion.

Tipping follows the club's management hierarchy, with some exceptions. For example, an expected tip to a DJ is between $5 and $10, but if he makes an introduction to a patron, provides smoke and special lighting to enhance stage dances, or otherwise accommodates a dancer during her shift, it is with the expectation of a higher tip. Failure to meet gratuity expectations frequently results in negative sanctions, such as the DJ's future refusal to accommodate lighting requests, or unfair treatment in the stage rotation. Tips to bouncers are generally the lowest (for example, $1 to $2 for escorting the dancer to her vehicle at the end of her shift—a practice that may be required by the club both for the dancer's safety and to ensure the bouncer receives a tip). Similar to DJs, if a bouncer has provided a profitable introduction, then the dancer's tip is expected to reflect it. The tip to the house, delivered to the manager, is the highest and should be based on overall earning from the dancer's shift.

Hustle club management, in particular, relies on dancers tipping in good faith, thus illustrating trust as an element of leadership. The convention in this type of strip club of allowing dancers to set their own prices for dances and champagne room hours restricts management's knowledge of a dancer's monetary intake for the time worked. In many cases, they rely on estimates from bouncers, DJs, bartenders, and champagne room hosts regarding a dancer's activity over the course of the shift, but this is complicated by the size of hustle clubs, the sheer number of dancers present throughout an evening, and allowing dancers to determine their own schedules. With new faces appearing daily and known ones seen irregularly, it can be difficult to recognize and track specific people.

Recruitment and Anticipatory Socialization

Dancers are recruited into strip club work in a variety of ways. Informal networking is one of the most frequently cited methods by which both male and female dancers are recruited into the industry (Dressel & Petersen, 1982; Forsyth & Deshotels, 1997; Skipper & McCaghy, 1970; Sweet & Tewksbury, 2000; Thompson & Harred, 1992). Dressel and Petersen also note that male strippers tend to drift into the work, while women may be coaxed into dancing through liquor, flattery, bribes, economic threats, or peer pressure (Barton, 2006). Simmons (1998) describes women as being "economically compelled, lured by false claims, or duped" into the work (p. 129). Dancers frequently describe the process of being socialized into club etiquette and processes by other dancers once on the job. Anticipatory socialization, however, has been found to occur during the recruitment and interview process (Stone, 2014). Future dancers are taught about and encouraged to conform to the norms and values of the club by the manager conducting the interview, in hopes of easing the transition into the new role. Management uses the job interview to provide education on a number of work-related necessities: salesmanship, time and money management, appearance expectations, and desensitization via alcohol.

LEADERSHIP AT CHAMPAGNE DELIGHTS: A CASE STUDY

This section explores the author's experiences as a dancer at Champagne Delights and her negotiation of the hierarchical system in which even patrons and other dancers enacted leadership roles at times. Champagne Delights is best described as an upscale hustle club. The gender makeup of its staff followed that of the majority of other clubs described in the extant literature. Dancers were exclusively female. Bartenders and champagne room hosts were primarily female. All of the managers, bouncers, and DJs were male. The main floor was a large multistoried room with an elevated main stage, a circular side stage enclosed by poles, a long social bar at the entry, and a private elevated champagne bar at the rear near the main stage. The couch dance rooms were out of view of the main room but in the line of sight of the DJ booth. On the second story, looking down on the main floor, were four champagne rooms. A high standard of luxury was communicated by furnishing (for example, couches and chairs were plush velvet) and staff uniforms (for example, bouncers wore tuxedos). Dancers were not employed by the club but worked as independent contractors. At any given time there were more than 200 dancers on the roster. There was no regular schedule or shift rotation. A dancer need only access her locker once per month to remain in good standing. Beyond that she was free to work as many or as few times per week as she chose. The amount of time she spent working was her choice as well, as long as she paid the stage fee and tipped the appropriate parties. There were no established starting or ending hours for shifts, although stage fees and tipping expectations increased for those beginning work after 6pm. Dancers negotiated their own fees for couch dances and champagne room hours, with the rare exception of specials announced by the DJ (for example, two-for-one dances, $1 one-minute lap dances). Tipping by patrons at the stage was more of an indication of their interest than a source of serious revenue. Patrons were expected to pay for dancers' drinks, but dancers made no profit from this transaction, as they would have in a social club.

Dancing at Champagne Delights was an opportunity to examine the numerous faces of leadership in a hustle club environment. In many ways, management there functioned autocratically. Dancers with past behavioral issues and those who were underage were restricted from drinking alcohol, and this was made visible to bartenders, staff, and patrons by an arm bracelet. Platform-heeled shoes were required in order to work. Dancers were expected to maintain high standards of grooming and attire. Any dancer whose attire and/or appearance were inappropriate was asked to remediate the situation or leave. Once on the floor, dancers had to sign in with the DJ for main and side stage rotations. DJs selected the music to which the dancers danced on stage. Dancers were expected to listen for stage cues, inform the DJ when their stage rotation was affected by couch dances or champagne room engagements, and respond to sale announcements. When on stage, dancers had to be completely nude by the second song. All employees monitored dancers' compliance with this requirement, even other dancers, who would inform on an offending dancer to someone above her in the hierarchy. DJs usually enforced the rule with an overhead announcement, often played off as a joke, reminding the dancer to remove her clothing. Occasionally a bouncer would be sent by the stage to give a direct warning. Managers were rarely out on the floor and did not intervene until there had been repeat offenses. Their verbal reprimands were delivered in private. Money, however, was managed in a very different manner.

A laissez-faire management style takes a relaxed approach, with little supervision. Champagne Delights' management employed this tactic with dancers in one area: capital. A great deal of lenience was afforded to dancers in terms of what Mount (2016) described as spreading the wealth. Dancers earned money that they were then expected to give away to others employed by the club, but this management style had the advantage of making those decisions feel as though they were the dancers' decisions rather than mandates. It fostered a climate in which the majority of workers went out of their way to promote positive relations with the expectation of financial remuneration. Tips to the DJ, the bouncer who acted as an escort to your vehicle, and the "house" (that is, management) were mandatory. Minimums were assumed but never stated. Managers repeatedly encouraged dancers: "If *you* have a good night, we should *all* have a good night." Frequently, newcomers looked to other dancers for guidance regarding tipping expectations. This could have been an unintended consequence of the laissez-faire management style, or perhaps it was management taking advantage of an opportunity to allow dancers to feel a modicum of autonomy in an otherwise autocratic system. Certainly the relaxed nature of scheduling was directly related to capital. The club kept a large roster of dancers in order to ensure that the floor would never be empty and save them from having to require dancers to keep specific hours.

The only fixed monetary amounts in the club were dancers' stage fees and drink costs (for example, beer, cocktails, shots, a bottle of sparkling wine in a champagne room). Bottle sales, essentially the club's room rental fee, merited the patron access to a champagne room for one hour. Prices varied according to the brand of sparkling wine; the rules of the champagne room and the amount of time did not vary. A token economy had been created to offset stage fees by rewarding top-dollar champagne room sales. Sales in excess of $300 (the least expensive bottle available during the evening hours) earned a stage fee coupon of $10 per $100. Dancers each paid a predetermined stage fee assessed according to the time of club entry. Begin working during the first (and slowest) hour of the day and the fee would be waived; begin working after 8pm on a Friday or Saturday evening and the highest possible fee of $40 would be required.

All other costs (for example, tips, price of dances, hourly dancer fee for the champagne room—in addition to the club's bottle fee) were determined by the dancer. Dancers were not locked into charging an amount set by the club. They could raise or lower their prices as they saw fit. They were also responsible for collecting and storing money until they left the club, which carried with it risks of nonpayment, loss, and theft. While affixing a price to oneself provides a dancer with the opportunity to empower herself financially ("I am worth *this* amount of money"), that thought itself is the beginning of a lesson in the commodification of her time and body. This can be good for management because it produces efficient workers who earn higher profits that should result in larger tips to the house. Managers never asked dancers how much they made for the period of time they spent in the club, but they had several ways of tracking their earnings. Just as Murphy (2003) described, there were cameras installed throughout the facility. The main screen was housed in the manager's office and displayed 24 views simultaneously. Bouncers, the DJ, and hosts recorded dancers' activities and reported in to management. Regardless, the club was frequently very busy and there was no limit on the number of dancers who could work at one time. On a weekend night there could be as many as 50 dancers on the floor simultaneously. A dancer could take care to manage her transactions privately. For instance, champagne room hosts were privy to the hourly fee charged by the dancer if the patron paid with a credit card, but not when he paid with cash.

A dancer's accountability for tipping is not always to those in positions of authority. Other dancers sometimes monitor tipping out. During one evening, a coworker and I had a multiple-hour champagne room. Spending several hours in a champagne room during an evening earns the expectation of higher tips from all parties. At the end of our night, she tipped the champagne host accordingly but gave the manager an amount based on a typical night's intake. We tipped out together, leaving me with a difficult decision: do I out my coworker, whose trust and support I needed in the club, by tipping the appropriate amount, or do I follow her example and risk alienating the manager? In the short term I sided with my coworker, earning me nothing more than a stern look from the manager. The next time I worked, however, I tipped him more than the difference and apologized.

This instance illustrates the relative fluidity of authority in the club setting. The leadership of management was, at least temporarily, undermined by that of a person on the same tier of the hierarchy as I was. Generally, managers commanded the most power, followed by bouncers and the DJ. Champagne room hosts' influence was limited to that area and exclusively related to money. At Champagne Delights, bartenders held no authority over anyone. Had it been a social club, that would not have been the case. Other dancers could exert a great deal of weight on one's decisions not related to money as well. The guidance of dancers, particularly to a newcomer, was crucial to navigating regular patrons and difficult staff, meeting unspoken expectations of management, and getting through emergency situations. Although they had no official authority, following the lead of key dancers could significantly impact a dancer's experience in the work environment. Patrons of Champagne Delights also played a leadership role. They frequently dictated what (for example, shots versus a cocktail) and how much a dancer had to drink (although there are certainly ways of circumventing the quantity factor), the nature of the conversation, and even details as mundane as the color of a dancer's clothing. In a world based on catering to consumers, their preferences become the dancer's responsibility.

Champagne Delights exemplifies many aspects of management and leadership styles discussed in this chapter. The power structure of strip clubs can be complicated, and their main source of revenue, the dancers, are led by a variety of entities within the club environment—sometimes even those at the same level of the hierarchy, and regardless of gender. Leadership also comes from outside the club, in the form of influence from patrons without whose financial input the club would not exist. Money is involved at every level of strip club organization and labor. Dancers negotiate with patrons and follow rules set by the club environment in order to generate revenue, which is then redistributed to those who are higher in rank and authority than they are. It is capital, then, that truly leads every facet of the strip club.

REFERENCES

Barton, B. (2006). *Stripped: Inside the lives of exotic dancers.* New York: New York University Press.

Bott, E. (2006). Pole position: Migrant British women producing "selves" through lap dancing. *Feminist Review, 83,* 23–41.

Bradley-Engen, M. S., & Ulmer, J. T. (2009). Social worlds of stripping: The processual orders of exotic dance. *The Sociological Quarterly, 50*(1), 29–60.

Brents, B. G., & Sanders, T. (2010). Mainstreaming the sex industry: Economic inclusion and social ambivalence. *Journal of Law and Society, 37*(1), 40–60.

DeMichele, M. T., & Tewksbury, R. (2004). Sociological explorations in site-specific social control: The role of the strip club bouncer. *Deviant Behavior, 25*(6), 537–58.

Deshotels, T. H., & Forsyth, C. J. (2006). Strategic flirting and the emotional tab of exotic dancing. *Deviant Behavior, 27*(2), 223–41.

Deshotels, T. H., Tinney, M., & Forsyth, C. J. (2012). McSexy: Exotic dancing and institutional power. *Deviant Behavior, 33*(2), 140–8.

Dressel, P. I., & Petersen, D. M. (1982). Becoming a male stripper: Recruitment, socialization, and ideological development. *Work and Occupation, 9,* 387–406.

Egan, R. D. (2006). Resistance under the black light: Exploring the use of music in two exotic dance clubs. *Journal of Contemporary Ethnography, 35*(2), 201–19.

Egan, R. D., & Frank, K. (2005). Attempts at a feminist and interdisciplinary conversation about strip clubs. *Deviant Behavior, 26*(4), 297–320.

Forsyth, C. J., & Deshotels, T. H. (1997). The occupational milieu of the nude dancer. *Deviant Behavior, 18*(2), 125–42.

Frank, K. (2007). Thinking critically regarding strip club research. *Sexualities, 10*(4), 501–17.

Gutek, B. (1985). *Sex and the workplace.* San Francisco: Jossey-Bass.

Kelly, R. M. (1991). *The gendered economy: Work, careers, and success.* Thousand Oaks, CA: Sage.

LaPointe, E. (1992). Relationships with waitresses: Gendered social distance in restaurant hierarchies. *Qualitative Sociology, 15*(4), 377–93.

Lavin, M. (2013). Rule-making and rule-breaking: Strip club social control regarding alcohol and other drugs. *Deviant Behavior, 34*(5), 361–83.

Lavin, M. (2014). If you want it, you can get it right here: Space and drug use in strip clubs. *Humanity & Society, 38*(2), 132–57.

Lerum, K. (2000). Doing the dirty work: Emotion work, professionalism, and sexuality in a customer service economy. Dissertation, University of Washington.

Lewis, J. (2000). Controlling lap dancing: Law, morality, and sex work. In R. Weitzer (Ed.) *Sex as work: Prostitution, pornography, and the sex industry* (pp. 203–16). New York: Routledge.

Lewis, J. (2006). "I'll scratch your back if you'll scratch mine": The role of reciprocity, power and autonomy in the strip club. *The Canadian Review of Sociology and Anthropology, 43*(3), 298–311.

Loe, M. (1996). Working for men—at the intersection of power, gender, and sexuality. *Sociological Inquiry, 66*, 399–421.

MacKinnon, C. (1980). Women's work. In D. A. Neugarten & J. M. Shafritz (Eds.), *Sexuality in organizations* (pp. 59–66). Oak Park, IL: Moore Publishing.

Mestemacher, R. A., & Roberti, J. W. (2004). Qualitative analysis of vocational choice: A collective case study of strippers. *Deviant Behavior, 25*(1), 43–65.

Mount, L. (2016). "Behind the curtain": Strip clubs and the management of competition for tips. *Journal of Contemporary Ethnography, 45*(1), 1–28.

Murphy, A. G. (2003). The dialectical gaze: Exploring the subject–object tension in the performances of women who strip. *Journal of Contemporary Ethnography, 32*(3), 305–35.

Philaretou, A. G., & Young, C. L. (2007). The social construction of female sexuality in a sexualized work environment (SWE): The case of a comedy club. *Sexual Addiction & Compulsivity, 14*, 41–62.

Price, K. (2008). "Keeping the dancers in check": The gendered organization of stripping work in The Lion's Den. *Gender & Society, 22*(3), 367–89.

Price, K. (2010). *Strip club: Gender, power, and sex work.* New York: New York University Press.

Ronai, C. R., & Ellis, C. (1989). Turn-ons for money: Interactional strategies of a table dancer. *Journal of Contemporary Ethnography, 18*(3), 12–22.

Simmons, M. (1998). Theorizing prostitution: The question of agency. *Sexuality and Culture, 2*, 125–49.

Skipper, J. K., & McCaghy, C. H. (1970). Stripteasers: The anatomy and career contingencies of a deviant occupation. *Social Problems, 17*(3), 391–405.

Stone, M. (2014). "This could be a good avenue for you": Influential strategies in the hiring of exotic dancers. *Deviant Behavior, 35*(9), 727–41.

Sweet, N., & Tewksbury, R. (2000). Entry, maintenance, and departure from a career in the sex industry: Strippers' experiences of occupational costs and rewards. *Humanity and Society, 24*, 136–61.

Thompson, W. E., & Harred, J. (1992). Topless dancers: Managing stigma in a deviant occupation. *Deviant Behavior, 13*(3), 291–311.

Trautner, M. N. (2005). Doing gender, doing class: The performance of sexuality in exotic dance clubs. *Gender and Society, 19*(6), 771–88.

Tewksbury, R. (1994). A dramaturgical analysis of male strippers. *Journal of Men's Studies, 2*(4), 325–42.

Williams, C. L., Giuffre, A., & Dellinger, K. (1999). Sexuality in the workplace: Organizational control, sexual harassment, and the pursuit of pleasure. *The Annual Review of Sociology, 25*, 73–93.

Wood, E. A. (2000). Working in the fantasy factory: The attention hypothesis and the enacting of masculine power in strip clubs. *Journal of Contemporary Ethnography, 29*(1), 5–31.

8. Training religious leaders in sexually related issues

William R. Stayton

As a parish minister for a small New England congregation 50 years ago, I was asked by the youth of my senior high school if I would provide them a sex education course. There was nothing available in the local public schools. I asked another minister and the local rabbi if they would join me. Among the three congregations were about 60 youth. We planned a four-session Sunday night course. We asked our youth to come with signed notes from their parents. More than 400 youth showed up, supposedly with signed notes, so we had to move to the sanctuary of the church we met in. The kids were eager learners and the course was very successful. The event was even written up in our local newspaper.

Six weeks later the local Board of Education asked me if the religious community could offer another course, for middle school students. I agreed as long as their parents could also be invited to the course. Soon I was being asked by other communities to offer similar courses. After I provided these courses to young people, adults from my parish and from the greater community began coming to me with their sexual issues, many of which I had never heard of. While I had always been curious about sexuality, I got nothing helpful in seminary; I then went on to get a doctorate in psychology and counseling, but still did not receive information on anything other than pathological issues in sexuality.

What follows is a sample of the various types of pastoral care situations I encountered during my first five years in the pastorate. I had been offered no preparation to assist me in being helpful to parishioners or others.

INTERSEXUALITY

A young couple, following the birth of their first child, were told that their child was born with ambiguous genitalia. Although genetically a male, the doctor told them it would be easier, healthier, and in the best interests of the child to surgically reassign the child as female. The surgery was for cosmetic purposes only. Not having any knowledge about intersex children, I agreed they should follow the doctor's advice, which I would not have done today.

GENDER EXPRESSION

The husband in a couple was a crossdresser. The wife was okay with his crossdressing at home, but their concern was whether they should tell their two prepubertal children about the crossdressing before puberty or following it. I did not even know about crossdressing. I learned a lot from them.

SEXUAL ORIENTATION

A popular minister in a neighboring community had an affair with his male associate. Both were married and their wives were aware of their relationship. The minister wanted to remain with his congregation, but the associate decided to leave that church, take another church, get a divorce, and live as a gay man. I learned from him that he had become happier and more fulfilled as a person, and ended up with the support of his family and his wife. Their love was stronger than their marriage vows and both were able to move on in their separate lives with the support of the other.

LIFESTYLE

I realized that within my congregations, several couples were living alternative lifestyles, such as open marriages, swinging, secret affairs, nonmarital relationships, and same sex extramarital affairs. I was asked to give a plenary on alternative lifestyles at an international family life conference. In my research, I learned that strict sexual exclusivity, "till death you do part," is in fact a minority lifestyle in our culture. I was given no tools in seminary or my graduate counseling courses to be helpful to those following an alternative lifestyle and seeking advice.

OTHER SEXUAL VALUE ISSUES

A family from a neighboring parish came to see me. The daughter, who had just turned 13, was pregnant. While abortion was against their religious belief system, they talked together, prayed, searched their hearts, and finally, unanimously, decided she would have an abortion. The father said several factors influenced their decision. The first consideration was the daughter's age. Second, she was a brilliant student and had a promising academic future. Third, she was not sure who the father was, as she had had consensual sex with five classmates at the same time. This was in the era before DNA testing. The family felt that going through the pregnancy and having the child would be harmful to her emotional health and her future pursuits. The decision was even more difficult because her father was the leader of a local "right-to-life" group in our community, believed in the views of that community with all his heart, and wanted to remain as its leader; however, he believed that in this instance it was not relevant to their particular situation. They wanted to discuss their processing with me. I agreed with their decision on the abortion because it was what their daughter really wanted. I felt the agony of her parents and know that it caused a lot of reflection and value clarification. I don't remember the father's final decision about his role in the antiabortion movement.

SEXUAL FUNCTION AND DYSFUNCTION

A couple with two teenage children had a sexless marriage. They loved one another very much and did not want to end their marriage. The wife had a high sex drive while the husband had no sex drive or sexual interest. The wife had an extramarital relationship with the husband of another couple where the wife had no desire and the husband had a high sex drive. While both felt guilty, they believed that their relationship saved both marriages. They consulted me regarding their guilt, not about ending the affair. They believed that if their spouses knew, it would end both marriages; therefore, they chose not to tell them.

Offering several sexuality-related courses and counseling many adults convinced me that people were eager to learn about their sexuality. I also became convinced of the way in which religion and sexuality are so intricately interwoven in our society. Many people that I counseled blamed their sexual issues and problems on their religious upbringing. It was from these experiences that I was led to choose human sexuality as my vocation, and especially the training of religious leaders and teachers.

There are at least four historically new phenomena that also challenge the core values of most religious institutions, especially in the United States (Stayton, 1998, p. 27).

(1)   There is a biblical admonition in Genesis to "be fruitful and multiply." This has been the biblical formula for human survival, which is now the formula for human disaster. It took human beings from their beginnings until 1850 just to populate the planet with 1 billion people. Between 1850 and 1950, another 3 billion were added. In 2016, more than 7 billion people lived on the earth. Humans are reproducing at geometric rates.

(2)   Reliable birth control methods, such as the condom, separated out recreational sex—or sex for pleasure only—from procreational sex. Christianity has not developed a sex ethic for recreational sexual relationships, particularly nonmarital ones, except to communicate such behavior as immoral and sinful.

(3)   Adolescence is a new historical phenomenon in the life cycle. In biblical times there was no such thing as adolescence. Persons were often married either just before or just during puberty. By 1850, the average youth was going through puberty at 15 or 16. They were often married by 17 or 18, thus adolescence was a period of about two to four years. It made sense to recommend abstinence so the young person could adjust to their developing body, emotionally, spiritually, and physically. In 2016, the average age of puberty was 11 or 12, and for many even younger—9 or 10. Youth are partnering later, often in their late 20s or early 30s. This means that often the period between puberty and marriage can be as much as 10–15 years—the time when the young person is at their reproductive and hormonal height. Our religions have not been resourceful in helping their youth to navigate their sexuality in a healthful or responsible way.

(4)   Most couples are not prepared for the admonition in most marriage vows of "till death do us part." In the early 1900s, life expectancy, according to actuarial rates, was 47/48 years. In 2016, life expectancy was 78/79. In 1900, the average marriage, if a couple stayed together, would last 25–30 years, just long enough to raise any of their children to young adulthood. In 2016, marriage meaning "till death do us part" could last more than 50 years. We in religious institutions need to give our young people the necessary skills to maintain a relationship for 50 or more years.

While there is a long history of the relationship between religions and sexuality, documented in history as well as the Bible and the Quran, there is little on religious leaders' training to speak out objectively on sexuality issues (Turner & Stayton, 2012). There were pre-scientific admonitions against and prohibitive statements on particular sexual behaviors, but, as in the Hebrew Bible, these were based on family, intermarriage, and/or inheritance factors.

In this chapter, I discuss the history of some of the programs and projects that have been developed and found to be most rewarding in religious leaders' training in sexuality. I have applied methods that have been helpful in training to develop competence in creating a comfort level regarding sexual subjects, building science-based knowledge regarding various sexual behaviors and practices, building skills to respond appropriately to sexual questions and concerns, and making proper referrals when needed. Suggestions for future training of religious leaders in sexuality education are forthcoming.

The Marriage Council of Philadelphia at the University of Pennsylvania Medical School, where I was then a postdoctoral fellow, received some sexually explicit films from Glide Memorial Methodist Church in San Francisco, which asked us to research the use of these films with individuals and couples. The explicit films featured regular people from the local community as well as from the Glide Memorial Methodist Church. This was unusual in that, rather than using adult sex industry performers, local members of the community and of the church joined the mission, believing that films of real people in real relationships would be more helpful and educational than erotica produced by professional actors.

This same church had used these films to set up a Sexuality Attitude Reassessment (SAR) program at the University of Minnesota Medical School for both medical and theological students. For the research, the University of Pennsylvania sent me to the University of Minnesota to learn about the SAR program. I discovered that showing and discussing these explicit sexual films did indeed help people explore their own attitudes, values, and behaviors regarding sexuality. This is especially important to religious leaders, in order to ensure they do not inadvertently pass their own attitudes on to their congregants (Stayton, 1978, 1998).

The films covered some very common sexual behaviors and issues that most people experience in life: sexual self-image, self-pleasuring, sexual identity and expression, sexual orientation, sex and disability, the variety of sexual lifestyle options, and sex and aging. Each film topic segment was followed by small group processing sessions. As well as viewing the films, either a speaker or a panel representing the subject presented an exploration of myths and misunderstandings regarding each of these sexual issues.

In order to measure any changes brought about by the SAR program, Lief and Reed, of the University of Pennsylvania, developed the Sex, Knowledge and Attitude Test (SKAT) regarding experienced sexual behavior, sexual attitudes, and sexual knowledge. The SKAT test was found to be a valid and reliable instrument (Lief & Reed, 1972). When offering a SAR program, a pre and post SKAT (split half method to test internal consistency of the SKAT) was given. The results consistently illustrated significant positive changes on all the measures: sexual behavior, sexual attitudes, sexual knowledge, and self-acceptance (Miller & Lief, 1979).

Over the past 45 years, as a postdoctoral fellow and then as a professor at the University of Pennsylvania, I have conducted more than 700 SAR programs with high school and college students, clients, supervisees, various religious institutions, medical schools, families, clergy couples, dentists, neighbors, parents, psychiatrists, seminary faculty and students, nursing school faculty and students, social workers, teacher training summer camps, and many continuing education programs. Feedback was and is very positive.

Based on the University of Pennsylvania research and that of the University of Minnesota, the American Association of Sexuality Educators, Counselors, and Therapists (AASECT) made SAR experience a requirement for certification as a sexuality educator, counselor, or therapist. This requirement is still in effect (AASECT website).

THE SAR AND SEMINARY EDUCATION

In 1973, Harold I. Lief, a University of Pennsylvania psychiatrist and director of the Marriage Council of Philadelphia, conceived the idea for a Center for Sex Education in Religion, based on the existing Center for Sex Education in Medicine (1967), to be part of the Marriage Council of Philadelphia (now the Council for Relationships). The mission of the Center for Sex Education in Religion was to inform religious systems of the best in sexuality science-based research, education, and practice with the goal of implementing and networking sexuality education in seminaries. At this point a Center had not been created.

The National Council of Churches of the United States underwrote three workshops for seminary professors with the aid of several member denominations. These four-day seminary workshops were held in Boston,

MA (east coast), St. Louis, MO (midcontinent), and San Anselmo, CA (west coast), and were led by myself and other University of Pennsylvania/Marriage Council of Philadelphia faculty. Each program was a SAR event consisting of explicit films, minilectures, and small group discussion covering a variety of topics: male and female genitalia, masturbation, homosexuality, heterosexuality, disability, and aging.

While these programs were well received on a personal level, there were questions about how they could be introduced in each of the seminary education programs represented, whether in liberal or conservative seminaries. The major lesson learned was that each seminary needed to be represented by more than one person, but also by more stakeholders—such as a student, faculty member, and hopefully a member of the board of trustees—to bring about the desired institutional change. The SAR events were personally rewarding for those who attended, but not helpful in gaining institutional support. Many years later we provided the SAR and education program to more representatives from each seminary. There were changes in the seminaries represented.

THE CENTER FOR SEXUALITY AND RELIGION

Nothing more was done about a Center for Sex Education and Religion until 1986, when the Rt. Rev. David Richards, the Bishop of Pastoral Care for the Episcopal Church, in consultation with Dr. Harold Lief about clergy and sexuality issues, suggested resurrecting the idea of a Center to help with sexuality issues faced by denominations, seminaries, and individual clergy. They contacted me about our original center idea and model.

The first task was to explore the need and make the case for establishing a Center for Religion and Sexuality. With the help of a gracious donor and some small grants from several foundations, an exploratory consultation, bringing together about 50 seminary professors, denominational representatives, and sexologists, was planned. We all thought it was important to begin the gathering with a SAR experience to highlight the issues of sexuality and religious reactions. This first gathering was painful and contentious, because many of the sexologists were hostile toward religionists, and the religionists were suspicious of the motives of sexologists. There was also a lack of diversity in both the planning group and the invited representatives, with few women or people of color invited. For the religionists, undertaking a SAR program alongside the sexologists, who were well experienced with it, was also very threatening and anger-provoking. These were important lessons learned.

Education and Dialogue without SAR Experience

For the next gathering, more women and persons of color were added to the planning and implementation team. Changes were made. Personal time was provided at the beginning for participants to get acquainted with each other, with no SAR experience included. This resulted in more creative dialogue between the sexologists and theologians, who concluded that it was important to bring the two disciplines together to discuss and strategize the important issues facing both sexologists and religionists, such as lack of preparation for marriage and other sexual relationships; unplanned pregnancy, especially among teenagers; the proliferation of sexually transmitted diseases; and concerns regarding sexual abuse by clergy. Thus, there was strong support for developing a Center for Sexuality and Religion (CSR), which was incorporated in 1988, with the mission "to inform religious systems with the best science in sexuality research, information, education, and best practices." Its goal was "to promote sexual health and responsible sexual behavior in denominations, theological education, pastoral ministry, individual faith communities, and the family" (CSR, 2002).

Over the years, several of the lessons from and accomplishments of CSR led to important contributions to training religious leaders and informing religious systems regarding sexuality issues:

- A survey of seminaries carried out as part of a dissertation confirmed that sexuality was not a part of the core curriculum but, if offered, was only available as part of an existing course such as moral theology and ethics. Future pastors were given little opportunity to identify their own sexual values and behavior.
- In 1994, after denominational executives from 28 different faith communities met—for the first time in history—to consider sexuality issues, two important issues challenging every denomination were identified. These were the issue of homosexuality, which was tearing at the fabric of each faith community, and the issue of clergy sexual misconduct, which had the potential to demoralize and bankrupt every denomination.
- A conference for midlevel denominational persons responsible for responding to any charges of sexual misconduct by clergy was held at the University of Minnesota. More than 200 persons attended this conference. Denominational representatives and church insurance companies informed the group about the consequences of clergy sexual misconduct and provided suggestions for preparing seminarians in ethics, including sexual ethics, and spiritual formation.

- A four-day conference on contemporary sexuality issues faced by religious systems was held at the University of Minnesota for the first 50 responding seminaries in the United States and Canada to send a representative from their teaching faculty. Approximately one third of the delegates were from Roman Catholic seminaries, one third were from conservative and evangelical seminaries, and one third were from theologically moderate seminaries. This program was very well received; however, in following up, the Center learned again that the majority of delegates could not implement sexuality education in their seminary, because, they reported, there was no support system to assist on their return.
- Members of the Center for Sexuality and Religion Board undertook a number of speaking and teaching engagements at various seminary and denominational meetings (Stayton, 2006).

It is important to understand some aspects of history that affected the work of the Center for Sexuality and Religion. During the 1980s and 1990s, some very important historical events were taking place in the field of sexuality that played an important part in furthering the need for training religious leaders in human sexuality, such as the emphasis in public education on "abstinence until marriage," the HIV/AIDS epidemic, and the trend toward more conservative views of human sexuality.

First, there was an absence of positive sexuality education, which is important to healthy and responsible living. Critical problems including violence against women; unplanned pregnancies; relationship breakups; sexually transmitted infections, including HIV/AIDS; abortion rates; and child sexual abuse and trafficking resulted in the World Health Organization and the United States' Surgeon General taking action on these matters. Our religious institutions were critical in helping to meet the challenges presented by the World Health Organization and the Surgeon General's Call to Action.

Second, in the early 1990s, the World Health Organization (WHO) asked the World Association for Sexual Health (WAS): are there universal sexual rights? WAS is a multidisciplinary, worldwide group of scientific societies, nongovernmental organizations (NGOs), and professionals in the field of human sexuality. It promotes sexual health throughout the lifespan and supports sexual rights for all people. WAS developed a Declaration of Sexual Rights that was first presented in Valencia, Spain, in 1997 and then ratified in Hong Kong in 1999, with a final revision in 2014 (WAS, 2014; see www.worldsexology.org).

Basically, the Declaration of Sexual Rights affirmed the universal central role that sexuality plays in all of human life, "encompassing sex, gender identities and roles, sexual orientation, eroticism, pleasure, intimacy, and reproduction. Sexuality is experienced and expressed in thoughts, fantasies, desire, beliefs, attitudes, values, behaviors, practices, roles, and relationships." Further, the WAS Declaration stated that equality for all people must include no prohibitions "on the basis of race, ethnicity, color, sex, language, *religion*, political or other opinion, national or social origin, property, birth or other status, including disability, age, nationality, marital and family status, sexual orientation and gender identity, health status, place of residence, economic and social situation." Finally, WAS declared 16 universal sexual rights that have been referred to the WHO for implementation. For an explanation of the meaning of each "Right," visit the WAS website (WAS, 2014).

These "sexual rights" are profound and call for a transformation of world societies and religions. They are the result of the WHO/WAS response to the spread of unscientific and uninformed sexual information and the high societal degree of sexual violence, especially to women; unintended pregnancies; sexual diseases; and sexual dysfunction. Members of WAS knew that some governments and religions would have problems with most of these sexual rights—for example, anything that had to do with homosexuality, transgender issues or any other expression of gender identity, consensual sexual practices, and access to birth control and services for reproductive health. The rights also include the right to comprehensive sexuality education that is age appropriate, culturally competent, and scientifically accurate, and the right to marry and/or divorce or to form similar types of sexual relationships based on equality. WAS believed that both governments and religions needed to be challenged to address the unhealthy sexual practices in their communities and to propose solutions for developing a sexually healthier world order.

Third, aware that WHO and WAS were working on the above sexual rights, the US Surgeon General, David Satcher, MD (1998–2002), decided that, as the US doctor responsible for public health issues, his major contribution would be to develop *A Call to Action to Promote Sexual Health and Responsible Sexual Behavior* (2001). The *Call to Action* recognized that sexuality and religion are deeply connected and that sexual health in the United States would benefit from leadership from religious as well as other agencies with deeply held beliefs relating to sexuality:

> The integration of sexual health, with mental/emotional, physical, relational, and spiritual health are foundational for the future health of religious institutions and public health in addressing sexual health. Religions contribute

decisively to the cultural context for the public understanding of sexuality and sexual health and provide the basis for ethical guidance regarding sexual behavior and expectations. (Satcher Health Leadership Institute, 2009, Case Statement)

Training religious leaders in sexuality has become critical to accomplishing the achievement of sexual rights, which are human rights, for all people, as well as in the promotion of sexual health and responsible sexual behavior.

TWENTY-FIRST CENTURY CHALLENGES TO SEXUALITY AND RELIGION

To return to the Center for Sexuality and Religion: confronted with the new phenomena mentioned at the start of this chapter (Stayton, 1998) and the information that arose through the work of WHO/WAS on sexual rights and Surgeon General Satcher's Call to Action, the need to train religious leaders in the area of human sexuality had become even more evident. CSR responded with a Sexuality and Seminary Initiative workshop in 2008, but expanded it with the latest science and technologies of the twenty-first century.

Newer, updated films were introduced for SAR. Various sexual values systems represented in theological faculties, local religious institutions, and seminary boards of trustees, funders, and students had to be understood.

With a budget of almost $100,000—because all participants' expenses were paid—the first "21st Century Challenges to Religion and Sexuality" workshop for seminaries was held at San Francisco State University in January 2008. Ten seminaries from across the United States, representing different theological perspectives, were invited and asked to send a professor, an administrator, and a second-year seminary study. Two evaluators from the National Council of Churches—an American Baptist Protestant theologian and a Roman Catholic Sister who was a professor of moral theology—were also invited to attend. The goals for this three-day workshop were to provide opportunities to:

- Become more aware of the latest available information and scientific findings related to diversity within human sexuality;
- Become more aware of the life experiences of human beings with diverse sexual backgrounds and orientations;

- Become more aware of personal reactions and understandings about sexuality and sexual diversity in their communities; and
- Identify potential first step strategies for incorporating increased dialogue and education about sexuality into their seminary teaching.

There was and is a need to be upfront about sexual health and a sexuality-affirming approach, which is described as "a state of physical, emotional, mental, spiritual, and social well-being related to one's sexuality and sexual activities. Sexually healthy individuals integrate sexuality into their lives, while avoiding and reducing harmful consequences for themselves and the community" (National Consensus Process on Sexual Health and Responsible Sexual Behavior, 2006, p. 7).

The subjects of this three-day experience can be utilized for the most comprehensive training of religious leaders.

"Circles of Sexuality"

The "Circles of Sexuality" involve the following definitions:

- *Sensuality* is the physiological and psychological pleasure derived from one's own body and/or the bodies of others.
- *Intimacy* is the experience of emotional closeness to another human being and having that closeness returned.
- *Sexual identity* includes both the sense of who one is as a sexual person, including a sense of maleness and femaleness (gender), and the sense of whom one is erotically and emotionally attracted to (orientation).
- *Sexual health and reproduction* is the biology of the body and the sexual and reproductive systems. Education in this area includes care of the organs, the health consequences of sexual behaviors, and the biology of producing children.
- *Sexualization* refers to the use of sexuality to influence, manipulate, or control others.
- *Spirituality* is a natural connectedness with the self and all else that is created.

All of these circles of sexuality involve attitudes, values, and feelings of the individual, as well as family, cultural, religious, legal, professional, institutional, scientific, and political considerations (as per Dan Dailey, 1981, and Pam Wilson of the UUA/UCC, Our Whole Lives curriculum; see Turner and Stayton, 2012, p. 495).

Differing Sexual Value Systems within Our Religious Communities

In Stayton's words, "Basically, there are three types of sexual value systems" (2007, p. 80). Value system A is most commonly associated with religious institutions. It is based on the primary concept that sex is for procreational purposes. Because procreation is the basis for the sex act, the purist will rule out birth control, abortion, masturbation, homosexuality, bisexuality, and nonmarital and alternative lifestyles. The Bible and the Quran are often interpreted as supporting this view of sexuality. In other words, this system is totally about the "Acts of Sex" as holding moral and immoral values in relation to sexuality. Value system C is also seen as scripturally based, but it is not as concerned about the acts of sex so much as the "Nature of Relationships." This system holds that one's relationships to God, self, neighbors, and possessions are all important (see Matthew 22:36–40). This view centers on the principles of love, justice and equality.

Value system B takes from either A or C depending on one's comfort with, acceptance of, or deeply held belief regarding the particular sexual behavior. For example, one may accept A's view of birth control, premarital sex or abortion, but be against C's view of homosexuality. There is no consistent theological base for B's value system, yet this is the value system that seems to be held by the majority of people in the United States.

While denominational groups, such as the Roman Catholic Church or fundamentalist Christianity, hold to value system A, individual members may hold to any one of the three value systems. Similarly, denominations such as the Unitarian/Universalist, Episcopal Church or the United Church of Christ may hold value system C as a denomination, but individual members may hold one of the other value systems. Interestingly, Islam's teaching from the Quran falls under value system B, with some individual members also falling under any of the other value systems.

The Effects of Internet Depictions of Sex

A troubling issue for many parents and some other adults is the effect of explicit sexual behaviors, chatrooms, and internet hookups on the sexuality of children, youth, and adults. For example, how should adults react when they find their child or partner is viewing sexually explicit sites on the internet? My answer now is to avoid shaming or placing guilt on the viewer, but for the parent to use this as an opportunity to calmly explore and explain adult sexual communication and behavior. For the adult, it is an opportunity to explore and improve communication with their adult partner.

The Subject of Intersexuality

The fact is that one in every 2,000 births is an intersex child. This is not always evident at birth and may only be discovered later in the person's development. When providing training, it is important to involve an intersex person or parents of an intersex child, or show a film on how intersexuality is dealt with in a family and often in the medical community.

Here is a sample scenario for discussion after the presentation. A family in your church has an intersex child and the pastor is the only one who has been told. What is this family going to experience within your church? How would your church respond if it knew? What sexual value system will this family come up against in your church? What kind of love/support will this family and child get?

Gender Identity and Expression

In training on the topic of gender identity and expression, not only is it important to discuss what is known about the gender spectrum, but it is best to have this followed by a film on the subject or a talk by someone who crossdresses and a transsexual person, who can tell their stories and describe their faith journey with their religious community.

Sexual Orientation: Heterosexuality, Homosexuality, and Bisexuality

A powerful way to address this topic is to screen a film(s), follow this with gay and/or lesbian, bisexual, and heterosexual speakers telling the story of their lives growing up in a faith community, and finish up with a small group discussion with similar relevant questions to those described above.

Other important modules that are helpful are Sexuality and Aging, Sexuality and Disability, and Diversity of Lifestyles and Relationships (something found in every faith community). I have found it important to include the new phenomena challenging religion, as discussed in the opening section of this chapter. The small group discussion can center on how the church or seminary prepares leaders to meet these issues and facilitates their church's response. A conundrum for each seminary is whether sexuality education should be a separate course or instead be integrated into other parts of the core curriculum. It is helpful if each seminary can then present an action plan.

SATCHER HEALTH LEADERSHIP INSTITUTE

When Dr. David Satcher left the post of Surgeon General of the US, he became the Interim President of Morehouse School of Medicine (MSM) in Atlanta, Georgia, and MSM established the Satcher Health Leadership Institute (SHLI) in his honor.

In 2008, CSR merged with SHLI and Morehouse School of Medicine to develop an endowed chair in sexuality and religion within an educational institution. It became the David E. Richards and the Marta S. Weeks Endowed Chair in Sexuality and Religion. The mission of the Endowed Chair is to reach out to different faith communities, especially in underserved areas, on the topic of sexuality education (Sexual Health Leadership Institute, 2009, Case Statement). An important project of the religious initiative was to have training programs for seminaries, similar to the one at San Francisco State University outlined above. The philosophy has been to promote dialogue among religious leaders in Hebrew, Christian, and Islamic traditions, as well as with those religious communities not identifying with any of the above traditions, to build a knowledge-based and skill-developed methodology for training religious leadership in science-based sexuality.

Since the founding of CSR, three other training programs in sexuality and religion for religious leaders have been established. Having served as a consultant on all of these programs, I can highly recommend each. They are not competing programs, but complementary to SHLI at MSM and each other.

The Unitarian Universalist Association and the United Church of Christ denominations have partnered on a project, Our Whole Lives, which considers human sexuality from kindergarten through adulthood. The curriculum provides science-based information, and offers a creative methodology for implementation at every age level. Everyone who teaches this curriculum must go through the project's excellent experiential education training program (see www.UUA.org/owl).

The Religious Institute, founded by the Rev. Dr. Debra Haffner, has been a leader in sexuality education for 15 years. Its work is mostly with progressive Jewish and Christian pastors/rabbis, churches/synagogues, denominations, and seminaries. The emphasis is on sexuality activism, with training and excellent publications for clergy and religious communities (see www.religiousinstitute.org).

The Incarnation Institute for Sex & Faith, founded by the Rev. Beverly Dale, provides "education that empowers people of faith to value all sexual bodies as beautiful—in whatever form, color, or shape—and to embrace sexuality in all its diverse expressions. They believe in grace, forgiveness, and abundance, teaching pleasure, goodness, and wonder." The Institute teaches sexual pleasure, sexual diversity, and sexual freedom which is based on a science-friendly Christianity. The training is mostly with progressive-minded clergy (see www.incarnationinstitute.org).

SUMMARY OF LEARNING FROM TRAINING

In my years of training religious leaders on sexuality-related issues, I have learned:

(1) Religious leaders generally feel the need for better education and skills in dealing with the sexual issues in their congregations. If they are involved with their congregation, this need becomes very apparent by the time they have been with a congregation for several years.

(2) Clergy are consistent in wishing that sexuality education was a part of their seminary training and/or continuing education offerings.

(3) Because most seminaries are struggling financially, it has not been easy to either train their professors or include sexuality courses in the core curriculum. There is little problem ensuring seminary involvement when there is no cost to the seminary. Thus finding funding for seminary sexuality education is absolutely necessary.

(4) Foundations and individual donors are required that can be convinced to meet the need for sexuality education in seminaries.

(5) A part of a university community—such as, for example, CSR being a part of Morehouse School of Medicine—may be more attractive to donors and funders than a standalone institute.

(6) Religious leaders and/or lay leaders need to ask that their budgets include training in science-based sexuality. This is necessary for both their clergy and their religious education directors and staff.

(7) Denominational and church religious leaders and their staff need to approach their publications to provide regular articles on science-based sexuality information, available training programs, and other important resources.

(8) Information on clergy sexual ethics and conduct needs to be easily available.

(9) It is helpful to offer a SAR program, when possible, to help participants to explore their own attitudes, values, knowledge, and behaviors before seeking to be helpful to others.

As the former Surgeon General of the US, David Satcher, concluded in his Introduction to the *Call to Action to Promote Sexual Health and Responsible Sexual Behavior* (Office of the Surgeon General, 2001):

> We need to appreciate the diversity of our culture, engage in mature, thoughtful and respectful discussion, be informed by the science that is available to us, and invest in continued research. This is a call to action. We cannot remain complacent. Doing nothing is unacceptable. Our efforts not only will have an impact on the current health status of our citizens but will lay a foundation for a healthier society in the future.

BIBLIOGRAPHY

Center for Sexuality and Religion (CSR). (2002). *The case for comprehensive sexuality education within the context of seminary human and theological formation: A report to the Ford Foundation.* Wayne, PA: CSR.

Dailey, D. (1981). Sexual expression and aging. In F. Berghorn & D. Schafer (Eds.), *The dynamics of aging: Original essays on the processes and experiences of growing old* (pp. 311–30). Boulder, CO: Westview Press.

Lief, H. I. and Reed, D. M. (1972). *Sex knowledge and attitude test.* Pennsylvania: University of Pennsylvania, Dept. of Psychiatry.

Miller, W. R. and Lief, H. I. (1979). Sex knowledge and attitude test. *Journal of Sex and Marital Therapy*, 5(3), pp. 282–7.

Office of the Surgeon General. (2001). *The Surgeon General's call to action to promote sexual health and responsible sexual behavior.* Washington, DC: US Government Printing Office.

Satcher, David MD, PhD. (2006). *The National Consensus Process on Sexual Health and Responsible Sexual Behavior: Interim report.* Morehouse School of Medicine, Atlanta, GA.

Satcher Health Leadership Institute. (2009). *Educating leaders to effectively address community sexual health issues: Case statement.* Atlanta: Morehouse School of Medicine.

Stayton, W. R. (1978). The core curriculum: What can be taught and what must be taught. In Norman Rosenzweig & F. Paul Pearsall (Eds.), *Sex Education of the Professional* (pp. 51–61). New York: Grune & Stratton.

Stayton, W. R. (1998). A curriculum for training professionals in human sexuality using a SAR (sexual attitude restructuring) model. *Journal of Sex Education and Therapy*, *23*, 26–32.

Stayton, W. R. (2006) *Proposal for the Board of Directors of the Center for Sexuality and Religion.* Unpublished report.

Stayton, W. R. (2007). Sexual value systems and sexual health. In Mitchell Tepper and Annette Owens (Eds.), *Sexual health*, vol. 3. New York: Praeger Publishers (pp. 79–96).

Turner, Y., & Stayton, W. (2012). The twenty-first century challenges to sexuality and religion. *Journal of Religion and Health*, *53*(2), 483–97.

PART III

The sexuality of leaders

9. "Stupid is as stupid does" or good Bayesian? A sympathetic and contrarian analysis of Bill Clinton's decision to have an affair with Monica Lewinsky

James K. Beggan

"I did not have sexual relations with that woman"—Bill Clinton, denying to
the American people his affair with Monica Lewinsky

"It constituted a critical lapse in judgment and a personal failure on my part
for which I am solely and completely responsible"—Bill Clinton,
apologizing to the American people about denying his affair
with Monica Lewinsky

"Stupid is as stupid does"—Forrest Gump, from the movie *Forrest Gump*

It seems to have evolved into a truism in leadership in business and politics that sex and work do not mix. "Sex in the workplace has become a political and legal hot potato" (Halpern, 2002, p. 118), partly because relationships between coworkers are now viewed in terms of imbalances in power with the potential for exploitation, rather than in terms of mutual attraction and the potential for romance (Boyd, 2010). Leaders and stakeholders, afraid of being sued, preemptively take steps such as banning romantic and sexual relationships between coworkers, especially when there is arguably a power difference between participants, even if the relationships are mutually consensual (Wilson, 2015). Advocates of workplace romance or those who support permitting relationships where a clear power difference exists are often dismissed as presenting either fringe perspectives or barely concealed attempts to rationalize self-serving and inappropriate behavior (Abramson, 2007).

The go-to example for the idea that leaders should not use their influence to find sexual partners would have to be Bill Clinton and his affair with Monica Lewinsky. In an edited volume called *Why Smart People Can Be So Stupid*, Bill Clinton has the honor of being the case study in two separate chapters. With regard to the affair, Halpern (2002, p. 107) states: "there does seem to be at least one example where most people can agree that a seemingly smart person made some really dumb mistakes." In another chapter in the same volume, Sternberg (2002, p. 233) suggests that Clinton's behavior could be understood as a form of "foolishness" that resulted from defects in accurately reading the environment. These defects stemmed from Clinton seeing himself as omniscient, omnipotent, and invulnerable, due, in part, to social processes derived from the privileged way that leaders, such as presidents, are treated by others.

In thinking about whether or not Bill Clinton was stupid, it is important to distinguish two different questions: was he stupid to have the affair, or was he stupid in the way he tried to deny having the affair? Willis (2017) called the decisions "monumentally dumb" and "even dumber," respectively. In the speech in which Clinton acknowledged the affair, he apologized for both. In the present chapter, I would like to focus on the first question but take a counterintuitive stance and ask: "Was it really so stupid of Bill Clinton to have a sexual relationship with Monica Lewinsky?" In the current climate of political correctness and fears about microaggressions, it might be argued that any attempt to engage in workplace romance is unwise, whether at a business-first practical level or due to questions about the ethics of such activity. Of course, to be fair to Bill Clinton, we need to ask the question from the perspective of 1995, which is when the relationship started, and not from the perspective of 2017, when this chapter is being written.

I intend to approach the question of apparent stupidity using the economics-based concept of expected value. The expected value of a choice can be viewed as a product of the outcome's value multiplied by the likelihood of obtaining it. An extension of expected value theory, called subjective expected utility theory (SEUT), modifies the basic concept of expected value by acknowledging that people, as decision makers, may not perfectly use probability and may assign a weight to the value of a commodity or outcome in a subjective way (Luce & Raiffa, 1957). As a result, subjective expected utility theory replaces probability and value with the more subjective concepts of a personal probability and a utility function, respectively. It is generally considered unwise to approach someone "out of your league," for example the iconic Victoria's Secret supermodel, especially if the approach carries costs (such as paying for dinner, drinks, and a movie). The sexual pleasure might be high but the likelihood of obtaining it is low. As such, the overall subjective expected utility is low.

We can extend the decision-making process to recognize that a choice might carry several values, some positive and some negative, each of which might be associated with a different subjective probability. Consider, for example, someone such as Bill Clinton who is contemplating having an affair. For a variety of reasons, he might place a great deal of value on the pleasure associated with a sexual encounter. Given his status as President of the United States, it is not hard to imagine that someone would want to have sex with him, for reasons ranging from a genuine attraction, to a what-the-hell curiosity, to a self-serving "this could be good for my career." The pleasure of the sexual encounter might be quite great and the likelihood of obtaining sex might be quite high. As such, the expected subjective utility would be large. But a decision maker might also be influenced by possible downsides, such as the scandal that might follow in the wake of being discovered. For Bill Clinton, the possible scandal would stem from the power differential between him and an intern and from the fact he was married. Of course, the influence on his decision making of the unpleasantness of being found out would be lessened to the degree that being discovered was highly unlikely.

In the present chapter, I examine whether Bill Clinton was stupid on the basis of a subjective expected utility model of his decision making. To do so, I develop a Bayesian analysis of the perceived risk of having an affair on the basis of prior probabilities. Subsequently, I examine the perceived value of the sexual encounter, using evolutionary pressures that operate on leaders—in fact, on all human beings—and argue that the sexual experience was sufficiently appealing such that the subjective expected utility of the affair was relatively high, or "worth the risk," and from this perspective a good decision.

The basis for this argument involves the assessment of and tolerance for risk that operates with regard to having marital infidelity found out. I suggest that, contrary to what might be expected, the likelihood of being found out was relatively low. In addition, I suggest that the very traits that make someone a good leader will also make them more willing to take risks. In some cases, it is the double standard our culture applies to sexuality and the expected behavior of leaders that is problematic, rather than the affair itself.

THE THREAT OF SCANDAL

The threat of scandal for someone having an affair, such as was the case for Bill Clinton, is represented in Table 9.1. The columns refer to whether or not an accusation is made. The rows refer to whether the accusation is believed. Table 9.1 represents an affair from the perspective of a third party observer—for example, the American public—and is premised on the assumption that the accused person actually is having an affair. As observers, we have to deal with a conditional probability. We want to know the likelihood that someone is having an affair, given that he or she has been accused.

Typically, when someone is accused, he or she will deny the allegation, or offer an innocent rationale for what seems like suspicious behavior. Unless the accused is caught *in flagrante delicto*, it is then up to the accuser to either accept or reject the explanation. An alternative approach is to admit guilt but then provide an apology on the basis of a rationale that includes atonement and asks for forgiveness (Grover & Hasel, 2015). Because the accusation was believed, Bill Clinton was in the upper, rather than lower, left-hand cell. Ultimately, he failed to spin the situation to convince people he was innocent and had to settle for atonement as a means for moving past the scandal. Of course, in the case of a celebrity, the scope of the "outing" greatly increases. Bill Clinton did not have to convince only a skeptical spouse and handful of friends. He had to persuade the entire world, including hostile Republicans with an ax to grind and professional reporters trained to dig for facts and looking for a story to tell.

The right-hand column describes the situation that exists for someone who is in fact having an affair, but is not accused. The best strategy is to preemptively minimize the likelihood that a future accusation will be made or believed by limiting potential accusers' ability to gather evidence in support of their claim. Some people may know or suspect an affair, but these beliefs exist as only background rumors. It is difficult to dispel rumors because the act of trying to deny nonaccusations draws attention to their possible validity. It is easy to imagine a variety of complex scenarios in which a spouse or other people might know but not let on. Hillary Clinton apparently knew of the affair prior to it being made public (Brower, 2015). As such, there could be a discrepancy between a public face (defends and/or appears to trust her husband) and private belief (is angry or sad because she knows he is guilty). A wife (or husband) may know (or strongly believe) a spouse is cheating and say nothing for a variety of reasons, such as preserving the marriage for the welfare of the children or to afford a large mortgage payment, or even to build a better case to present later.

The lower right-hand cell represents the condition in which the individual would feel most safe. He or she has not been accused and there is no reason to believe that anyone suspects anything. There is always the possibility of a future threat. The danger inherent in this situation is that a person grows complacent and ends up taking risks or being careless in ways that ultimately reveal the affair. Perhaps the best known case of unnecessary risk taking was that of Gary Hart, a US Senator who ran for president in 1988. He was married, but was also having an affair with Donna Rice (Bai, 2014). In an interview with E. J. Dionne, he said: "Follow me around. I don't care. I'm serious. If anyone wants to put a tail on me, go ahead. They'd be very bored" (Bai, 2014, p. 107). In the end, reporters were not bored, because they discovered the affair that effectively ruined Hart's bid for president.

Table 9.1 Are you thought to be having an affair, given that you are accused? (Observers' perspective)

	Accused	Not accused
Believed to be having an affair	Deny or apologize	Passive defense
Believed not to be not having an affair	Garner sympathy	Threat of growing lax

From the perspective of Table 9.1, the affair has already taken place. Table 9.1 involves the conditional: what is the probability of being perceived as guilty, given an accusation of being guilty, given that someone is guilty? But there is another way to think about an affair with the potential to be made public, and that is as a prospective event being contemplated. This situation is mapped out in Table 9.2. In Table 9.2, no affair has yet taken place. The actor has done nothing wrong (except perhaps in his or her thoughts). The situation described in Table 9.2 involves someone trying to estimate the likelihood of getting caught if he or she were to have an affair. In Table 9.1, the problem is one of plausible deniability. In Table 9.2, the problem is a perception of risk and the risk–benefit ratio. From Bill Clinton's point of view, when he was pondering having a sexual encounter with Monica Lewinsky, he had to decide whether it was "worth it." An "is it worth it?" judgment can be expressed as a trade-off between a risk and a reward (or punishment).

Table 9.2   Are you likely to be accused, given that you are having an affair? (Actor's perspective)

	Accused	Not accused
Having an affair	Regret	Persist, intensify
Not having an affair	Shock	Innocence

The two cells in the top half of Table 9.2 are most relevant. Being accused of having an affair when a person actually *is* having an affair is an accurate situation but represents a failure of the adulterer's deception skills. Not being accused of having an affair while having an affair represents a failure of the other's detection capacity but is the preferred state for someone having the affair. This cell is potentially unstable because there is always the possibility that an undiscovered affair will be discovered at some future time.

The situations modeled in Tables 9.1 and 9.2 are interrelated. To the extent that a leader feels that Table 9.2 best captures the decision-making situation and he or she answers in the negative, that is, that it is unlikely he or she will be accused of having the affair, the decision problem represented in Table 9.1 is rendered moot. People do not have to worry about whether their denial of the accusation is believed if they do not think they will be accused in the first place.

Halpern (2002) faulted Bill Clinton's decision to enter into the affair. After describing the way in which Bill Clinton's life (as President) would have been closely monitored by people like Secret Service and the press, Halpern (p. 108) asked: "Did he really believe that he could have multiple sexual encounters with a young woman at the White House without experiencing any consequences ... How can we explain this seemingly stupid behavior by an otherwise intelligent man?" My perhaps unexpected answer to that rhetorical question is: yes, it was quite reasonable to believe he could have the affair without undesired consequences. In other words, I am interested in Clinton's judgments of the likelihood of being found out, given the base rate for being found out as a prior probability. The reason I argue this is embedded in Halpern's own analysis of why Clinton believed he could get away with it: in addition to citing the machismo of the president's office and social mores that reflected a tolerance for infidelity, she notes Clinton's past history of engaging in extramarital affairs without repercussions.

THE BASE RATE FOR AFFAIRS

When asked about marital infidelity across a lifetime, estimates for men may range from a high of 40 percent to a lower bound of 23 percent (Allen & Atkins, 2012; Kinsey, Pomeroy, & Martin, 1948; Laumann, Gagnon, Michael, & Kolata, 1994; Wiederman, 1997; Whisman & Snyder, 2007). Estimates for women tend to be lower but still well above zero. On the basis of a large-scale nationally representative survey, Allen and Atkins (2012) reported that 23 percent of men and 14 percent of women reported at least one instance of extramarital sex across their lifetime.

Rather than think about infidelity in terms of a lifetime (that is, "have you ever cheated?"), some researchers ask respondents for incidences of cheating in the past 12 months. It has been found that for a given year, 2–4 percent of men and women report engaging in infidelity (Wiederman, 1997), though Whisman and Snyder (2007) found that with anonymous reporting through a computer rather than interviewer, the rate for women respondents increased to about 6 percent. It is possible that men's rates of admission of infidelity would be higher if the assessment process were anonymous, but given that men's sexuality seems less open to being stigmatized than women's, it is also possible that men's self-reports would not fluctuate on the basis of assessment method.

As a compromise figure, if we assume the rate of infidelity in any one year is 5 percent, we obtain a rather grim projection over time. Even if only 5 percent of marriages are characterized by an affair in any one year, the cumulative rate is much higher, given the way the multiplication rule works. When a couple first gets married, if we assume there is only a 5 percent likelihood that one of them will cheat, then the probability that there won't be infidelity in year 1 is .95. But if we consider the likelihood that cheating won't occur in year 1 or year 2, we take the product of .95 * .95, which is .9025. For three years, the number is .85. After seven years of marriage, the likelihood that no cheating will have occurred is the product of seven .95s, or .69. If the likelihood of not cheating across those seven years is .69, then the likelihood of cheating occurring in one or more years is .31. In other words, after seven years of marriage, the likelihood that there has been an indiscretion at least once is just over 30 percent.

Of course, a marriage involves two people, either of whom could cheat. The likelihood that one might cheat in that year is not necessarily independent of the likelihood that the other will cheat. For example, one spouse might sense the infidelity of the other, and that suspicion or dissatisfaction might influence an otherwise faithful spouse to also cheat. But if I make the simplifying assumption that both men and women will cheat at a 5 percent rate in a year of marriage, the likelihood of no cheating taking place is reduced from .95 for an individual to .9025 for a couple. In honor of the movie *The Seven Year Itch*, if I calculate across seven years of marriage, the likelihood of no cheating occurring is .49, so the likelihood of at least one partner cheating at least one time is .51, just a bit over half—that is, a coin flip.

THE BASE RATE FOR DISCOVERED AFFAIRS

In addition to the likelihood that someone will have an affair, it is necessary to take into account the likelihood that someone will get caught. Obviously, this kind of data is not easy to gather (Griffith, 2011). As with collecting data about extramarital affairs, those involved may be reluctant to admit to wrongdoing. Additionally, it may be impossible for someone having an affair to tell whether or not a spouse has gotten wise to the relationship. It is always possible that a knowing spouse will hide their knowledge. Similarly, some people will suspect their partners are cheating, but there is a set of an unknown size of people who are being cheated on by skillful deceivers without their awareness. As such, estimates of being discovered cheating, or reporting that one has been cheated on, probably underestimate the true likelihood of being caught. Despite these inherent problems, some data are available (Allen, Atkins, Baucom, Snyder, Gordon, & Glass, 2005).

In a study of wives' indirect exposure to HIV, Fals-Stewart, Birchler, Hoebbel, Kashdan, Golden, and Parks (2003) reported that 41 percent of wives were unaware that their spouses had engaged in extramarital sex. Lawson and Samson (1988) reported that 77 percent of women reported that infidelity had been relevant to their divorce. Using data collected from a random sample of all divorced or separated individuals in a geographic area surrounding Centre County, Pennsylvania, Spanier and Margolis (1983) found that 60 percent of men reported that their former spouse knew of their affair; the remainder believed it had not been discovered (34.3 percent) or were uncertain (5.7 percent). In a survey of college students who had been married between two and ten years, a majority indicated that they would reveal to their spouse that they had had extramarital sex and stated that they would want their spouse to do the same (Wiederman & Allgeier, 1996). Of course, these reported preferences are hypothetical.

A relevant study conducted by Allen and Atkins (2012) assessed base rates for the possible discovery of an affair using 16,090 cases from the General Social Survey, a large nationally representative survey. Individuals were asked about their own lifetime experience of extramarital sex and their current marital status and divorce history. It is possible to use divorce and separation as proxies for discovery. Despite certain limitations, the data reported in the Allen and Atkins paper represent one of the few efforts to identify the rate at which extramarital sex is discovered. They found that among those men who admitted to having had extramarital sex, 62 percent indicated they were previously divorced, currently divorced, or currently separated. About 33 percent of men who stated that they had had extramarital sex had never been divorced. The remaining percentage reported that their spouse had died. Although separation or divorce does not prove that the extramarital sex was discovered, it would be consistent with it. There is also ambiguity regarding whether the cheating spouse confessed the affair or only admitted it after being accused.

In summary, then, there appears to be a lot of extramarital sex going on and it seems to be found out on a pretty regular basis. In an attempt to synthesize the (albeit imperfect) results of the cited research, I assumed that 23 percent of men could be assumed to have engaged in extramarital sex in their lifetime. Given that the average age of a Congressperson is about 58 years (Manning, 2016), I assumed that most if not all of the people who might have been willing to have an affair had already done so at least once. I assumed that the conditional probability of being found out, presuming that a man had extramarital sex, was .62. I used the figure from the Allen and Atkins paper because it was derived from a large, representative sample of people and was not out of line with other estimates.

BASE RATES OF POLITICAL SEX SCANDALS

With regard to the behavior of important politicians, I considered the history of sexual scandal among members of Congress, as reported on Wikipedia (the entry "List of Federal Political Scandals in the United States"). To determine the base rate for sex scandals that might have influenced Bill Clinton's decision making, I considered the period between 1980 and 1989, roughly when he was governor of Arkansas. In that time frame, there were 13 sex scandals. Between 1990 and 1995 there were seven, with a total of 20 between 1980 and 1995. I cut off the search in 1995 because that was when the Clinton–Lewinsky affair began.

There are 100 Senators and 435 Representatives, a total of 535 individuals. Because the average length of service for members of the Senate is 10.2 years and that for members of the House of Representatives is 9.1 years (Roberts, 2013), more than 535 would have served across a 16-year period due to attrition caused by retirement, death, or a failure to seek or achieve reelection. I made the simplifying assumption that there were only 535 distinct individuals serving in Congress between 1980 and 1995. Although women represent a significant minority of members of Congress in the present, the number of women members of Congress in the past was much smaller. Women are involved in fewer sex scandals than men, so it is unclear whether the presence of women should alter base rate probabilities, but to simplify calculations, I assumed that every member of Congress was equally likely *a priori* to be involved in a sex scandal.

A total of 20 scandals out of 535 people yields a discovery base rate of $20/535 = .037$, or, for simplicity, .04. This relatively low number stands in contradiction to people's beliefs about members of Congress. Lacayo and Branagan (1998) reported that 37 percent of a random sample of more than 1000 people believed that members of Congress were more likely to engage in adultery than the average man. A total of 52 percent felt there was no difference. Only 7 percent felt that members of Congress would be less likely than the average man to act in an adulterous manner.

BAYES' THEOREM AND ESTIMATING THE LIKELIHOOD OF BEING DISCOVERED

The posterior, or after the fact, probability of a hypothesis can be calculated using Bayes' theorem. That is: the probability that a belief is true given the evidence is a function of the probability of the evidence given that the belief is true, the probability of the evidence, and the probability of the belief. The relationship is stated as: P(Belief is true/Evidence) = P(Evidence/Belief is true) * P(Belief is true)/ P(Evidence).

Stated with regard to the situation modeled in Table 9.2, this would mean the likelihood that a leader would be accused given that he is having an affair is equal to the product of the conditional likelihood that he was having an affair given that he was accused of having an affair and the likelihood that he was accused of having an affair, divided by the likelihood that he was having an affair. Bayes' theorem can be viewed as a powerful tool for understanding the behavior of leaders contemplating sexual infidelity because it addresses the way that a subjective degree of belief should change as a function of prior evidence.

On the basis of base rate estimates of affairs, I assumed that the likelihood of an affair was .23 and the likelihood of no affair was .77. One assumption of this analysis is that among those who have not been accused, their tendency to have an affair mirrors the proportions in the population as a whole. In other words, some people who have not been accused are in fact having affairs. I also assume that members of Congress are engaging in marital infidelity at a rate comparable to the population as a whole. Using the data about the number of sex scandals revealed for members of Congress, I assumed the likelihood of being accused was .04 and the likelihood of not being accused was .96, for those individuals having an affair. For someone not having an affair, I assumed that the likelihood of being accused is 0 and the likelihood of not being accused is 1.

We can express this Bayesian analysis in terms of a tree diagram (Figure 9.1).

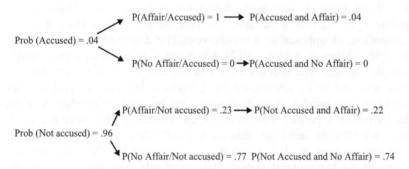

Figure 9.1   A Bayesian analysis of Congressman's likelihood of being accused of having an affair given they are having an affair

According to Bayes' theorem, the probability of being accused of having an affair, given that a person is having an affair, is .15. That value is derived from .04/(.04 + .22). Thus, the likelihood of getting caught is relatively small. What produces this small value is the significant number of people who are having affairs but are not being caught.

In contrast, if we consider data from the general public, the pattern is quite different (Figure 9.2).

Thus, among the general public, the likelihood of being accused, given that someone is having an affair, is .62/(.62 + .09) = .87.

If we compare the likelihood of getting accused, given that someone is having an affair, between the general public and high-ranking politicians,

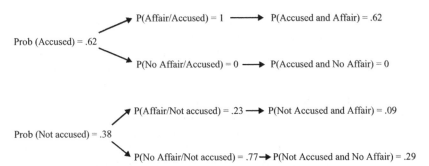

*Figure 9.2   A Bayesian analysis of an average man's likelihood of
               being accused of having an affair given he is having an
               affair*

we see that people in the general public are almost six times more likely
to be accused than senators and representatives. In interpreting these
results, it is important to keep in mind the distinction between being
found out privately and being found out publicly. For a leader in the
public eye, such as a senator, the real danger comes from a public
accusation, as opposed to a private one. The data on which I based my
analysis (Allen & Atkins, 2012) was from a large-scale, representative
sample and involved speculation about the rate at which extramarital sex
was revealed to or discovered by a partner. In contrast, political sex
scandals have two layers of disclosure. One has to do with whether or not
an individual's partner was aware of the infidelity. The other has to do
with whether the infidelity was made public. Sex scandals, such as the
one experienced by Bill Clinton, are only scandals because they are
revealed to the general public. The relatively low frequency of sex
scandals among members of Congress in relation to the general public
may occur because of the two layers of discovery required to become
public. Alternatively, it is possible that men in important positions are
better able to restrain themselves and are therefore engaged in marital
indiscretions to a much lesser degree than the general public. Although
there is evidence that important men with more to lose are more risk
averse with regard to sex (Ronay & von Hippel, 2010), a number of vivid
instances in which this assertion is contradicted might suggest otherwise
(Apostolidis & Williams, 2003).

   One way to understand Bill Clinton's behavior, at least with regard to
the perception of stupidity, is to recognize that from a Bayesian perspective, his behavior could be seen as representing a rational choice because
the likelihood of being found out could be considered a low probability

event. There is evidence that, while not perfect Bayesians, people's decisions do correspond, at least to a degree, to what Bayes' theorem would expect (El-Gamal & Grether, 1995). In conclusion, then, to the extent that leaders, such as Bill Clinton, are sensitive to base rates, it is not as surprising that they are willing to engage in extramarital sexual activities.

EVOLUTIONARY PSYCHOLOGY AND THE VALUE OF SEX

In addition to a probability component, subjective expected utility theory has a value component, that is, the need to assess how attractive the sexual experience would be. I use evolutionary psychology to think about the value element. Essentially, it is possible to ask, "How important is sex?" I echo many others in suggesting: "very important," especially for men. A significant body of evidence indicates that on average, men have a higher sex drive than women and will more readily take advantage of opportunities to engage in sex (Baumeister, Catanese, & Vohs, 2001; Clark & Hatfield, 1989). Further, I suggest that being in a leadership role actually plays a part in making sex even more important.

Evolutionary psychology examines the way in which biological differences between the way in which men and women reproduce encourage them to adopt different reproductive strategies which, in turn, lead to differences in social behavior (Buss, 2016). For women, reproduction is a much more expensive and risky enterprise, given that they have to physically carry the unborn child for nine months and then provide more postnatal care in the form of food and protection. Men's contribution to reproduction can be as small as a sexual encounter lasting a few minutes. The differential investment in reproduction has led to women being more selective about their sexual partners and as a result they are better able to defer sexual gratification than men. In other words, men value sex to a greater degree than women do.

Leaders may value sex to a greater degree relative to nonleaders through the mediating influence of testosterone. Leadership and testosterone may operate in a mutually reinforcing way, such that the competitive pressures to attain a leadership position may favor men with higher levels of baseline testosterone (Josephs, Sellers, Newman, & Mehta, 2006). Further, as a man's level of dominance increases, he may generate higher levels of testosterone, which might reinforce his desire for more authority. Clinton was perceived as more masculine after the Lewinsky scandal (Ducat, 2004).

An additional consideration is that as a man's level of dominance increases and he produces more testosterone, this may increase his sex drive (Pagano, De Fazio, Levy, RoyChoudhury, & Stahl, 2016). The inverse applies here as well. Unemployment, which can be viewed as a loss of authority, is associated with increased erectile dysfunction (Morokoff & Gillilland, 1993). Lippa (2006) found that as men's level of self-reported sex drive increased, they reported finding women more sexually attractive. Lippa called for future research to examine the degree to which the level of testosterone would increase sex drive, which would, in turn, increase attraction to women.

Marital status can influence testosterone production. Single men have a higher level of testosterone relative to married men (Mazur & Michalek, 1998) or men in long-term relationships (Gray, Chapman, Burnham, McIntyre, Lipson, & Ellison, 2004). Further, Gray et al. (2004) found that as the length of time in a committed relationship increased, the level of testosterone decreased. Although single men do better than married men in terms of testosterone production, men in the early stages of a relationship do better than both. The results of Gray and colleagues suggest an interesting possibility. A long-term married man (as we might expect members of Congress to be) would be expected to suffer the worst reduction in testosterone production. Having an affair would serve as a means of providing a testosterone boost, given research indicating that men in the early stages of a relationship do better than either single or long-term married men. The finding that men who have sex with more than one partner generate more testosterone in comparison to those who are limited to one partner also supports this idea (van Anders, Hamilton, & Watson, 2007).

From the perspective of Bill Clinton contemplating an affair with Monica Lewinsky, or any leader thinking about having sex with a coworker, the positive relationship between sex and the production of testosterone, and the subsequent influence of both on leadership, represents an incentive to the leader to engage in an affair. It is often assumed that subordinates may use sex as a means to advance their careers, or leaders may dangle the promise of career advancement as an unethical means of obtaining sex with employees. I suggest a different pattern: the leader may use sex with a subordinate to increase his own authority as a leader. To the extent that this is true, it is the subordinate, by virtue of his or her willingness to have sex with a supervisor, who exerts power over a leader.

EVOLUTIONARY PSYCHOLOGY AND THE TOLERANCE FOR RISK

Men and women differ in their tolerance for risk (Eckel & Grossman, 2002), with women being on average less risk seeking than men across a wide range of domains, including financial planning (Watson & McNaughton, 2007) and aggressive behavior (Campbell, 2004). From an evolutionary perspective, the differences between risk tolerance for men and that for women can be explained with regard to the likelihood of reproduction. Baumeister (2010) noted that, historically, roughly twice as many women as men have reproduced. Because women have a relatively high likelihood of reproducing, they can afford to adopt a risk-averse strategy and patiently wait to be approached. In contrast, because a smaller percentage of men will successfully reproduce, they are more desperate to obtain reproductive opportunities and, as such, may be more likely to take advantage of sexual opportunities (Clark & Hatfield, 1989). In addition, men may have to take greater initiative in order to stand out from competitors to attract mates. Historically, and from an evolutionary perspective, being in a leadership position entitled the leader to greater sexual access to females. As a result, in most cases men are descended from alpha males, that is, leaders, who have been willing to take risks. At least under certain conditions, there is a positive correlation between risk-seeking behavior and the production of testosterone (Apicella, Carré, & Dreber, 2015). One caveat is research indicating that risk seeking may be less likely in the case of men with power. Among men with power, having high testosterone is actually associated with less risk seeking (Ronay & von Hippel, 2010).

SUMMARY

In this chapter, I have considered the apparent foolishness of Bill Clinton's choice to have sex with Monica Lewinsky using subjective expected utility theory as my analytic framework. Rather than thinking of the affair as an instance of a smart person doing a stupid thing, I have argued that his choice can be seen as a rational way to maximize his own gain. With regard to the probability component, from a Bayesian perspective, the risk of getting found out appeared low. From an evolutionary perspective, the opportunity to have sex with a woman much younger than his wife would have represented a greatly valued opportunity with a high likelihood of being achieved. Given his status as President of the

United States, it was not unreasonable to assume that a woman would be willing to have sex with him.

Based on evolutionary theory, it is possible to argue that Bill Clinton's leadership role probably influenced the subjective value he assigned to the probability and values component. In addition to the objectively low likelihood of being found out, as a leader he had displayed a willingness to tolerate risks, a trait that has been selected for in men as a result of competition for mates. In fact, the willingness to take on risk was a contributing factor to becoming a leader in the first place. Moreover, his being in a leadership position may have increased the perceived attractiveness of a sexual encounter. It is reasonable to assume that Bill Clinton found the opportunities for sexual interaction with Monica Lewinsky, a woman much younger than his wife, very appealing.

Testosterone production can be viewed as an underlying contributor to creating and maintaining a feedback loop that keeps a leader's interest in sexual opportunities high. Testosterone increases an individual's aggressiveness, that is, their desire to take on a challenge such as becoming a leader. Being a leader also increases testosterone production. Increased levels of testosterone increase interest in sex, and increases in sexual activity fuel the production of greater amounts of testosterone.

DOOMED TO FAIL: PSYCHOLOGICAL PROCESSES MAKE IT DIFFICULT TO LEGISLATE AGAINST THE LURE OF THE LEADER

It seems that the dominant paradigm through which workplace relationships are understood has shifted to one that is defined as exploitation and involves possible differences in power between participants in even a consensual relationship. Although the workplace is, by definition, where work occurs, it can also be viewed as a place well designed to bring people together romantically and sexually. There is evidence that as many as ten million new workplace romances start each year (Pierce & Aguinis, 2009). Although other authors (for example, Boyd, 2010) suggest this number may be much smaller, it is still assumed to be rather large in an absolute sense (two or three million).

There are a number of reasons why the workplace will draw people together in a way that then allows romance to flourish. First is that one of the best predictors of whether people become friendly or romantically involved is propinquity (Finkel, Norton, Reis, Ariely, Caprariello, Eastwick, Frost, & Maniaci, 2015). Just being near each other increases the likelihood that an affair will take place. People who work together have an automatic degree of shared interest, and a shared interest can be the basis for attraction (Byrne, 1997). Similarly, having cooperative goals and a shared fate will bring people closer (Tjosvold, Johnson, & Johnson, 1981).

One strategy is to outlaw workplace romances (Boyd, 2010). Although this heavyhanded approach might superficially make sense, especially since it may allow the organization to avoid liability, it disregards certain realities about people. The act of outlawing a behavior may make it more tempting and more likely to be performed. One reason for this is the theory of reactance, which refers to the idea that people are motivated to assert control when their freedom of choice is taken away (Sinclair, Felmlee, Sprecher, & Wright, 2015). Another unintended consequence is that behaviors viewed as transgressive are also sometimes viewed as very appealing, and transgressiveness can fuel sexual desire (Ogas & Gaddam, 2011). Finally, the very act of trying to suppress thoughts can paradoxically make the thoughts more intrusive in the mind (Abramowitz, Tolin, & Street, 2001) and can lead to more difficulty resisting the temptation of the affair due to self-regulation fatigue (Ciarocco, Echevarria, & Lewandowski, 2012).

Of the millions of workplace romances that begin each year, only a percentage involve power differentials between the two participants, and only a percentage involve a relationship that has an inherent need for secrecy (for example, an affair between people where one or more are married). These conditions were satisfied by the Bill Clinton–Monica Lewinsky relationship. Workplace romances where the participants have unequal power are seen as especially problematic. At the same time, romances that involve power imbalances may be particularly enticing to the degree that the roots of the imbalance are associated with desired traits. For example, the traditional imbalance between the older, more powerful male supervisor and younger, less powerful female subordinate draws on the mate preferences that have evolved over time as a function of the different ways that men and women reproduce. Because of how they satisfy the desires of participants, they may be particularly hard to eliminate.

The atmosphere of political correctness and the overarching threat of lawsuits have made institutions extremely sensitive to being accused of creating a hostile work environment. A lens that views any romantic or sexual relationship in the workplace in terms of dominance and submission and as an opportunity for exploitation has made it permissible—even required—that large institutions insert themselves into the personal lives of employees. The validity of this interference is rarely challenged, despite the notion that it represents a paternalistic restriction of freedom (Barbella, 2010). In the few instances where cultural observers do challenge the status quo, they are often seen as fringe apologists for sexual harassers (Abramson, 2007).

CONCLUSIONS

The purpose of the present chapter was to critically examine an assertion that seems to go unchallenged: Bill Clinton's choice to have an affair with Monica Lewinsky represents the apogee of bad decision making. I adopt a contrarian opinion and suggest that his decision can be viewed as logical and "worth the risk," given what we can apply to it from a Bayesian analysis of the prior estimate of his getting caught and an evolutionarily based assessment of the value he may have placed on sexual gratification.

Previous scholars such as Halpern (2002) and Sternberg (2002) have distinguished between Clinton's choice to enter into the affair and his choice to cover it up after the fact, but have asserted that both components represented a highly intelligent and educated individual acting in a stupid or foolish manner. My analysis deviates from previous work by suggesting first that his choice to enter into the affair should not automatically be judged as an example of poor decision making, and second that his efforts to cover up the affair should not be viewed as unintelligent actions. Rather, I prefer to see his response to the scandal as a byproduct of societal hypocrisy about sexual behavior. Given Clinton's need to pander to the values of marital fidelity, he had no choice but to deny the affair once its existence was asserted. This pandering was required to salvage his career by conforming to the alleged values of marital fidelity, despite the overwhelming evidence that marriage as an institution does not operate as we expect. The high level of divorce rates and the high percentage of respondents reporting incidents of extra-marital sex speak to the failure of marriage as an institution when conceptualized as an almost magical bond between a man and a woman, or, more recently in the United States, between any two humans regardless of gender and sexual orientation.

The file drawer problem, which is the tendency not to publicize research with null findings, leads to underestimates of how often researchers fail to replicate previous results, and can be applied to the relative frequency of leadership sex scandals (Rosenthal, 1979). Although we can readily obtain information about sexual liaisons that go wrong, it is quite difficult to collect information about successful affairs due to their axiomatic secretive nature. As such, we may overestimate the likelihood of unwanted office romances between two people with different levels of power, mainly because those are the only ones that make it to the newspapers. In a climate that vilifies and ostracizes people who choose to engage in workplace romances, it is hard to find examples of leaders who are able to successfully navigate the dilemmas of an affair, not necessarily because they do not exist but because those participants may be reluctant to speak of their affair. Yet it leads to an interesting question: why are some leaders able to successfully start and end a romance without leaving bad blood between themselves and the person with whom they had the affair?

REFERENCES

Abramowitz, J. S., Tolin, D. F., & Street, G. P. (2001). Paradoxical effects of thought suppression: A meta-analysis of controlled studies. *Clinical Psychology Review*, *21*(5), 683–703.

Abramson, P. R. (2007). *Romance in the ivory tower: The rights and liberty of conscience*. Cambridge, MA: MIT Press.

Allen, E. S., & Atkins, D. C. (2012). The association of divorce and extramarital sex in a representative US sample. *Journal of Family Issues*, *33*(11), 1477–93.

Allen, E. S., Atkins, D. C., Baucom, D. H., Snyder, D. K., Gordon, K. C., & Glass, S. P. (2005). Intrapersonal, interpersonal, and contextual factors in engaging in and responding to extramarital involvement. *Clinical Psychology: Science and Practice*, *12*(2), 101–30.

Apicella, C. L., Carré, J. M., & Dreber, A. (2015). Testosterone and economic risk taking: A review. *Adaptive Human Behavior and Physiology*, *1*(3), 358–85.

Apostolidis, P., & Williams, J. A., eds. (2003). *Public affairs: Politics in the age of sex scandals*. Durham, NC: Duke University Press.

Bai, M. (2014). *All the truth is out: The week politics went tabloid*. New York: Knopf.

Barbella, L. (2010). Hot for teacher: The ethics and intricacies of student–professor relationships. *Sexuality & Culture*, *14*(1), 44–8.

Baumeister, R. F. (2010). *Is there anything good about men? How cultures flourish by exploiting men*. New York: Oxford University Press.

Baumeister, R. F., Catanese, K. R., & Vohs, K. D. (2001). Is there a gender difference in strength of sex drive? Theoretical views, conceptual distinctions, and a review of relevant evidence. *Personality and Social Psychology Review*, *5*(3), 242–73.

Boyd, C. (2010). The debate over the prohibition of romance in the workplace. *Journal of Business Ethics*, *97*(2), 325–38.

Brower, K. A. (2015). *The residence: Inside the private world of the White House*. New York: HarperCollins.

Buss, D. (2016). *Evolutionary psychology: The new science of the mind* (5th ed.). New York: Routledge.

Byrne, D. (1997). An overview (and underview) of research and theory within the attraction paradigm. *Journal of Social and Personal Relationships, 14*(3), 417–31.

Campbell, A. (2004). Female competition: Causes, constraints, content, and contexts. *Journal of Sex Research, 41*(1), 16–26.

Ciarocco, N. J., Echevarria, J., & Lewandowski Jr., G. W. (2012). Hungry for love: The influence of self-regulation on infidelity. *Journal of Social Psychology, 152*(1), 61–74.

Clark, R. D., & Hatfield, E. (1989). Gender differences in receptivity to sexual offers. *Journal of Psychology & Human Sexuality, 2*(1), 39–55.

Ducat, S. J. (2004). *The wimp factor: Gender gaps, holy wars, and the politics of anxious masculinity.* Boston, MA: Beacon Press.

Eckel, C. C., & Grossman, P. J. (2002). Sex differences and statistical stereotyping in attitudes toward financial risk. *Evolution and Human Behavior, 23*(4), 281–95.

El-Gamal, M. A., & Grether, D. M. (1995). Are people Bayesian? Uncovering behavioral strategies. *Journal of the American Statistical Association, 90*(432), 1137–45.

Fals-Stewart, W., Birchler, G. R., Hoebbel, C., Kashdan, T. B., Golden, J., & Parks, K. (2003). An examination of indirect risk of exposure to HIV among wives of substance-abusing men. *Drug and Alcohol Dependence, 70*(1), 65–76.

Finkel, E. J., Norton, M. I., Reis, H. T., Ariely, D., Caprariello, P. A., Eastwick, P. W., Frost, J. H., & Maniaci, M. R. (2015). When does familiarity promote versus undermine interpersonal attraction? A proposed integrative model from erstwhile adversaries. *Perspectives on Psychological Science, 10*(1), 3–19.

Gray, P. B., Chapman, J. F., Burnham, T. C., McIntyre, M. H., Lipson, S. F., & Ellison, P. T. (2004). Human male pair bonding and testosterone. *Human Nature, 15*(2), 119–31.

Griffith, J. D. (2011). The psychology of risky sexual behavior: Why politicians expose themselves. In A. Dagnes (Ed.), *Sex scandals in American politics: A multidisciplinary approach to the construction and aftermath of contemporary political sex scandals* (pp. 28–46). New York: Bloomsbury Academic.

Grover, S. L., & Hasel, M. C. (2015). How leaders recover (or not) from publicized sex scandals. *Journal of Business Ethics, 129*(1), 177–94.

Halpern, D. F. (2002). Sex, lies, and audio-tapes: The Clinton–Lewinsky scandal. In R. J. Sternberg (Ed.), *Why smart people can be so stupid* (pp. 106–23). New Haven, CT: Yale University Press.

Josephs, R. A., Sellers, J. G., Newman, M. L., & Mehta, P. H. (2006). The mismatch effect: When testosterone and status are at odds. *Journal of Personality and Social Psychology, 90*(6), 999–1013.

Kinsey, A. C., Pomeroy, W. B., & Martin, C. E. (1948). *Sexual behavior in the human male.* Bloomington, IN: Indiana University Press.

Lacayo, R., & Branagan, J. (1998). The big face-off. *Time, 151*(3), 46–8.

Laumann, E. O., Gagnon, J. H., Michael, R. T., & Kolata, G. (1994). *The social organization of sexuality: Sexual practices in the United States.* Chicago, IL: University of Chicago Press.

Lawson, A., & Samson, C. (1988). Age, gender and adultery. *British Journal of Sociology, 39*(3), 409–40.

Lippa, R. A. (2006). Is high sex drive associated with increased sexual attraction to both sexes? It depends on whether you are male or female. *Psychological Science, 17*(1), 46–52.

Luce, R. D., & Raiffa, H. (1957, rev. ed. 2012). *Games and decisions: Introduction and critical survey.* New York: Dover.

Manning, J. E. (2016). Membership of the 112th Congress: A profile. *Congressional Research Service, 4.* Retrieved September 18, 2017 from https://www.senate.gov/CRSpubs/c527ba93-dd4a-4ad6-b79d-b1c9865ca076.pdf.

Mazur, A., & Michalek, J. (1998). Marriage, divorce, and male testosterone. *Social Forces, 77*(1), 315–30.

Morokoff, P. J., & Gillilland, R. (1993). Stress, sexual functioning, and marital satisfaction. *Journal of Sex Research, 30*(1), 43–53.

Ogas, O., & Gaddam, S. (2011). *A billion wicked thoughts: What the world's largest experiment reveals about human desire.* New York: Dutton.

Pagano, M. J., De Fazio, A., Levy, A., RoyChoudhury, A., & Stahl, P. J. (2016). Age, body mass index, and frequency of sexual activity are independent predictors of testosterone deficiency in men with erectile dysfunction. *Urology, 90*(April), 112–18.

Pierce, C. A., & Aguinis, H. (2009). Moving beyond a legal-centric approach to managing workplace romances: Organizationally sensible recommendations for HR leaders. *Human Resource Management, 48*(3), 447–64.

Roberts, A. (2013). By the numbers: Longest-serving members of Congress. Retrieved September 18, 2017 from http://www.cnn.com/2013/06/07/politics/btn-congressional-tenure/.

Ronay, R., & von Hippel, W. (2010). Power, testosterone, and risk-taking. *Journal of Behavioral Decision Making, 23*(5), 473–82.

Rosenthal, R. (1979). The file drawer problem and tolerance for null results. *Psychological Bulletin, 86*(3), 638–41.

Sinclair, H. C., Felmlee, D., Sprecher, S., & Wright, B. L. (2015). Don't tell me who I can't love: A multimethod investigation of social network and reactance effects on romantic relationships. *Social Psychology Quarterly, 78*(1), 77–99.

Spanier, G. B., & Margolis, R. L. (1983). Marital separation and extramarital sexual behavior. *Journal of Sex Research, 19*(1), 23–48.

Sternberg, R. J. (2002). Smart people are not stupid but they sure can be foolish: The imbalance theory of foolishness. In R. J. Sternberg (Ed.), *Why smart people can be so stupid* (pp. 232–42). New Haven, CT: Yale University Press.

Tjosvold, D., Johnson, D. W., & Johnson, R. T. (1981). Effect of partner's effort and ability on liking for partner after failure on a cooperative task. *The Journal of Psychology, 109*(1), 147–52.

Van Anders, S. M., Hamilton, L. D., & Watson, N. V. (2007). Multiple partners are associated with higher testosterone in North American men and women. *Hormones and Behavior, 51*(3), 454–9.

Watson, J., & McNaughton, M. (2007). Gender differences in risk aversion and expected retirement benefits. *Financial Analysts Journal*, *63*(4), 52–62.

Whisman, M. A., & Snyder, D. K. (2007). Sexual infidelity in a national survey of American women: Differences in prevalence and correlates as a function of method of assessment. *Journal of Family Psychology*, *21*(2), 147–54.

Wiederman, M. W. (1997). Extramarital sex: Prevalence and correlates in a national survey. *Journal of Sex Research*, *34*(2), 167–74.

Wiederman, M. W., & Allgeier, E. R. (1996). Expectations and attributions regarding extramarital sex among young married individuals. *Journal of Psychology & Human Sexuality*, *8*(3), 21–35.

Willis, J. (2017). How to impeach a U.S. president (say, Donald Trump), explained. *GQ*. Retrieved September 18, 2017 from http://www.gq.com/story/impeachment-us-president-explained.

Wilson, F. (2015). Romantic relationships at work: Why love can hurt. *International Journal of Management Reviews*, *17*(1), 1–19.

10. Leading and following? Understanding the power dynamics in consensual BDSM

Emma Turley

INTRODUCTION TO BDSM

Bondage, discipline, dominance & submission, and sadism & masochism, or BDSM, is a term commonly used to describe a set of consensual sexual and erotic sexual practices that usually involve the application or receipt of intense physical and/or emotional sensations (Turley & Butt, 2015). The acronym BDSM refers specifically to bondage and discipline (B&D), dominance and submission (D/S), and sadism and masochism (S&M), although the term is often used to describe other consensual sexual practices that can be considered "kinky." The range of BDSM activities is vast and varied, and is limited only by the fantasies of those involved. Bondage and discipline consists of using physical or psychological restraints, dominance and submission involves the exchange of power and/or control, and sadism and masochism refers to enjoyment of the application or receipt of physical or psychological pain. Weinberg, Williams, and Moser (1984) identified five common practices that occurred as part of BDSM play: the impression that one partner controls the other, roleplay, shared beliefs, a sexual context, and consensuality.

BDSM is characterized by an eroticized exchange of power (Langdridge & Butt, 2005), with partners usually adopting the "top" or dominant role or the "bottom" or submissive role during the BDSM play. Less common are those individuals that like to "switch" between these roles depending upon the nature of the sexual scene (Turley & Butt, 2015). For the sake of clarity, this chapter will use the terms *dominant* or *top*, *submissive* or *bottom*, and *switch* throughout. It is a common misconception that BDSM play always must include some sort of pain.

This is not necessarily the case; however, there should be some psychological power exchange involved in the scene, and interestingly, BDSM does not always have to include sexual contact. Regardless of role or activity preference, BDSM play is highly subjective and nuanced (Turley, 2012), and it should be noted that proclivities vary from person to person. Individuals from across the sexual spectrum practice BDSM, along with transgender, cisgender (when gender identity matches birth sex), and nonbinary individuals. The available research indicates that BDSM occurrence in the general population is not particularly rare or infrequent. Moser and Kleinplatz (2006) estimate that around one in ten of the population enjoy participating in BDSM, while other estimates propose that 10 per cent of women and 14 percent of men had engaged in some form of BDSM at least once (Janus & Janus, 1993). It should be noted that it can be difficult to arrive at a consensus when estimating frequency due to the diverse nature of BDSM, stigma that affects reporting, and the varied nature of associated activities and practices.

The purpose of this chapter is to examine the power dynamics involved in consensual BDSM. Power and the ways in which power can be exchanged are central features in both BDSM and leadership. The common perception relating to BDSM is that the dominant partner is in control of everything relating to the play, from deciding on the theme or narrative of the scene to choosing which erotic activities occur, when, and for how long. The dominant partner seemingly holds all of the power and control, while the submissive partner is required to yield to their authority and will and relinquish their power, agreeing to be controlled by someone else. This chapter will examine the power dynamics in BDSM and discuss who is really in control during a BDSM scene. The chapter begins with an overview of BDSM and its practitioners, before presenting a discussion of the complex leader-and-follower relationship.

A common misconception relating to BDSM is that practitioners suffer from a psychological disorder(s) or psychopathology, are psychologically damaged in some way, or have been victims of abuse at some stage during their lives. This perspective stems from the early sexology literature of the nineteenth century, which positioned those with an interest in BDSM as "deviant," and BDSM practitioners are still frequently viewed from a forensic and/or psychomedical perspective. Indeed, the conflation of consensual BDSM and nonconsensual sexual violence remains apparent in the academic literature as well as in the mainstream media. Many of the practices associated with BDSM are defined as "paraphilias" in the Diagnostic and Statistical Manual of Mental Disorders (DSM-5), although the practices must cause distress to the person experiencing them in order to be considered a disorder by the

DSM. The research evidence, however, has found no evidence that individuals who practice consensual BDSM are any more likely to suffer from psychopathology than the general population. Despite dominant psychomedical discourses situating BDSM firmly within the realm of pathology, various research studies have concluded that BDSM practitioners are no more psychologically damaged or dangerous than those who do not participate in BDSM (Dietz, 1990; Cross & Matheson, 2006; Connolly, 2006; Yost, 2009; Stockwell, Walker, & Eshleman, 2010). Despite the lack of evidence, the dominant, pathologizing positions espoused regarding BDSM and its practitioners influence the perception of the general population, resulting in the perpetuation of common stereotypes and negative views (Turley, 2012); however, there is an increasing body of research literature aiming to challenge notions that BDSM is pathological (see Beckmann, 2001; Taylor and Ussher, 2001; Barker, Gupta & Iantaffi, 2007; Turley, 2016).

Practitioners of BDSM take notions of risk and safety seriously, and place safety and consent central to participation. The slogans "safe, sane and consensual" (SSC) and "risk aware consensual kink" (RACK) express the ethical code of conduct clearly (Langdridge & Barker, 2007). These codes acknowledge that the practitioners should be aware of the possible risks involved in the BDSM play, and that they are consenting to taking part. Risks are managed through a number of channels. Practitioners discuss and negotiate the development of the BDSM scene and their roles and interests before and sometimes during the play. Often BDSM practitioners use a system known as a safeword—a word or gesture that enables them to pause or stop the scene—and both dominant and submissive partners are able to use this safeword. Practitioners also use a traffic light system to describe activities that they enjoy (green), activities they might like to try (amber), and activities in which they would never engage (red); alongside this, practitioners may have "hard" and "soft" limits. Soft limits refer to activities, practices, and boundaries that individuals may like to explore with discussion and negotiation, while hard limits refer to boundaries that must not be violated.

DEMOGRAPHICS OF BDSM PRACTITIONERS

This section of the chapter will explore the demographics of BDSM practitioners, examining a range of factors, including socioeconomic, psychosocial and sexual identity dynamics.

Educational and Socioeconomic Demographics

Research has demonstrated that BDSM practitioners are a relatively homogenous group and tend to be white, highly educated (to undergraduate degree level), and middle or upper-class professionals (Sandnabba, Santtila, Alison, & Nordling, 2002; Langdridge & Barker, 2007), reflecting the demographic characteristics of individuals in Western leadership roles. Attendees at BDSM events, conferences, community meetings, and "play parties" are predominantly white (Sheff & Hammers, 2011). Given the expense involved in attending BDSM community and play events and purchasing appropriate clothing and toys, it is unsurprising that individuals with lower incomes or less disposable income are excluded from these environments. It should be noted that the majority of studies exploring BDSM consider Western participants and data due to the paucity of work investigating BDSM crossculturally, and therefore represent a culturally homogenous group of people. It is also the case that research studies are unlikely to be able to accurately capture the range of people involved in BDSM; for example, it is more difficult to reach individuals who practice BDSM privately rather than as part of a community.

PSYCHOSOCIAL AND PSYCHOLOGICAL CHARACTERISTICS OF BDSM PRACTITIONERS

Richters, de Visser, Rissel, Gulrich, and Smith (2008) used survey data from almost 20,000 people in Australia to study the psychosocial features of individuals who engage in BDSM. In this survey, 2.2 per cent of men and 1.3 per cent of women reported some involvement with BDSM over the past year, and lesbian, gay, and bisexual-identified people were more likely to be interested in BDSM than heterosexual individuals (9.3 per cent, 14.2 per cent, and 14 per cent, respectively). Those who engaged in BDSM reported more diverse sexual lives in terms of number and gender of partners, and in terms of sexual activities, than their heterosexual counterparts did. The data showed no link between BDSM participation and sexual coercion and no increased reporting of sexual difficulties when compared to non-BDSM individuals. Similar findings have also been described by others (see Cross & Matheson, 2006; Connolly, 2006; Moser & Levitt, 1987). Wismeijer and van Assen (2013) examined the core psychological characteristics of BDSM practitioners on a range of psychological characteristics, and compared them to a control group of non-BDSM practitioners with the aim of investigating any psychological differences between the two groups. The research concluded that BDSM practitioners are characterized by enhanced psychological strength and greater autonomy rather than by maladaptive characteristics, which again is reflective of those in leadership roles.

Sexual Identity and BDSM

Alison, Santtila, Sandnabba, and Nordling (2001) identified four sexual themes used to categorize and map sexual behaviors. Results indicated that heterosexual men and women engaged in significantly more behaviors related to the humiliation region of the map, while gay men engaged in significantly more behaviors related to the hypermasculinity region. Alison et al. (2001) concluded that the four sexual themes were qualitatively different, that the various facets of BDSM adopt different functions and meanings for men and women, and that sexual identity was a factor in preferred activities. Nordling, Sandnabba, Santtila, and Alison (2006) examined the relationship between sexual identity and "sadomasochistic" preferences. It was reported that gay men had their first BDSM experience at an older age than their heterosexual counterparts. There were clear differences in the preferences of gay and heterosexual men in this particular study, with gay respondents favoring leather, specialist equipment, wrestling, and uniform scenes. Heterosexual preferences were focused on verbal humiliation, sensory deprivation, crossdressing, and role playing. Gay men were sadistically oriented with a preference for masculinization of their sexual behavior, while heterosexual men adopted submissive roles more frequently, with an emphasis on humiliation and pain.

BDSM Roles, Activities and Interactions

Kleinplatz and Moser (2006) examined common manifestations of BDSM-related interactions. The manifestations identified were roles, that is, the adoption of the dominant or submissive role, with some participants opting to adopt these roles flexibly by switching. The researchers note that the adoption of the same label does not suggest that practitioners attach identical meanings to their labels, however. For example, it is noteworthy that some participants who use bondage enjoy tight bonds that prohibit movement while others favor looser restraints that allow struggle, highlighting the variation in the experience's personal meaning. According to Kleinplatz and Moser, discipline is a feature of a BDSM interaction, where the notion of being disciplined due to a violation of some prearranged rule is erotic. Another key manifestation is dominance and submission, and the feelings obtained from these roles can be the source of the eroticism. There must be a clear power dynamic that resonates with the participants in the experience. Physical pain is identified as a common manifestation, although this is a specific type of pain within the BDSM experience—pain outside of the sexual context is rarely eroticized. Kleinplatz and Moser (2006) contend that humiliation is the most problematic area of BDSM to accurately describe. The subjective nature of humiliation is emphasized, as what one individual considers to be deeply humiliating has no effect at all on another. Kleinplatz and Moser contend that the relationships involved in BDSM play a key part in the interaction. They contend that there is no typical BDSM relationship, and that any and all combinations are possible, including alternative relationship styles.

UNDERSTANDING ROLES IN BDSM

This section of the chapter will discuss the sexual roles adopted during BDSM. Broadly, these consist of: the top (also referred to as dominant), the bottom (also referred to as submissive), and the switch (an individual who enjoys assuming both roles at different instances). The roles involved in BDSM are usually more complex and nuanced than simply dominant, submissive, and switch, and further distinct definitions under the umbrella of the "dominant" role can include sadist, master, mistress, daddy, or dom/domme, while definitions under the umbrella of "submissive" can include masochist, slave, pet, boi, owned, and sub. The choice of role label or name is subjective to each individual involved in BDSM, and the terms used can vary. It should be noted that individuals who opt to describe their role using the same label will not necessarily participate in the same erotic BDSM activities. As mentioned, the meanings assigned to the labels and roles will differ between BDSM practitioners. There tend to be differences in assigned meanings among different countries, regions, groups, and sexualities (Moser & Kleinplatz, 2007).

BDSM is organized around the adoption and embodiment of roles related to a particular power dynamic, and the way that power is exchanged between those involved (Turley, 2016). Experimenting with the exchange of power is a fundamental feature of a BDSM experience, and it is this shift in status, either to the dominant or the submissive position, that is key to successful BDSM play. Generally it is the top, or dominant, partner that has the power during a BDSM scene, and this can mean that they decide on the activities and practices that occur within the context of the scene. The dominant partner's elevated status is often signified by a particular symbolic style of dress, manner of speech, and demeanor, among other things. Conversely, the bottom, or submissive, partner relinquishes power during the scene, meaning that they have limited or no input into events during the context of the scene. Again, the lower status can be signified by style of dress, rituals such as the placing of a collar around a submissive partner's neck, and the prohibition of speech and behaviors. Rituals and symbolic acts can play an effective role in facilitating the exchange of power between BDSM partners. These can range from formal "ownership" ceremonies to informal collaring rituals and serve to explicitly illustrate the exchange of power and a shift in the practitioners' status within the scene. They contribute to a sense of authenticity (Turley, 2012).

In terms of the dominant and submissive roles, there may be differences among the preferred activities of those that identify as belonging to the same subcategories, and an individual who identifies with/as a particular label will not necessarily participate in the same activities as another person who adopts that same label. A person who identifies as a submissive would primarily enjoy psychological domination, while someone with a preference for masochism will be interested in intense physical sensations and/or pain, while an individual who identifies as a slave will receive gratification from providing service. In terms of dominance, an individual who identifies as a sadist will enjoy inflicting intense physical and/or painful sensations; a dominant will enjoy restraining a submissive partner, either physically in bondage or psychologically, or both. These roles are not mutually exclusive and there will likely be some overlap between them. There are a range of relationship styles, types, and permutations in BDSM, and erotic encounters can be long-term or short-term arrangements, as well as more casual or one-off encounters. Relationships can be fluid, with a range of partners depending upon the erotic scene, or can adopt a more static state consisting of two or more regular partners. It is also the case that some BDSM practitioners practice polyamory and are involved with primary and secondary partners, while others do not. The diversity of BDSM relationships enables practitioners to engage in the types of BDSM activities they enjoy, and preferences are unique to those involved.

Submissive partners enjoy the process of demotion to a lower status during the power exchange, and the elevated status of the dominant partner can also be a source of eroticism. The implicit knowledge that the dominant partner possesses the power and can control the direction of the scene can be exciting for the submissive partner (Turley, 2012). The acknowledgement of this shifted power dynamic highlights the sub-missive's own lack of power and status in contrast to the dominant partner, and contributes to the multifaceted experience of submission in terms of both the psychological act of submission and the psychological and physical consequences of this act. Turley (2012) noted that a key element of submission is the removal of responsibility due to the submissive's lower status. In the submissive role, practitioners' autonomy is removed and placed in the hands of the dominant partner, meaning they are able to orchestrate the themes and content of the scene and the BDSM activities that take place. Submissive partners are not able to question or challenge these choices, given that the qualities of this role do not allow independence. The act of submission often leads to practitioners experiencing a range of contrary emotions during the scene, which can be an exciting and novel aspect of the play, as emotions which are not usually experienced together (for example, humiliation and sexual arousal) are blended. It must be remembered, however, that these roles are adopted only within the context of the BDSM scene and have already been negotiated and agreed upon by all individuals involved. In some cases submission has been found to be popular among individuals, particularly men, who have achieved high-status positions at work, in the community, and/or within the family group. Baumeister (1988) reports that adopting a submissive role may be a means of temporarily escaping from this position of power and authority. During submission, the focus shifts to the immediate moment and to visceral bodily sensations, leading to a deliberate loss of the usual high-level awareness of oneself as a powerful authority figure. The individual's identity can be transformed into a new, temporary identity of "powerless" "submissive," temporarily erasing their everyday position in the world (Baumeister, 1988). This symbolic transformation offers a temporary respite from the demands of occupying a high-status position in society, and the act of submission can create a fantasized identity for the duration of the BDSM scene. There is a shift away from the cerebral towards the corporeal, providing a space to shed the usual responsibilities of their everyday role and forget, if only temporarily, about the outside world (Turley, 2012). It should be noted, however, that not all powerful people who participate in BDSM enjoy submission. Some high-status individuals prefer domination, deriving pleasure from the eroticization of their power within the context of the sexual scene.

It may appear easier to adopt the dominant role during BDSM activities than the submissive role, but practitioners who assume this role face complex challenges in pleasing themselves, pleasing the submissive partner, maintaining control, and monitoring safety during the scene, all

while convincingly exercising power over the submissive. This is reflective of leadership processes that operate outside of BDSM within
different contexts of the wider world. Good leadership should come from
a position of care, and dominant partners are required to care about their
submissive partner(s) and are responsible for their physical and psychological welfare and wellbeing during and after a scene. One of the main
erotic features that dominants derive from this role is a sense of their own
all-powerful status and total control of the situation and of the submissive
partner. This mirrors the submissives' perception of their own lack of
control and autonomy and reinforces these philosophies during the scene.
Dominant partners are able to exercise the shift in status by dictating and
directing the submissive partner in ways that they desire, without feeling
constrained by societal norms and judgments. The adulation and reverence a dominant partner receives from their submissive is often a central
feature of the experience of domination for practitioners; this, coupled
with the knowledge that the submissive partner respects them and wants
to please them, forms the basis for satisfying domination. Choice is a
feature of this role: dominant partners are the engineers of the scene and
have the power to choose the activities, the instruments, and the narrative
within the negotiated context of the scene. These choices, in reality, are
constrained by the submissive partner's previously negotiated limits,
highlighting the complex and nuanced power dynamics between the
dominant and submissive partners. The dominant partner is the director
of the BDSM scene and enjoys making decisions and controlling choices,
which can ensure their own desires are met within the fantasy of
perceived unlimited opportunities for satisfaction. As is the case for all
successful leaders, dominance requires a level of creativity and innovation in order to engineer a scene that pleases everyone. Accessing
personal power is a key feature of effective leadership, and given that
everyone responds differently to having power, the dominant partner
must use their power responsibly for the benefit of everyone involved in
the scene. The quality of a leader's relationship with his or her followers
is an important factor in determining a good-quality relationship, and this
can be impacted by the leader's behavior (Howell & Shamir, 2005). For
leaders both outside of and within BDSM, fostering a sense of collective
identity and mutual goals between leaders and followers is crucial for
maintaining productive and successful relationships. Interpersonal
dynamics are important, and followers' needs and expectations should be
met effectively by leaders (Shamir, 2007); dominant partners should
therefore ensure others' needs are met during the scene as well as their
own, in order to ensure a successful and fun BDSM scene. Charismatic
leaders can form a transformational relationship with their followers

(Avolio, 1999), and collective investment in outcomes coupled with a transformational leader enables followers to perform beyond their initial capacities and positively influence followers' attitudes and behaviors (Liao & Chuang, 2007). Submissives often report that they want to please their dominant partner by exceeding their limits of endurance with each scene, to achieve a more pleasing outcome for both.

This chapter has focused on BDSM that occurs within a specified and negotiated scene or context. Some practitioners of BDSM chose to engage in a permanent BDSM relationship that lasts beyond context-ualized scenes, which is known as a 24/7 relationship. It can be argued that these relationships are qualitatively different from the BDSM inter-actions discussed in this chapter, and therefore it is beyond the scope of this work to elucidate the power dynamics involved in these relationships.

WHO IS REALLY IN CONTROL OF A BDSM SCENE?

This section of the chapter will explore the power dynamics in BDSM and examine various perspectives regarding who is actually in control during a scene. A traditional, and perhaps superficial, idea is that the dominant partner is in total charge of the BDSM scene. Given what has been outlined in the chapter so far, the dominant partner appears to have all of the control and the submissive partner appears to have none. The dominant partner is the one who is able to exert their sexual will over the submissive partner, while the latter simply endures the challenges of submission and attempts to please their dominant. The dominant partner is the "do-er," doing things to others, while the submissive partner is being "done to." However, BDSM roles and interactions are more complex than they initially appear; it is *assumed* that the dominant partner has all of the power, but this is not necessarily the case.

The general consensus among BDSM practitioners is that the power is equal but is exchanged during the scene (Hébert & Weaver, 2014; Moser & Kleinplatz, 2007), and the qualities and traits synonymous with effectual leadership are exhibited by both the dominant and the submis-sive partners. This can be interpreted as a form of shared or collective leadership, which is dynamic and relational and evolves throughout the lifespan of a group or team (Avolio, 2007; Pearce and Sims, 2002). This mutual relationship involves the development of a pattern of reciprocity that deviates from traditional hierarchical leader–follower dynamics. The successful outcome of the BDSM scene is a collective endeavor, and elements of leadership are distributed among the individuals involved.

Whether the preference is for the dominant or the submissive role, engineering the scene is a collaborative effort, and each individual has a set of responsibilities to create and maintain the erotic fantasy and contextual framework of the scene.

Easton and Hardy (2001) contend that submissive partners do not have to relinquish their individuality, strength, or power during BDSM, and state they should be mindful of the specific responsibilities entailed in being a sub. These include being aware of their own limits and boundaries and communicating these clearly to the dominant partner, along with supporting the dominant partner and meeting their needs effectively. It is also important that the submissive partner cooperates with the dominant to establish a cocreated fantasy (Turley, 2012) and that honest feedback is provided to partners during and after a scene (Sophia, 2007). There are other forms of power held by the submissive partner that are far from straightforward. Newmahr (2011) reports on "badass bottoming," where the submissive partner approaches BDSM competitively—competing either with themselves by attempting to endure more than they have done previously or to go further than they have done before, or with the dominant partner by trying to outlast the latter's physical or psychological limits. Moser and Kleinplatz (2007) describe "dominant bottoms" who authoritatively direct their partner to stimulate them in specific ways with detailed instructions, and submissive individuals who "top from the bottom" by subtly guiding the scene and the activities that occur within it. The ability to endure and overcome physically difficult or psychologically challenging scenes is considered a source of power for submissives (Easton & Hardy, 2001; Turley, 2012), along with being able to accept feelings of vulnerability and fear. Concepts of strength, toughness, and endurance are not often considered when thinking about submission; however, these are important features that also illustrate the ways in which submissive partners display leadership skills, despite adopting the perceived "powerless" role. It is also the case that submissive partners excel in "soft" leadership skills, such as resilience. Submissive partners demonstrate resilience during the act of submission through the endurance of unpleasant or painful BDSM practices, as outlined above.

As mentioned earlier in this chapter, negotiation is a cornerstone of BDSM, and it is during negotiations that the submissive partner can decide on the degree of power they are prepared to exchange. It is not often the case that the submissive partner relinquishes all of their power during BDSM; rather, there are degrees of power that are given up depending upon the circumstances of each individual scene. The aim of the negotiations is to ensure all participants' needs are met and each individual has a satisfying and fulfilling experience (Sophia, 2007). Hard and soft limits and boundaries are set by the submissive partner, yet are important for the dominant partner to understand as they have a duty of care to their submissive partners—and tops who go beyond agreed limits are not tolerated in the BDSM community (Sophia, 2007). Negotiation usually takes place prior to the beginning of a BDSM scene, though often there will be forms of in-scene negotiation, meaning that the submissive partner is able to have some input despite the illusion of complete powerlessness. It can be difficult to strike a balance between an overtly planned scene and an adequately negotiated one that satisfies everyone involved—it is not exciting for participants when scenes feel unspon-taneous or stale, or when authenticity is compromised (Turley, 2012). Submissive partners have the power of the safeword, and therefore the ability to pause or stop the scene if necessary. Although some prac-titioners choose not to use a safeword during play for fear of breaking the illusion of powerlessness, safeword use is common for submissive partners in BDSM. This is arguably the greatest power of all—the ability to bring a halt to the entire BDSM scene—and it is difficult to argue that submissives are powerless if a safeword is involved. Excellent communi-cation is a very important skill in effective leadership, and it is the submissive's responsibility to be able to explain and negotiate their hard and soft limits, along with other preferences and dislikes about the scene's contextual framework.

In conclusion, the concept of power and power exchange within BDSM is a multilayered dynamic, and it would appear that power within the scene and outside of the context of the scene are different, as are the ways in which the roles interact with power within and outside of the scene different. Despite the outward impression that the dominant partner is all-powerful, both roles involve mastery of various leadership qualities in order to create an exciting and erotic sexual scene. Both dominant and submissive partners have equal responsibilities and influence in BDSM play; however, the dominant partners have control, while the submissive partners have power.

REFERENCES

Avolio, B. J. (2007). Promoting more integrative strategies for leadership theory-building. *American Psychologist, 62*, 25–33.
Avolio, B. J. (1999). *Full Leadership Development: Building Vital Forces in Organisations*. Thousand Oaks, CA: SAGE.

Alison, L., Santtila, P., Sandnabba, N. K., & Nordling, N. (2001). Sadomaso-chistically oriented behavior: Diversity in practice and meaning. *Archives of Sexual Behavior, 30*, 1–12.

Barker, M., Gupta, C., & Iantaffi, A. (2007). The power of play: The potentials and pitfalls in healing narratives of BDSM. In D. Langdridge & M. Barker (Eds.), *Safe, Sane and Consensual Contemporary Perspectives on Sadomaso-chism* (pp. 197–216). Basingstoke: Palgrave Macmillan.

Baumeister, R. (1988). Masochism as escape from self. *Journal of Sex Research, 25*(1), 28–59.

Beckmann, A. (2001). Deconstructing myths: The social construction of "sado-masochism" versus "subjugated knowledges" of practitioners of consensual "SM." *Journal of Criminal Justice and Popular Culture, 8*(2), 66–95.

Connolly, P. (2006). Psychological functioning of bondage/domination/ sadomasochism (BDSM) practitioners. *Journal of Psychology and Human Sexuality, 18*(1), 79–120.

Cross, P. & Matheson, K. (2006). Understanding sadomasochism: An empirical investigation of four perspectives. *Journal of Homosexuality, 50*(2/3), 133–66.

Dietz, P. E. (1990). The sexually sadistic criminal and his offences. *Bulletin of the American Academy of Psychiatry and the Law, 18*(2), 163–78.

Easton, D., & Hardy, J. W. (2001). *The New Bottoming Book.* San Francisco: Greenery Press.

Howell, J. M., & Shamir, B. (2005). The role of followers in the charismatic leadership process: relationships and their consequences. *Academy of Management Review, 30*, 96–112.

Hébert, A., & Weaver, A. (2014). An examination of personality characteristics associated with BDSM orientations. *Canadian Journal of Human Sexuality, 23*(3), 106–15.

Janus, S., & Janus, C. (1993). *The Janus Report on Sexual Behaviour.* New York: John Wiley & Sons.

Kleinplatz, P., & Moser, C., eds. (2006). *Sadomasochism: Powerful Pleasures.* New York: Harrington Park Press.

Langdridge, D., & Barker, M. (2007). Situating sadomasochism. In D. Langdridge & M. Barker (Eds.), *Safe, Sane and Consensual Contemporary Perspectives on Sadomasochism* (pp. 3–9). Basingstoke: Palgrave Macmillan.

Langdridge, D., & Butt, T. (2005). The erotic construction of power exchange. *Journal of Constructivist Psychology, 18*(1), 65–73.

Liao, H., & Chuang, A. C. (2007). Transforming service employees and climate: A multilevel, multisource examination of transformational leadership in build-ing long-term service relationships. *Journal of Applied Psychology, 92*, 1006–19.

Moser, C., & Kleinplatz, P. (2006). Introduction: The state of our knowledge on SM. *Journal of Homosexuality, 2/3*, 1–15.

Moser, C., & Kleinplatz, P. (2007). Themes of SM expression. In D. Langdridge & M. Barker (Eds), *Safe, Sane and Consensual Contemporary Perspectives on Sadomasochism* (pp. 35–54). Basingstoke: Palgrave Macmillan.

Moser, C., & Levitt, E. E. (1987). An exploratory-descriptive study of a sadomasicistically oriented sample. *Journal of Sex Research, 23*(3), 322–37.

Newmahr, S. (2011). *Playing on the Edge: Sadomasochism, Risk and Intimacy.* Bloomington, IN: Indiana University Press.

Nordling, N., Sandnabba, N.K., Santtila, P., & Alison, L. (2006). Differences and similarities between gay and straight individuals involved in the sadomasochistic subculture. *Journal of Homosexuality* (Special Issue: Sadomasochism: Powerful Pleasures), *50*(2–3), 41–57.

Pearce, C. L., & Sims, H. P. (2002). The influence of vertical vs shared leadership on longitudinal effectiveness of change management teams. *Group Dynamics: Theory, Research, and Practice, 6*, 172–97.

Richters, J., de Visser, R. O., Rissel, C. E., Grulich, A. E., & Smith, A. M. (2008). Demographic and psychosocial features of participants in bondage and discipline, "sadomasochism" or dominance and submission (BDSM): Data from a national survey. *The Journal of Sexual Medicine, 5*(7), 1660–68.

Sandnabba, N., Santtila, P., Alison, L., & Nordling, N. (2002). Demographics, sexual behaviour, family background and abuse experiences of practitioners of sadomasochistic sex: A review of recent research. *Sexual and Relationship Therapy, 17*(1), 39–55.

Shamir, B. (2007). From passive recipients to active coproducers: Followers' roles in the leadership process. In B. Shamir, R. Pillai, M.C. Bligh, & M. Uhl-Bien (Eds.), *Follower Centred Perspectives on Leadership* (pp. ix–xxxix). Greenwich, CT: Inform Age.

Sheff, E., & Hammers, C. (2011). The privilege of perversities: Race, class, and education among polyamorists and kinksters. *Psychology & Sexuality, 2*(3), 198–223.

Sophia, S. M. (2007). Who is in charge in an SM scene? In D. Langdridge & M. Barker (Eds.), *Safe, Sane and Consensual Contemporary Perspectives on Sadomasochism* (pp. 271–6). Basingstoke: Palgrave Macmillan.

Stockwell, F. M. J., Walker, D. J., & Eshleman, J. W. (2010). Measures of implicit and explicit attitudes towards mainstream and BDSM sexual terms using the IRAP and questionnaire with BDSM/fetish and student participants. *The Psychological Record, 60*, 307–24.

Taylor, G., & Ussher, J. (2001). Making sense of S&M: A discourse analytic account. *Sexualities, 4*(3), 293–314.

Turley, E. (2012). "It started when I barked once when I was licking his boots!" A descriptive phenomenological study of the everyday experience of BDSM. Unpublished doctoral thesis. University of Huddersfield.

Turley, E. L. (2016). "Like nothing I've ever felt before": Understanding consensual BDSM as embodied experience. *Psychology and Sexuality, 7*(2), 149–62.

Turley, E., & Butt, T. (2015). BDSM—bondage and discipline; dominance and submission; sadism and masochism. In C. Richards & M. J. Barker (Eds.), *Palgrave Handbook of the Psychology of Sexuality and Gender* (pp. 24–41). Basingstoke: Palgrave Macmillan.

Weinberg, M. S., Williams, C. J., & Moser, C. (1984). The social constituents of sadomasochism. *Social Problems, 31*(4), 379–89.

Wismeijer, A. A. J. & van Assen, M. A. L. M. (2013). Psychological characteristics of BDSM practitioners. *Journal of Sexual Medicine, 10*(8), 1949–52.

Yost, M. (2009). Development and validation of the Attitudes about Sadomasochism Scale. *Journal of Sex Research, 47*(1), 79–91.

11. Does the "zipless dance" exist? Leadership, followership, and sexuality in social dancing

James K. Beggan and Scott T. Allison

"Dancing is a perpendicular expression of a horizontal desire"—
George Bernard Shaw

What do you think of when you hear the word "dancing?" Lithe and supple ballet dancers in tutus and slippers moving with the rhythm of classical music? Musicals from the 1950s such as *Singin' in the Rain*, featuring legendary performers such as Gene Kelly, Fred Astaire, and Ginger Rogers? The highly stylized routines featured on *Dancing with the Stars*? One important aspect of these examples is that the dancing they feature is choreographed and well rehearsed ahead of time. Another element is that the people in these examples are well-trained professionals.

This chapter focuses on another type of dancing—social dancing, where ordinary people get together to express themselves at the local dance studio. Unlike what transpires in *Singin' in the Rain* and *Dancing with the Stars*, social dancing is not planned out in advance and participants' skill levels can range from first-time beginner to seasoned 30-year veteran. Social dancing can be considered a form of serious leisure (Stebbins, 2007), with some participants spending thousands of dollars and hundreds of hours on lessons, costumes, and travel to and from dance events (Brown, 2007). Most people have heard of the main types of social dances, even if they have never done them or seen them performed. Examples of social dance styles include swing, salsa, foxtrot, tango, waltz, and cha-cha.

Although it might not seem so at first pass, social dancing is saturated with examples of leadership and strong overtones of sexuality. In fact, the leadership and sexuality elements are heavily intertwined on the basis of three social dance conventions. The first convention is that for a coordinated dance effort between two people to take place, someone has to be designated as a *lead*, and as a result the partner has to adopt the role of *follow*. The second convention is that during the dance, the lead and the follow usually hold each other in an intimate embrace, even if they are complete strangers to each other. Third, the roles of lead and follow are assigned almost exclusively on the basis of biological sex: men lead and women follow (Ericksen, 2011). Peters (1991) views couples dancing as a form of dance that "depends on the simultaneous execution of movement by two dancers locked in intimate body contact, but how those movements are performed and where the focus lies depends entirely and absolutely on whether one is male or female" (pp. 147–8). Despite some efforts to challenge the sex-based conventions of social dancing (Johnson, 2005), in general the heterosexist perspective strongly dominates. One type of challenge is to permit or even encourage men and women to learn the opposing role. As such, sometimes women will learn to lead and men will learn to follow. Another way in which dance conventions are challenged is for same sex couples to dance together.

We conceptualize social dancing as a form of nonverbal communication geared toward creating the coordinated movement of two people done in time, and over time, to musical accompaniment. Two key elements of this definition are worthy of comment. First, social dancing involves nonverbal communication that is carried out on the basis of the physical connection between the lead and follow. The main point of connection is the lead's right hand on the follow's left shoulder blade. The lead sends signals based on shifting their weight from one foot to another and moving forward, backward, or to the side. The follow must decode the messages and respond in turn. Of course, as with any form of communication, there is a reciprocity and interdependence that develops as the dance—as an expression of a conversation—continues. If a lead realizes a follow does not have the skill level needed to perform certain moves, he should not require the follow to attempt them. A good follow can stylize and a good lead will give her both adequate physical space and time to carry out those stylings.

Second, social dancing involves coordinated movements over space and time. The space can range from three square meters, as in the case of nontraveling dances, to 50 or more square meters, as in the case of traveling dances. These socially coordinated movements imply the use of a cognitive script that both the lead and the follow must share for the dance to proceed successfully. These scripts contain beliefs and expectations about what each person will do and how they will do it (Fiske & Taylor, 2013). Dancers possess scripts for various dance steps, of course, but they also have a script for what constitutes a good dance partner. The lead has a script for a good follow and the follow has a script for what represents a good lead. These social expectations can be the source of either great satisfaction or dissatisfaction with the dance. Although a social dance need not imply any sexuality, the rhythmic, intimate, coordinated activity between a lead and a follow shares many of the features of sexual intercourse (Riva, 2016).

Representations of what it takes to be a good lead are consistent with stereotypes about masculinity (Hoyt, 2014). A good lead needs to be *agentic* (Carli & Eagly, 1999). A 2006 film about ballroom dancing featuring Antonio Banderas is actually called *Take the Lead* (Godsick & Friedlander, 2006). Traditionally, the man initially takes the lead by asking a woman to dance. Once the dance begins, a good lead has to be decisive about what move or pattern to lead next. Good leads are described as "strong," though the use of the term "strong" can often create hardship for women. Beginning male dancers often view the term "strong" in terms of being forceful, which is not correct. In reality, in the context of dancing, a strong lead is "clear" because he sends a strong— that is, exact—signal. Weak leads send messages that are ambiguous and therefore create uncertainty among follows.

A good follow needs to be responsive to signals from the lead. In the film *Strictly Ballroom* (Miall & Luhrmann, 1992), during a competition, a young and ambitious male ballroom dancer gets boxed into a corner. To escape, he carries out a series of unorthodox dance moves which are considered shocking to the audience watching the performance, as well as to his dance partner. Although an unwilling participant, she is constrained by the rules of dance to go along with his radical steps. She explains her acquiescence with the statement: "Where the man goes, the lady must follow." The idea that a woman acting as a follow has to conform to the requirements of the lead is consistent with stereotypes about women as passive and compliant. However, to be effective as follows, women also have to be sensitive to the signals they receive, a trait consistent with a view of women as sympathetic and empathic.

Sex enters into social dancing in two distinct ways. The first way is through the assignment of the lead and follow roles on the basis of biological sex (Marion, 2008). This arrangement is rarely challenged on the social dance floor (Beggan & Pruitt, 2014). In more than a decade of dancing, neither of the authors of this chapter has ever been asked if he wants to lead or follow. It is always assumed he will lead. Most social dancers do not contest this conventional arrangement. When it's talked about, the assignment of lead and follow on the basis of sex is often rationalized by the assertion that men are bigger and stronger than women. This is often the case, true, but even in cases when women are the same size or taller than a lead, participants do not rethink their roles.

Part of the reason that dance roles are rarely disputed or debated is that most male dancers do not know how to follow and most female dancers do not know how to lead. Because of the specialized nature of what most men and women learn, there is a disincentive for the average social dancer to attempt to act out the complementary sex's dance role. Most women who dance as follows would prefer to have a male lead, partly because women often do not think that other women are as effective as men as leads. Given a choice between dancing with a man or a woman, most men would rather dance with a woman. As such, a dancer who chooses to dance against their role will be less likely to get dances, the *raison d'etre* for attending a dance. Any concern over ideology is overruled by the desire to dance.

The second way that sex enters into dance has to do with the role of sexuality and sexual attraction (Hanna, 2010). If you observe what happens at a dance with the neutral eye of an anthropologist, social dancing violates many norms. Despite the importance that people place on personal space (Evans & Howard, 1973) and the ease with which violations of personal space can become unpleasant, in the idioculture of social dance, two people who have never met before can within seconds adopt a very intimate embrace (usually) without any discomfort or embarrassment. Of course, different dances have different standards of closeness. For example, waltz and foxtrot are danced much less closely than balboa, blues, bolero, or Argentine tango. In the film *Alive and Kicking*, Sharon talks about the origins of blues dancing, stating: "Historically, was more about the sort of thing you did late at night at a house party, when you'd been drinking, in a private juke joint ... it was never a ballroom dance." Evita says, "Blues dancing was of course a very intimate dance that was supposed to be done with your sweetheart."

People who dance with each other may or may not even exchange names. In the classic novel *Fear of Flying*, Erica Jong (1973, pp. 14–15) coined the term *zipless fuck*, which she defined as:

> absolutely pure. It is free of ulterior motives. There is no power game. The man is not "taking" and the woman is not "giving." No one is attempting to cuckold a husband or humiliate a wife. No one is trying to prove anything or get anything out of anyone. The zipless fuck is the purest thing there is. And it is rarer than the unicorn. And I have never had one.

We propose that this notion of the zipless fuck can be extrapolated to the concept of the *zipless dance*, a dance that is absolutely pure and free of ulterior motives, especially those of a sexual nature. Dancers promulgate the existence of the zipless dance among themselves as well as among nondancers. For example, in *Alive and Kicking*, Andrea states:

> There's an incredible intimacy that forms among strangers. You meet someone
> for the first and by the end of the song you feel like they're finishing your
> sentences. If I had that kind of connection with someone I met in the grocery
> store I'd ask him for his number. But it's not like that. In a swing dance, you
> just move on and find the next person.

John, another dancer in *Alive and Kicking*, says: "Frankie [Manning, one
of the founders of Lindy Hop] always called it like three-minute
romance. You're just going to be in love with this person you're dancing
with for three minutes and it's going to be amazing. And you do it again,
and again, all night long." The key element of these quotes is that
the connection is intense but brief and exists only on the dance floor. The
attraction rarely moves to real life. It can happen, of course, but the
unspoken code of the social dance world is that the three-minute
norm-violating intimate series of coordinated movements must only be
viewed as temporary, platonic fun.

From our perspective, we question whether the zipless dance actually
exists or, at the very least, whether it is as common as people present it
as being. In other words, we inquire about the degree to which the
"purity" of the lead–follow role is contaminated by real-world sexual and
romantic feelings. Female dance teachers in particular acknowledge that
part of their ability to attract customers—that is, male customers—relies
on creating the appearance that they may be romantically interested
without ever actually acting on that appearance (McMains, 2006). Our
inspiration for this analysis is the previously mentioned swing dance
documentary *Alive and Kicking* (2016), which details the experiences of
several dance couples and includes candid interviews in which participants discuss their feelings about dancing.

The existence of the zipless dance is especially relevant for dancers
with a spouse or significant other who does not dance. In these
asymmetrical situations, there is a real possibility that the intimacy of
dancing, which is experienced unilaterally, can lead to a psychological, if
not physical, infidelity. In fact, it is possible that the nondancer may think
of the act of his or her romantic partner dancing with someone else as
infidelity in and of itself. This possibility is consistent with the famous
actor–observer difference in social psychology (Jones & Nisbett, 1971).
Observers of behavior tend to assume that the behavior of an actor
reflects the true desire of the actor, whereas the actor herself sees her
own behavior as guided by norms and situational forces. Thus, a husband
who is a nondancer may mistakenly assume that his wife, dancing with a
stranger, harbors positive feelings for the man. The wife knows that her
close embrace with the stranger is the result of mere convention, but the
husband is left watching the behavior and assuming emotional infidelity.

Some dancers acknowledge the intimacy involved in the connection that exists between two people dancing as a couple. In *Alive and Kicking*, Andrea states, "I needed to hold people's hand and I needed to, like, hug people ... and I just wasn't doing that before Lindy Hop." Similarly, Evita says, "Physical contact and touch has got to be the most powerful gift that we could give to each other. I think people are afraid to physically contact each other because maybe it's too intimate. And it's really easy to distance ourselves."

In *Alive and Kicking*, a dancer comments on the mental connection that can occur between dancers: "It's sincerely what happens all the time with this dance. You'll find someone and you'll just hit it off with them, and it doesn't mean you're going to marry them. But there is a sincere spark." Evita comments on the closeness of blues dancing: "Lots of people are afraid of it because of how intimate it can be. There's a stillness while you're pressed up against someone else." Another actor states, "Every dance feels like sharing a joke or having like a little secret conversation. And I think that connectedness to another person is enough to like break the doldrums ... makes you realize that things are okay."

Although we agree that a special magic can occur between two people sharing a dance, we also suggest that this "magic" has an illusory quality brought about by the narrow parameters of the shared dance. When one is dancing, the real world does not enter into the equation. In *Alive and Kicking*, dancers note that when they dance they can forget about problems related to paying their bills and so on. A dance floor romance has none of the baggage associated with a real-world relationship that might include mundane problems such as who washes the dishes or takes the kids to the dentist. In this way, a zipless dance can be considered an erotic illusion—a situation that feels good, perhaps even great, because it exists in a bubble isolated from the real-world problems that inevitably become attached to any real-world relationship. After the dance, there is also the allure of mystery; the possibility, however remote, that the person with whom you shared rhythmic intimacy harbors some forbidden attraction for you. Social psychologists have only recently begun to identify the processes associated with the allure of mystery in romance and in leadership (Goethals & Allison, 2018).

The possibilities for two people involved in a romantic relationship who are also connected to social dancing can be broken down into four distinct situations. For simplicity and because of the heterosexist bias inherent in the social dance community, we refer to the two actors as husband and wife. The possible situations are presented in Table 11.1.

Table 11.1   *Possible outcomes for a husband and wife who do or do not dance*

	Wife dances	Wife does not dance
Husband dances		
Husband does not dance		

Unfortunately for the people in these relationships, the only condition that seems free of possible conflict is when neither party dances. With the other conditions, the interplay between certain aspects of dance, as well as certain realities about men and women as sexual beings, can lead to conflicts that may be difficult to resolve. What is perhaps surprising is that even the situation in which both parties dance is not necessarily free of strife.

NO DANCER IS AN ISLAND

Dancers' comments in *Alive and Kicking* imply that the dance floor is an isolated space that remains unattached from the real world. It is possible, however, that the personal and romantic feelings that can be experienced on the dance floor can transfer to other aspects of a dancer's life. John states that a dance with someone is a three-minute experience with discrete beginning and end points. Although he states that the dancer moves on to the next experience with a different partner, in reality, people can cycle back to a previous dance partner. They can remember dancing with a previous partner and use that experience as a standard to compare new dances and dancers.

For dancers who pursue the hobby seriously, the ability to dance becomes an important point of connection socially and emotionally. Dancers want to dance and because they do, they need to seek out other people with whom to dance. It only makes sense that dancers will become friends with each other, seek out each other's company, and develop emotional attachments to each other. When one partner dances and the other does not, the nondancing partner is excluded from a wide range of experiences. The couple then faces the problem of coordinating a romantic relationship between a dancer and a nondancer.

Probably the nondancer's strongest reaction is jealousy related to the fear of missing out. As noted by Jane Austen (1813) in *Pride and Prejudice*, "To be fond of dancing was a certain step towards falling in love" (p. 7). The act of dancing with someone may create an emotional connection that could feel like romantic attraction, even love, and act as a lure that might take the dancer away from the nondancer. Couples can engage in certain strategies to ameliorate the negative consequences of an asymmetrical relationship. The problem with these solutions is that while they may work in the short term, they can then create new kinds of problems.

Perhaps the most obvious solution is for the nondancer to learn to dance. The problem with this solution is that the nondancer may not want to learn. In our experience, the most common scenario is that a woman dances and her husband, boyfriend, or potential boyfriend does not. In this case, the man will often make an effort or, more likely, the illusion of an effort to learn. The woman, who might often be a very good dancer, makes a sincere effort to help him improve. As a result, she limits herself to dancing only with him, which then costs her dance opportunities with the better dancers with whom she intended to dance. An additional problem is that most women who act out the role of a follow do not possess the necessary skills to teach someone to lead. As a result, despite being well-intentioned, she can only help a little bit. A further difficulty faced by a male nondancer is that learning to lead is quite challenging. There is a high cost of effort which represents a significant barrier to entry. The nondancer loses interest rapidly and says he is happy just to watch. Of course, just watching further fuels his jealousy as he watches the woman he is interested in dance with other men who possess a skill that he lacks.

In our experience, the nondancing partner tends to pull the dancer away from the dance scene. The process behind this withdrawal is difficult to resist because of the asymmetry of interests between the dancer and nondancer. For the nondancer, dancing represents an activity which does not interest him. For the dancer who wants to dance, there are other possible nondancing activities that would be interesting to pursue, and dancing gets replaced by other pleasant, albeit nondancing, activities. Ultimately, the nondancer pulls the dancer away from dancing. We suspect that the sexual and romantic aspects of social dancing are the root cause of the issue, and we leave it to future research to illuminate the leadership and negotiation processes that underlie this relationship conflict.

When the woman is a nondancer, the dynamics of an initial exposure to dancing tend to run more favorably. A man, acting as a lead, can teach a woman, acting as a follow, a few basic principles of following, and then make her feel like she has accomplished something. Other men can show her new moves, either by explicitly teaching her or by just leading her through them. Overall, women seem more excited than men at the thought of a date that involves dancing.

Unfortunately, even when both partners in a relationship are dancers, there is room for discomfort. One reason is that one member of the partnership is likely to be more serious about or better at dancing than the other. As with the frequency of sexual intercourse in a couple, the frequency with which a couple attends social dances may be an uneasy compromise between each person's levels of desire. Unfortunately, the equilibrium they reach, like any compromise, might be ultimately unsatisfying to both sides. The partner who likes dancing more finds that his or her frequency of dancing is driven down by the lower level of dance desire displayed by the partner. Yet the latter partner is dancing more than he or she would like.

Another source of discomfort can stem from the personal characteristics of the two partners. One person may be less secure in the relationship than the other. Our experience tells us that in this case, either the relationship doesn't last or the secure dancer stops attending dances to appease their insecure partner. At times a physical disability may prevent one person in a relationship from dancing. We have seen instances in which there is no overt relationship stress when the physically able person continues dancing without the other, but we have also seen physically able dancers discontinue their dancing because of their partner's limitations. Again, additional research is needed to determine how these negotiations proceed among couples where there is an asymmetry in social dancing interest and ability.

Finally, the specifics of the dance scene itself may fuel potential dissatisfaction or discomfort. If there is an imbalance in the number of men or women at a social dance, the partner in the numerical minority will find himself or herself in greater demand. In the dance scenes we have experienced, the numerical imbalance manifests itself in the male partner dancing as much as he wants and the female partner sitting out a number of dances because of a shortage of leads. Sitting around and waiting for a dance could be viewed as a chance to rest and recover or as an opportunity for jealousy to be fueled.

THE COMMODIFICATION OF DANCE

"The commodification of dance" refers to the benefits accrued to people who possess the ability to dance. We argue that having dancing skills can be viewed as a valuable resource that can enhance a person's perceived attractiveness. Our experience tells us that both on and off the dance floor, women tend to gravitate toward males who are perceived to possess social dancing skills, especially strong ones. This attraction need not be romantic but it can be. Although men who do ballroom dancing are stereotypically thought to be gay (Stossel & Binkley, 2006), we have personally not encountered any negative fallout from such a stereotype. We should also note that we are both heterosexual—a fact that has served us well, for unexpected reasons. Heterosexuals with social dancing skills are viewed by many as individuals who are especially bold, counter-cultural, and healthily in touch with both the feminine and masculine sides of their personalities.

Women who dance, and especially those who dance (and follow) well, are also highly sought after by heterosexual male dancers. Most men like to lead (Baumeister, 2010), and they especially enjoy leading women who follow their signals well. As mentioned earlier, a social dance featuring a strong lead and a strong follow can be perceived as "magical" by one or both parties. As women often outnumber men at social dances, men's choices about whom to ask to dance can reveal their primary motives for dancing. In our experience, there are three types of male social dancers: the *gentleman*, the *scoundrel*, and a *hybrid* of the two. Gentlemen dance with all the ladies, regardless of their level of attrac-tiveness and their skill level. The gentleman is the true heroic leader (Allison & Goethals, 2013) on the dance floor, showing communion with all and no romantic motives for his dancing. The scoundrel chooses only young, attractive women as his dance partners, revealing his sexual motives for dancing and also his profound ignorance of the fact that everyone can see what he is doing and disapproves of it. The hybrid is the category of male social dancer that we see in the greatest numbers. The hybrid may be driven by romantic or sexual motives to attend social dances, but possesses enough gentlemanliness to dance occasionally with less desired women and also enough self-awareness to know the import-ance of not being labeled a scoundrel.

We do believe that one's desire or need to have dancing skills *a priori* can be a significant barrier to attending social dances. Many of our friends will never attend dances because they lack the skills, and of course they lack the skills because they never attend. We've also noted that it is harder for neophyte men to learn to lead than it is for neophyte women to learn to follow. Men who overcome this initial barrier to social dancing reap rich rewards in acquiring leadership skills and in enhancing their social and romantic lives.

Why do more women attend social dances in greater numbers than men? There are several reasons why this sex-based imbalance occurs. One reason is that women are more comfortable than men with moving their bodies gracefully and on dance floors. As children, more women than men have experience with forms of dance such as ballet, tap, and jazz dancing. Men also may associate gracefulness with weakness or homosexuality (Stossel & Binkley, 2006). Males may tend to avoid performing a task, such as ballroom dancing, that can threaten their masculinity. Worse yet, the idea of failing at such a task can only compound that threat.

Another, but related, reason is that many men see dancing as a feminine activity, and therefore men who dance as effeminate and possessing a threatened masculinity. Of course, an irony of this assumption is that men who dance socially encounter and develop stronger connections to more women than men who do not. As experienced social dancers, we both know of many male friends and family members who complain about how hard it is to meet women, yet these same individuals eschew social dancing as they would cyanide. Whether it is due to shyness, homophobia, fear of failure, or an unconscious desire to be lonely, these men contribute to the gender imbalance problem seen in most dance studios.

One way to think about this gender-based barrier is in terms of the relationship between a *social fence* and a *social trap* (Messick & Brewer, 1983). A trap operates by the lure of a reward that then brings about misfortune. A mouse trap works because it tempts the mouse with cheese, but in the end the quest for the reward brings about capture. In contrast, a fence represents a barrier to some greater good that must be overcome. A man who could overcome his pathological shyness with women could learn a skill that could allow him to start conversations with potentially many new women. In his analysis of shyness, Zimbardo (1990) discusses many ways in which shy people avoid situations that could cure their shyness, thereby entering into a self-perpetuating cycle.

Attractiveness becomes a commodity that makes someone more likely to attract dance partners, which then increases the likelihood that someone will get dances and thus more opportunities to dance and learn more. The self-fulfilling prophecy, a robust phenomenon in the social sciences, is thus clearly at play here (Jussim, 2012). The norms of the social dancing world place women at a large disadvantage with regard to commodification. An undesirable male can have as many dances as he likes, as males are in shorter supply and as males are also expected to take the lead in asking women to dance. But an undesirable woman must wait for the few gentlemen in attendance to ask her to dance. She is destined to get fewer dances and thus fewer chances to hone her dance skills, thus perpetuating her undesirability. As social dancers, we favor the practice of encouraging men and women to be equally responsible for extending invitations to dance. While it seems reasonable for practical purposes to assign one gender the role of lead and the other the role of follow, there is no practical reason for the convention of assigning one gender the role of inviter and the other gender the role of invitee.

STRATEGIES TO REDUCE JEALOUSY

Perhaps the most common strategy to deal with the myth of the zipless dance is to accept the veracity of the myth without question. The dance community creates a shared reality and operates as if this shared reality is objectively correct. The implicit strategy here is that members of the dance community tell each other the myth and adhere to it without challenge. The problem with this method is that ultimately its adherents are living a lie, which can lead to self-doubt as well as the doubting of a partner.

Another strategy is for dancers to only date or marry other dancers. The assumption here is that mixed marriages do not work. The problem with this strategy is that by attempting to satisfy this criterion, an individual severely limits his or her pool of potential partners. A further problem is that if there is a gender imbalance (and there most likely will be), then one gender has to go outside the dance scene to find a partner. A third problem is that when people meet, connect, and then partner up, they often ultimately separate. The question then becomes: how do the people involved, as well as the scene as a whole, deal with the fallout of the breakup? Who gets custody of the dance scene?

Even if two people are both dancers, they still may have to deal with problems of jealousy related to the number of dances they have relative to their partner. One solution is to create rules governing how often partners engage in extradyadic dances. Couples may create rules such as "we always dance the first (or last) dance together" or "we dance every third dance together." At its most extreme, of course, the rule would be to only dance with one's romantic partner. The problem with this solution is its ultimate inability to provide novel dance experiences. Voluntarily cutting oneself off from possible dance experiences can fuel resentment, especially if one partner sees himself or herself as making greater concessions. An underlying issue associated with creating these kinds of rules is that they serve as an indirect reminder of the underlying sexuality of dance. If there is no problem of possible abuse, then why would we need to enact rules in the first place?

One solution to the myth of the zipless dance is to engage in voluntary restraint. The partner who wants to dance or who wants to dance more will cut themselves off from dancing. The limitation of this solution is that it can build resentment. This draconian solution can backfire because, paradoxically, the act of denying oneself the activity or a partner ("I won't dance with that highly attractive other") can make the forbidden or self-denied activity all the more attractive, a phenomenon we can term the *Romeo and Juliet effect*. It is a well-known psychological fact that the more one consciously suppresses a desired action, the more desirable the action becomes (Wegner, 1989).

CONCLUDING COMMENTS

As social scientists who have enjoyed social dancing for a long while, we have been struck by the paucity of research on the psychology and sociology of an activity that is replete with phenomena that have long attracted scholarly interest. We have seen in this chapter how social dancing creates a context for the unique expression of leadership skills and followership skills. As male leads, we have both experienced our fair share of women who are outstanding follows as well as women who are wretched at the task. Moreover, women tell us the same thing, namely, that some men are born to lead in dancing while others should never step on a dance floor again. What distinguishes good dance leads and good dance follows from poor ones? What role do romantic and sexual motives and behaviors play in the development and expression of good leads and follows? We leave it to future research to sort out these issues.

Let us return to the concept of the zipless dance, a dance that enjoys freedom from ulterior motives, especially those of a sexual nature. Is it as rare as a unicorn? Inasmuch as males are considered to be more sexual beings than women (Baumeister, 2010), we suspect that men are more likely to enter the dance community with ulterior motives. We also suspect that men are likely to publicly endorse the philosophy of zipless dancing while privately hoping that their Argentine tango intrigues the woman they are embracing. Women are rarely so naïve as to fail to pick up on a dance lead's true motives, as research has shown that females are superior to males at detecting and decoding nonverbal communication (Gulabovska & Leeson, 2014). Good leadership places the wellbeing of everyone ahead of the wellbeing of the self (Allison & Goethals, 2013). Social dancers who heed this general principle will undoubtedly prosper as dancers, in their romantic relationships, and as members of their dancing communities.

We have put forward an analysis of social dancing as a case study that applies to a broader range of issues associated with leadership and sexuality. Many of the issues at the intersection of sexuality and leadership, such as sexual harassment in schools or the workplace or the oppression of certain groups, have larger stakes than a leisure activity does. One reason for this is that, in many instances, issues related to sexuality and leadership occur in a context where the people involved do not have the option to opt out. It might be quite difficult to quit a job, even in the face of sexual harassment, because of people's financial dependence on employment. At the same time, however, we feel the leadership and sexuality issues that percolate beneath something as seemingly benign as social dancing represent an important thin slice (Ambady & Rosenthal, 1992) of human behavior because they appear at first pass minor, but in reality speak to important social issues.

REFERENCES

Allison, S. T., & Goethals, G. R. (2013). *Heroic leadership: An influence taxonomy of 100 exceptional individuals.* New York: Routledge.

Ambady, N., & Rosenthal, R. (1992). Thin slices of expressive behavior as predictors of interpersonal consequences: A meta-analysis. *Psychological Bulletin, 111*(2), 256–74.

Austen, J. (1813/1918). *Pride and prejudice.* New York: Charles Scribner's Sons.

Baumeister, R. F. (2010). *Is there anything good about men? How cultures flourish by exploiting men.* New York: Oxford University Press.

Beggan, J. K., & Pruitt, A. S. (2014). Leading, following and sexism in social dance: Change of meaning as contained secondary adjustments. *Leisure Studies, 33*(5), 508–32.

Brown, C. A. (2007). The Carolina Shaggers: Dance as serious leisure. *Journal of Leisure Studies, 39*(4), 623–47.

Carli, L. L., & Eagly, A. H. (1999). Gender effects on social influences and emergent leadership. In G. N. Powell (Ed.), *Handbook of gender and work* (pp. 203–22). Thousand Oaks, CA: Sage.

Ericksen, J. A. (2011). *Dance with me: Ballroom dancing and the promise of instant intimacy.* New York: New York University Press.

Evans, G. W., & Howard, R. B. (1973). Personal space. *Psychological Bulletin, 80*(4), 334–44.

Fiske, S., & Taylor, S. E. (2013). *Social cognition: From brains to culture.* New York: Sage.

Gulabovska, M., & Leeson, P. (2014). Why are women better decoders of nonverbal language? *Gender Issues, 31*(3–4), 202–18.

Glatzer, S. (Producer & Director). (2016). *Alive and kicking* [Motion Picture]. United States: Magnolia Pictures.

Goethals, G. R., & Allison, S. T. (2018). *Mystery and meaning making: How people extrapolate from hints of heroism and villainy.* Unpublished manuscript, University of Richmond.

Godsick, C. (Producer), & Friedlander, L. (Director). (2006). *Take the lead* [Motion Picture]. United States: New Line Cinema.

Hanna, J. L. (2010). Dance and sexuality: Many moves. *Journal of Sex Research, 47*(2), 212–41.

Hoyt, C. L. (2014). Social identities and leadership: The case of gender. In G. R. Goethals, S. T. Allison, R. M. Kramer, & D. M. Messick (Eds.), *Conceptions of leadership: Enduring ideas and emerging insights.* New York: Palgrave Macmillan (pp. 71–91).

Johnson, C. W. (2005). "The first step is the two-step": Hegemonic masculinity and dancing in a country-western gay bar. *International Journal of Qualitative Studies in Education, 18*(4), 445–64.

Jones, E. E., & Nisbett, R. (1971). *The actor and the observer: Divergent perceptions of the causes of behavior.* New York: General Learning Press.

Jong, E. (1973). *Fear of flying.* New York: Penguin Books.

Jussim, L. (2012). *Social perception and social reality: Why accuracy dominates bias and self-fulfilling prophecy.* New York: Oxford University Press.

Marion, J. S. (2008). *Ballroom: Culture and costume in competitive dance.* New York: Berg.

McMains, J. (2006). *Glamour addiction: Inside the American ballroom dance industry.* Middletown, CT: Wesleyan University Press.

Messick, D. M., & Brewer, M. B. (1983). Solving social dilemmas: A review. In L. Wheeler & P. Shaver (Eds.), *Review of personality and social psychology,* vol. 4 (pp. 11–44). Beverly Hills, CA: Sage.

Miall, T. (Producer), & Luhrmann, B. (Director). (1992). *Strictly ballroom.* [Motion Picture]. Australia: Ronin.

Peters, S. (1991). From eroticism to transcendence: Ballroom dance and the female body. In L. Goldstein (Ed.), *The female body: Figures, styles, speculations* (pp. 145–58). Ann Arbor, MI: University of Michigan Press.

Riva, L. (2016). Do people social dance for the sex? Retrieved May 12, 2017, from http://www.danceplace.com/grapevine/do-people-social-dance-for-the-sex/.

Stebbins, R. A. (2007). *Serious leisure.* New Brunswick, NJ: Transaction Publishers.

Stossel, J., & Binkley, G. (2006). Gay stereotypes: Are they true? Retrieved May 13, 2017, from http://abcnews.go.com/2020/story?id=2449185&page=1.

Wegner, D. M. (1989). *White bears and other unwanted thoughts: Suppression, obsession, and the psychology of mental control.* London: The Guilford Press.

Zimbardo, P. G. (1990). *Shyness: What it is, what to do about it.* Boston, MA: Da Capo Press.

12. Heroic leadership in *The Walking Dead*'s postapocalyptic universe: The restoration and regeneration of society as a hero organism

Scott T. Allison and Olivia Efthimiou

The Walking Dead (*TWD*) is a critically acclaimed postapocalyptic horror television series that follows the lives of a group of survivors as they encounter various challenges in a world overrun by zombies, in the aftermath of the infection of the human race by a deadly plague. Although the zombie apocalypse is a central feature of the series, in many ways it acts as a backdrop to the dramatic twists and turns of the characters' lives as they struggle to reclaim a sense of humanity in an inhumane world.

There is a curious scene, and one that is telling with regard to *TWD*'s vision of humanity, in its seventh season episode entitled *Sing Me a Song*. The most horrific villain in the series' history, Negan, is seen playing with a two-year-old child named Judith. Negan is a sociopath best known for pulverizing the heads of his enemies with his baseball bat. As Negan holds Judith in his lap, it becomes clear that the scene is oddly lacking in tension. In her two short years, Judith has had near-death encounters with zombies, cannibals, and crazed gunmen. She is one of the very few young children remaining on the planet, and she clearly carries the mantle of humanity's future. Even in the murderous hands of Negan, viewers know that Judith is in no danger—a striking testament to *TWD*'s commitment to maintaining a sliver of hope that human civilization can rebuild from the ashes of apocalyptic devastation.

In this chapter, we describe an important yet overlooked aspect of heroic leadership demonstrated by the survivors of the postapocalyptic world of *TWD*. We focus on the heroic self-sacrifice of bringing children into a world of lawlessness, hunger, and brutality. Sexual behavior in *TWD* has necessarily occupied a peripheral role, as such behavior represents a luxury in a world where food and safety are always paramount. Yet the series has dared on two occasions to showcase the decision to reproduce, and we argue that this decision illustrates heroism and heroic leadership at two different levels of analysis. First, the choice to have children in the postapocalyptic world reflects heroic self-sacrifice on the part of the individual decision maker. A woman who chooses to have a child in a world with no formal healthcare system risks her own physical well-being. Second, we propose that the choice to repopulate the broken world of *TWD* also reflects a systemwide societal drive toward regeneration and restoration. We thus conceptualize the decision to reproduce as the heroic embodiment of human society as an organism intent on surviving, and even flourishing.

To develop this argument, we adopt a model of heroism as applicable to "hero organisms not only in the human species, but beyond, revealing a vast network of life grounded in heroic properties and evolution" (Efthimiou, 2017, p. 155). The organism metaphor places heroic actors in their biological, psychological, social, and cultural contexts as living entities that grow, respond, and regenerate within complex systems (Efthimiou, 2017; Allison, Goethals, & Kramer, 2017). The heroic actor is a "functioning biological organism that can perceive, move within, respond to, and transform its environment" (Johnson, 2008, p. 164). Embedded within this organism framework is the additional metaphor of *regeneration* or *restoration*, an acknowledgment of an organism's ability to grow, heal, and recreate itself. From this perspective, an understanding of heroism and heroic leadership goes far beyond prosocial behavior or an exemplar of a moral ideal. Heroic leadership is "a deeply personal, multi-sensorial and transrational experience" (Efthimiou, 2017, p. 148).

LEADERSHIP AND CHILDREN IN *THE WALKING DEAD*'S UNIVERSE

Not surprisingly, children who have survived *TWD*'s zombie apocalypse are seen as valuable human capital, requiring special attention and protection. Leaders of various groups and communities in *TWD* show great sensitivity to the need to keep children out of harm's way. Although the majority of this protective behavior toward children is shown by the heroic characters of Rick, Dale, Hershel, and Tyreese, we also witness villainous characters such as the Governor take actions to save and protect a child. In the first few seasons of *TWD*, the focus of attention is placed many times on the survival and well-being of central protagonist Rick Grimes' young son, Carl. When Carl is accidentally shot in a hunting accident, several episodes are devoted to emergency surgery performed on Carl and to obtaining necessary medical supplies for him to recover. Later, after Carl has recovered from his injuries, there are many occasions on which Carl's parents, Rick and Lori, make their child's safety the number one priority of their group's activities.

Two of the more heartwrenching episodes of *TWD* feature scenes of children who do perish. In season 2's *Pretty Much Dead Already*, viewers were shocked to discover that Sophia, the only child of another central character, Carol Peletier, had succumbed to the zombie plague. Equally jarring was the bullet to Sophia's head delivered by the group's leader, Rick, who does much of the mercy killing on *TWD*. Another emotionally charged episode featuring the death of a child is season 4's *The Grove*. In this episode, two young sisters named Mika and Lizzie are being cared for by Carol and Tyreese. Lizzie harbors a strange affinity for the zombies and views the transformation from human to zombie as something to be desired. When Lizzie murders Mika, Carol realizes that Lizzie presents a danger to all human survivors and makes the agonizing decision to execute the child. These scenes involving children's deaths are portrayed with far greater poignancy than scenes of adults dying, a fact that underscores the precious value of children's lives in the zombie apocalypse.

Attempts to protect and save the lives of children meet many of the definitional standards of heroism and heroic leadership (Allison & Goethals, 2011, 2013; Franco, Blau, & Zimbardo, 2011; Kinsella, Ritchie, & Igou, 2015a, 2015b). These definitions of heroism center on performing actions that enhance the greater good, involve risktaking, and require self-sacrifice (Allison et al., 2017). In the zombie apocalypse, protecting and preserving children is every surviving group's highest priority, demonstrating that concern for future generations must also be considered a significant attribute of heroic leadership (Rohr, 2011). A central metaphor guiding heroism research has focused on human development and transformative growth that can only come about from the resolution of various crises across the lifespan (Allison et al., 2017; Erikson, 1994). These are usually personal crises, but they can also be societal crises and tragedies along the scale of a worldwide apocalypse not unlike the disaster featured in *TWD* (Allison & Goethals, 2017). Crises and disasters are the soil from which the seeds of heroism and heroic leadership germinate (Allison & Goethals, 2011).

In season 3 of *TWD*, Lori gives birth to a daughter, Judith. Although Rick is unsure whether he is the father of the child, he recognizes the necessity of placing the child's well-being ahead of his need to know the true paternity. Rick knows that Lori had an affair with his law enforcement partner, Shane, and even with this knowledge he is able to instantly forgive all parties involved, with the goal of raising Judith to the best of his ability. Later in the series, Rick admits that the baby is likely Shane's, yet this fact never diminishes his devotion to caring for Judith. It takes heroic leadership to dare to have a baby in the zombie apocalypse. Maggie Rhee (née Greene) is another character who makes this decision, choosing to carry her husband Glenn's child to term. The decisions of Rick and Lori and of Glenn and Maggie to reproduce in the midst of the zombie apocalypse are sometimes met with disbelief from other characters in the series. Several characters react with scorn, accusing Lori and Maggie of reckless decision-making. As a baby's crying can attract zombies, Lori is accused of selfishness by a few characters who believe that her having a child will jeopardize the safety of the entire group. Most members of Rick and Lori's group, however, support her decision to have the child and work together selflessly to attend to the child's needs while also working on the entire group's behalf—a mark of heroic leadership.

THE TERROR WITHIN: DISEASE, MUTATION, AND MONSTROUS BIRTH

In the first season we get a rare glimpse into the actual science behind the virus that has infected humanity, when Rick and the group make it to the Center for Disease Control in Atlanta, Georgia. Doctor Edwin Jenner, the last remaining scientist, visually describes what happens to the body when invaded by the virus. The infection kills its carrier; shortly after, however, the brain is reactivated and the human corpse is reanimated, but only capable of base functions, in effect erasing any trace of human consciousness. The virus has a devastating effect on the organism, causing irreversible mass neurological degeneration and "extensive brain alterations" which affect "all the motor control regions of the brain very diffusely" (Zehr & Norman, 2015, p. 41). In short, this resurrected body—the zombie, or "walker," as characters refer to it—is a mere empty container of its former self, devoid of what makes you "you."

A virus, by its very nature, seeks to self-propagate and secure its "immortality." Once it comes into contact with a cell, it binds itself to it and injects its DNA into it. The DNA then uses our own cellular engineering to reproduce new virus molecules which continue to attack. A virus turns our very cells into "mini-copy machines" to replicate itself into a grand biological army (Dubner, 2017). The body turns into a battleground; in *TWD*, infection is accompanied by a hellish fever. In biological terms, this signals the body is trying to fight back. Antibodies are likely being deployed to heal the infected cells and restore the body's well-being (Dubner, 2017). However, in this case, it seems to be to no avail, as the human organism succumbs again and again, resulting in the inevitable monstrous transformation into a walker. Our human organism has become host to a disease-causing mutation passed on through biting, scratching, and other close contact. But, importantly, it is passed on through sexual reproduction resulting from the mutation of a single gene, similar to other genetic diseases such as cystic fibrosis and sickle cell anemia. It thus resides deep within us, as the enemy within.

Life in *TWD* is in many ways an exemplary state of Edmund Burke's *sublime*. For Burke (1757, as cited in Byrne, 2006, p. 24) the "ruling principle" to the sublime, which ignites a more "powerful and unique emotional" reaction than the conventional beautiful, is "identification with terror." It is arguably the ability to come to terms with their mortality and hang onto life by a bare thread that makes our characters all the more heroic (Franco, Efthimiou, & Zimbardo, 2016; McCabe, Carpenter, & Arndt, 2015). The ability to love, live, hope, feel, and fight the good fight in the face of danger, pain, and terror for one more day becomes the apotheosis of the sublime and heroic leadership in the *TWD* universe. A newborn child, as the symbol of new life and a vessel of hope on the one hand, and a carrier of both terror or the genetic mutation of the deadly virus on the other, is also the apotheosis of the sublime for the entire human race. Here, then, *life*, its preservation and restoration, becomes more precious than ever as both a means and an end, in and of itself.

For Burke (1757, as cited in Shusterman, 2006, p. 223) the sublime is necessarily accompanied by "some (albeit muted) sense of menacing self-destruction, which links … [it] to our strongest instinct, that of self-preservation." In this case, the menacing self-destruction is the unbeatable zombie virus which all human organisms carry. Keeping yourself and those you love alive is the most important goal in *TWD*'s postapocalypse. But there are times when facing the inevitable is the only thing left to do. At that point, there are only two choices—accepting the monstrous within (by choosing to transform into a walker beyond death), or destroying it (by inflicting trauma to the brainstem to rule out any chance of "coming back"). At least a couple of our characters at the cusp of transformation, albeit in two very different circumstances, are haunted by images of tearing flesh and the insatiable cannibalistic appetite of the undead. This haunting occurs with Jim in season 1, and also prior to Shane's "rebirth" into a walker after he was killed by Rick in a dramatic Western-style showdown in season 2.

The monstrous in *TWD* is nowhere more pronounced than in the maternal body. Falling pregnant in this terrifying world seems ludicrous and irrational. As mentioned, a number of characters comment on this "insane" choice, namely in relation to our two mothers-to-be, Lori and Maggie: when Maggie and Carol are captured by members of Negan's group, the Saviors, in season 6 and one of them discovers that Maggie is pregnant, she comments, "You're some kind of stupid getting knocked up at a time like this." Back in season 2, in a heartwrenching private conversation when Rick finds out that Lori is pregnant after she re-gurgitates abortion pills, she exclaims:

> You want me to bring a baby … into *this*?! To live a short, cruel life?! … Not when its life will hang by a thread from the second it's born … Not when every cry will put it, and Carl, and everyone we care about into danger. That's not right.

As they both try to grapple with the enormity of this decision, Rick pleads with Lori that "not even giving it a chance isn't right either" (*TWD*, season 2, episode 6). A baby can be seen as a harbinger of hope, as we discuss throughout this chapter. Indeed, as we will argue, the choice to carry a pregnancy to term in such a world is a heroic one, fraught with risk. In this sense, Lori and Maggie, or the female *womb*, are symbols of boundless female energy and universal creation from which a new start for the human race may spawn—nothing short of a sacred hero organism.

Nonetheless, these women also walk a fine line between the heroic feminine and Barbara Creed's "monstrous feminine," a common motif in horror. Creed's (1986, p. 45) work explores Julia Kristeva's theory of abjection as a way of separating the human from the nonhuman form. In *TWD* the monstrous is "produced at the border between … man and beast" (Creed, 1986, p. 49). Here, it takes on the form of the walker or zombie. The walker represents the "other" within—it exists at the permeable borders of the self, as a primal symbolic figure (Kristeva, 1982, as cited in Cranny-Francis, Waring, Stavropoulos, & Kirkby, 2003, p. 65). Most significantly, *TWD* incorporates a number of the seven "faces" of the monstrous feminine, including "castrating mother," "mon-strous womb," and "archaic mother" (Creed, 1993, p. 7).

The womb holds a prominent place in horror. As Creed (1993, p. 53) points out, for Sigmund Freud the womb is a representation of an "other" or the uncanny in film: that "familiar/unfamiliar place" and "the subject's 'former home'." Creed (1993, p. 53) argues that the "womb is repre-sented in the horror film in at least two main ways: symbolically in terms of intra-uterine settings and literally in relation to the female body." In *TWD* the womb, in its literal sense, becomes a powerful space in which the human race can be reborn anew, or, conversely, devoured and cast into the abyss.

The fear of a monstrous birth becomes a preoccupation, especially for Lori. She confides her concerns to Hershel, Maggie's father, after Rick reveals the shocking truth passed on in secret by Dr. Jenner—that everyone carries the deadly virus, irrespective of whether they have been bitten or not, and reanimates shortly after death: "It's the baby, I think I lost it ... If we're all infected then so is the baby ... So what if it's stillborn? What if it's dead inside me right now, what if it rips me apart?" Equally, for us viewers the idea of a fetus eating its mother alive from the inside is the epitome of the grotesque, echoing the representation of the womb in other horror films in which the female body becomes the vessel of an "inhuman offspring" (Creed, 1993, p. 56).

Just as horrifying is the reverse possibility: the mother eating her baby. In the sixth season episode *Twice as Far*, when the group's doctor, Denise, accompanies main characters Daryl and Rosita on a run to an apothecary, she discovers a female walker trapped in a back room who appears to have eaten her infant. This is the image of the maternal subject, the devourer, and Creed's (1993) castrating mother. That is why childbirth is such a heroic act in this reality, because there is terrible risk. As such, the maternal figure in *TWD* can either ascend to a *sublime hero organism* or descend to a *monstrous organism*, depending on the out-come. The concept of the monstrous feminine is centered on blood, flesh, and devouring, especially of the male (Creed, 1986). Symbolically and literally, in this monstrous scenario the male is devoured, as the female eats the future of the human race alive.

REBIRTH AND REGENERATION: AN ESSENTIAL INGREDIENT OF A DYSTOPIAN UNIVERSE

So why would anyone want to bring a child into a world like that of *TWD*? Irrespective of its horror, the abject must be endured, for what threatens to extinguish life also helps define it (Creed, 1986, p. 46). Regardless of what choices our characters make, there is only one thing certain in this chaotic reality – that the cycle of life and death will go on, with or without them. As Morgan Jones, another *TWD* survivor, aptly puts it in season 6, "everything gets a return."

Rebirth and regeneration go hand in hand with destruction in dystopian postapocalyptic fiction. The duality that is indispensable to the schizophrenic condition and human nature overall is critical to understanding the gravity of *TWD*'s universe from a heroic perspective. In volume 8 of his *Collected Works*, Carl Jung (1953, as cited in Adams, 2004, p. 90) remarks that "[t]he delusional systems of schizophrenics are … 'aiming at something'." There is a logic to madness, and so too do "visions of the end of the world" (Perry, 1987, as cited in Adams, 2004, p. 122) serve a purpose—in volume 12 of the Standard Edition of his *Complete Psychological Works*, Freud (1953, as cited in Adams, 2004, p. 121) asserts that the formation of such "notions about a 'world catastrophe' … *'is in reality an attempt at recovery, a process of reconstruction'*."

Does humanity need to arrive at the brink of destruction in order to generate the conditions it requires to redefine itself and evolve? Does it seek its own self-dissolution to attain a unified state? According to Wiener (1948, as cited in Bynum, 2010, p. 424) "entropy," or the "irreversible loss of physical information," is *"the greatest natural evil."* Each "physical object or process, consequently, participates in a creative 'coming-to-be' and a destructive 'fading away'"—all "information objects" in the universe, and by extension hero organisms, "are subject to ultimate decay," as life must constantly give way to new forms of existence as a means of naturally regenerating itself (Wiener, 1948, as cited in Bynum, 2010, p. 424). Hershel comments to Rick in the season 2 finale: "I can't profess to understand God's plan. Christ promised a resurrection of the dead. I just thought he had somethin' … a little different in mind," hinting at the regeneration and rebuilding of the human race.

The paradox of all creation myths is the cycle of birth-death-rebirth. The theme of "world renewal" (Perry, 1987, as cited in Adams, 2004, p. 122) in creation myths as indispensably tied into a cataclysmic event has been most notably represented in the myth of the phoenix (Gardiner & Osborn, 2006). This legendary bird has been the symbol of resurrection and rebirth in a number of mythical accounts throughout history: "for just as the phoenix was reborn out its own dead self … so again and again the spiritual nature of man [sic] rises triumphant from his [sic] dead physical body" (Hall, 1928, as cited in Gardiner & Osborn, 2006, p. 109). According to Gardiner and Osborn (2006, p. 118), humanity is "unconscious of this spiritual source and these life-death-rebirth processes"—the realization of this paradoxical integrative cycle of opposites will inevitably "initiate a collective rebirth." Arguably, then, the most significant aspect of this myth is that both individual and collective ascension is not possible without the occurrence of some form of self-destruction—to live anew one must die as one's current self, whether symbolically or literally, rendering catastrophe in some form a *pre-requisite* to personal and societal regeneration.

How do we begin to conceive of what a regenerated world would look like beyond the horrific reality that is *TWD*'s universe? If the idea of rebirth is fundamentally linked to both individual and collective transformation, then any discussion on the renewal of civilization raises questions of biological, social, and psychological evolution (Efthimiou, 2017). In *TWD* the chance of a new beginning is grounded in bodily experience, both with the sacred sexual union of man and woman to seed humanity's preservation and the transformation of the species, and with the maternal figure. Dadoun (1977, pp. 55–6) refers to the archaic maternal figure as a "totalizing, oceanic mother, a 'mysterious and profound unity', arousing in the subject the anguish of fusion and of dissolution"; she is "an omnipresent and all-powerful totality, an absolute being," existing beyond the phallus by predating its knowledge.

The desire to protect Maggie and Lori, as primeval mother figures, and their offspring is thus a "desire to return to the original oneness of things, to return to the mother/womb" (Creed, 1986, p. 63). This primordial need is inextricably wedded to the heroic. As Fisher (2017) observes, the heroic is an innate impulse driving us to connect with the "Mother" of all creation:

> Just as plants have the impulse to photosynthesis encoded in every one of their cells, heroes are compelled to heal that which is broken and unite those who have lost their way. In an entropic universe, where our life energy and time is ever-depleting, this mission is promethean.

A baby becomes a symbol of this primordial process of creation and return. It becomes the void from which the universe is "seeded into being" (Gardiner & Osborn, 2006, p. 162), and marks the return to the mother/womb as the ultimate purification of the abject in horror (Creed, 1986). Judith, Carl, and Maggie's unborn child are the surviving humans' "symbolic reference to their … 'new beginning' in a 'newly created world', after what … [has] been a worldwide cataclysm" (Gardiner & Osborn, 2006, p. 163). They represent Corbin's (1964, p. 10) "resurrection body" or "*imaginal body*" as encountered in Eastern myth, demonstrating once again the centrality of destruction as an integral element of creation myths and personal regeneration.

The "maternal imaginary" is critical to the process of the female journey of becoming (Irigaray, 1985, 1987, as cited in Sempruch, 2007, p. 334). Both Judith and Maggie's baby are a *reimagining* and a *reinvention* of the species—but first, there must be destruction and disease. In this sense, *TWD* stays true to other postapocalyptic narratives by illustrating the necessary coexistence of utopias with dystopias, and catastrophe with creation. These narratives often allude to the notion that "[h]umans sleep. It is when they die that they awake" (Corbin, 1964, p. 8). The disease forces us to awaken—interestingly, Rick's journey into "the new world" (to which he makes reference in the midseason finale of season 6, while Carl is unconscious after losing his eye) begins with awakening from a coma.

At the same time, a deeper significance is hinted at—Rick's awakening is a symbol for humanity's awakening into something much larger than each one of us alone. In season 2 Hershel urges Rick to take a moment to take stock of what has happened to him, making reference to pivotal points of "resurrection" and rebirth throughout his early journey:

> Lori told me your story ... How you were shot, the coma. Yet you came out of it somehow. You do not feel God's hand in yours? ... In all the chaos you found your wife and boy, then he was shot, and he survived. That tells you nothing? (*TWD*, season 2, episode 4)

Coyne (1999, p. 13) argues that a prominent reading of the Oedipus myth is as an attempt "to return to a state of childhood innocence ... when we were omnipotent participants in a whole"—at the sublime edge of hope and despair that comprises the *TWD* universe, a child represents the possibility of a return to a state of wholeness, and a testament to the awesome power and ultimate unfathomability of the creator.

TRANSFORMATION, GENES, AND EVOLUTION: THE HEROIC LEADERSHIP PATH

As we have seen, the zombie virus in *TWD*'s postapocalyptic reality results in an irreversible transformation in the organism's DNA structure, in turn transforming one's worldview, social relations, and personal agency forever. The biological, social, and psychological human landscape as we know it will never be the same again. But biological and "natural genetic transformation" is an indispensable part of our biological experience, especially since the discovery that "transformation may be a powerful mechanism of horizontal gene transfer in natural bacterial populations" (Lorenz & Wackernagel, 1994, p. 563). Transformation is a natural state of our species, whether malignant or transcendent. Procreation is a chance to restore the genetic/biological, social, psychological, and planetary balance of transformation.

A brief discussion of archetypes and heroism is pertinent here. Carl Jung posited the idea that archetypes, including the heroic, are innate. MacLennan (2006, p. 9) explains:

> *The archetypes are psychical correspondents of human instincts.* That is, when you are behaving instinctually, you experience yourself to be in an archetypal situation. Activation of an instinct structures an animal's perception and behavior, and when *you* are that animal, you experience a myth unfolding in which you are a key actor.

Reanimated humans, or walkers, are certainly operating on animalistic instinct and undeniably represent a type of transformation and, indeed, archetype. A walker must fight to stay alive, as a living human must. But they cannot be said to possess heroic leadership, in the conscious and complex senses of which a living human would be capable. That is, one form of transformation can be said to be degenerative or malignant (the walker's) and the other aimed at transcendent action (the human/hero organism). In this sense, an archetype has a powerful, almost primordial urge to reproduce itself as a unique unit of information and behavior.

In the process of transformation, we are not powerless to affect our fate—this is where heroic leadership and heroic agency become paramount in the evolution of our species as hero organisms. According to Aboitiz (1989, p. 87), "behavior is … the most fundamental cohesive factor in the morphological evolution of animals." Aboitiz (1989, p. 93) points out that Lamarck was "the first to suggest that habits, or the function of an organ, would be causal factors determining its growth and shape, both in the individual and in the 'race' (in modern terms, phylogeny)." *TWD* provides a critical "scenario for evolutionary change" (Aboitiz, 1989, p. 89)—it is a unique opportunity for humans to utilize their innate traits (if they are truly that, as we argue here, and as the innateness of archetypes hypothesis describes) as hero organisms and impact on the course of human evolution in both a biological reproductive and social sense.

Hurley (2013, p. 3) describes how "[a]ccording to the new insights of behavioural epigenetics, traumatic experiences … in our recent ancestors' past, leave molecular scars adhering to our DNA." On the flipside, this can also be true of the heritability of "strengths and resiliences" in positive and enlightening experiences in our ancestral past (Hurley, 2013, p. 3). In his theory of "gene keys," Rudd (2013, p. 74) takes this a step further to include the heroic as a means of unlocking our true DNA potential as part of the genetic gift of strength:

The 34th Gift is the gift of heroes and heroines. It is one of the greatest and oldest of human archetypes. True heroism occurs without awareness and is a wholly individual act. This is why every human being alive feels deep resonance to the heroes of myth or the heroes of contemporary culture. Heroism denotes strength.

Our *TWD* characters are in a prime setting to "imprint" heroic action, through their biology and the environment—the latter through heightened actions and observation in daily life—onto the next generation, and unlock the gift of heroism and the heroic archetype that resides within.

The walker virus has thrown quite a wrench in the works for the human race. Rick's "resurrection" from his coma is critical in various senses—both in a literal biological sense and in a symbolic sense, he is thrust into a violent awakening. He is forced to adapt to this new reality and given the opportunity to become a heroic leader, which would never have been likely in the old world. This is arguably both a gift and a curse. In *TWD*, humanity is being forced to adapt to reach its next stage of evolution. In biological terms, "an adaptation is a mutation, or genetic change, that helps an organism, such as a plant or animal, survive in its environment" (National Geographic, 2017). Due to the helpful nature of the mutation, it is passed down from one generation to the next. This must be done at both the environmental level—through daily acts of heroic leadership—and at the biological level—through procreation.

These daily acts of heroism begin to slowly alter the biochemistry of the living organism, passed onto the next generation through genetic code *and* lived experience—heroism and heroic regeneration become truly embodied in *TWD*'s postapocalyptic universe. Even as the horrors endured by our characters throughout the series amplify, Hershel still invokes a bigger plan at play:

Hershel: "I still think there's a plan. There has to be a reason."

Rick: "You think it's all a test?"

Hershel: "Life was always a test, Rick."

(*TWD*, season 4, episode 5)

This larger plan may indeed mean evolving as a hero organism and breathing new life into the degradation of the barren and violent human landscape. The virus brings about the kind of suffering necessary for heroic transformation (Allison & Setterberg, 2016). Moreover, the virus is biology's way of calling us to our heroic archetypal birthright.

RISK AND SACRIFICE: GIVING BIRTH AS THE ULTIMATE GIFT TO HUMANITY

With the incorporation of survival as a fundamental element in its materialization, *TWD* as an expression of the sublime *necessarily* incorporates risk. But with great risk potentially comes even greater reward. Babies and youth are miracles. When Morgan holds baby Judith in his arms for the first time, he marvels in awe at this precious creature; when he was lost in hopelessness, his mentor, Eastman, had told him he would one day be able to hold a baby in his arms again, like a holy grail-type reminder of the value of life. Judith is the sheer embodiment of the whole human species and its future, in a single life. In the words of the great poet William Blake, a child in such a horrific universe allows us "To see a World in a Grain of Sand/And a Heaven in a Wild Flower/Hold Infinity in the palm of your hand/And Eternity in an hour." Every time we see baby Judith on the screen it is a reminder for us, the audience, that there is still hope; that all the pain will somehow be worth it if she remains alive. For her to be killed would leave a gaping hole in the hearts of our beloved characters as well as in our own hearts, the echoes of which will be felt far and wide. That same hope is felt as we watch characters in the RV pass around an ultrasound picture of Maggie and Glenn's unborn baby on their way back from the Hilltop in the sixth season episode *Knots Untie*.

The maternal figures (Lori and Maggie), Carl, and baby Judith continue to inspire and energize heroic actions throughout the series, as is characteristic of heroic leadership (Allison & Goethals, 2014). The group tries to find Lori, Carl, and baby Judith a stable and safe home, moving from the farm (season 2), to the prison (seasons 3 and 4), to the walled-off safe zone community in Alexandria, Georgia (season 5–present); this is practically their modus operandi throughout the various challenges they face. Rick clears out an entire prison full of walkers to do it in season 3. Earlier on, at the farm, he tries desperately to handle the tense situation between Shane and Hershel, in order to persuade the latter to let them stay now that Lori is pregnant: "I'm a father," he says to Hershel; "he's [Carl] the one thing I don't wanna fail." In season 6, Rick and the group go to great lengths to get Maggie to a doctor when complications develop during her pregnancy, and because of that, beloved characters Glenn and Abraham die.

What is more, many characters commit unspeakable and torturous acts to *protect life*. In season 2, while the group is at the farm, Shane sacrifices farm resident Otis, who offers to help get medical supplies for

Carl after inadvertently shooting him while hunting a deer Carl has paused to admire in the forest. Shane shoots Otis and leaves him as bait while they are pinned down by walkers in the local school where the supplies are held, to get the medicine Carl needs to survive the operation that can save his life.

So potent is this innate knowledge of the importance of bringing new life into this decimated world and preserving it that, in perhaps the greatest act of heroic self-sacrifice in the series, Lori gives up her life to bring baby Judith into the world. In the aptly named third season episode *Killer Within*, experiencing birth complications as she, Carl, and Maggie are surrounded by walkers inside the prison, Lori realizes she needs to make a choice between herself and her baby. Despite Carl's and Maggie's pleas, Lori is adamant about the importance of this act for a purpose far greater than her own life. She begs Maggie to deliver her baby using Carl's knife: "My baby has to survive ... please ... my baby ... *for all of us ... Please! Maggie!*" Lori shows unimaginable strength as Maggie cuts her open to perform a C-section without anesthetic. Lori's piercing cries cannot be unheard in this visceral scene, before she expels her last breath. Shortly after, Carl shoots his mother to prevent her from "turning." With this ultimate sacrifice, Lori has transcended into a sublime hero organism, ensuring there is no possibility of she or her baby transforming into the monstrous lurking within. Life prevails despite all odds, for the greater good of the group, and the entire human race.

Baby Judith inspires constant heroic action. In the highly confrontational scene mentioned earlier on, Carol makes the impossible decision to shoot young Lizzie to keep Judith safe, after she and Tyreese discover Lizzie has stabbed Mika. This is further exemplified in one of Rick's toughest decisions in the series—his choice not to fight the Saviors, in order to keep Judith, Carl, and those he loves safe. He explains to his new partner, Michonne, after revealing the circumstances of Judith's conception:

> I know Judith isn't mine ... I know it ... I love her, she's my daughter ... but she isn't mine. I had to accept that. I did. So I could keep her alive. I'll die before she does, and I hope that's a long time from now so I can raise her, and protect her, and teach her how to survive. This is how we live now. I had to accept that too so I could keep everyone else alive.

In this scene, we feel the unbearable weight of the burden of being a heroic leader in such a heightened environment. Baby Judith becomes a compass that informs Rick's heroic leadership. The enormity of the decision and the strength it takes to *not* fight is the mark of Rick's leadership in this instance, in his choice to preserve the precious lives that have escaped the horrors of Negan's wrath. Judith, Carl, and Michonne energize Rick to keep going, even if this mean not acting, if that is what it takes to protect life and love—a core function of heroic leadership. At the same time his words reveal the epistemic function of heroic leadership (Allison & Goethals, 2014) in his drive to teach Judith everything he has learned, in order to ensure her survival. In a world of terror and chaos, a child truly is the ultimate gift that brings the heroic out in us.

FINAL THOUGHTS: THE PARADOX OF LIFE, DESPAIR, AND HOPE IN *THE WALKING DEAD*

When Carl is fighting for his life at the farm after being shot, Lori begins to accept that he would be better off dead than having to face a short and cruel life in such a reality. Overcome by anguish and despair, she asks Rick: "Tell me why it would be better, the *other* way [if he survived the wound]?" Soon after, when Carl regains consciousness momentarily, the first thing he mentions is his deeply mesmerizing, if not transcendent, experience with the deer in the forest, seconds before he is shot. Unable to answer Lori's question initially, later on Rick narrates the story of Carl and the deer to Lori—his words mirroring perfectly the edge of despair and hope on which our characters live:

> That's what he was talking about when he woke up—not about getting shot, or what happened at the church. He talked about something beautiful, something living … Why is it better for Carl to live even in this world? He talked about *the deer. Lori—he talked about the deer.*

This renewed faith becomes a catalyst for their joint decision, a few episodes later, to carry their second child to term.

By breathing new life into their decaying and infected physical bodies through the act of procreation, Lori and Maggie as maternal subjects become harbingers of hope, in turn breathing new life into the rest of the decaying world of rotting flesh and spirit—they literally embody the heroic body/hero organism in this biological act, from which the broader social and spiritual (and so forth) restoration and healing effect of the heroic act can be felt. This signifies the hero's journey as a cycle of fertility and creation in our evolution and its mythical origins (Campbell, 1949). One could say this is the ultimate act of resistance against the hopelessness that pervades the postapocalyptic order. In the end, in the wise words of Morgan, "all life is precious."

The symbolism of beginning and ending the seventh season finale, *The First Day of the Rest of Your Life*, with flashbacks of Maggie and her close friend Sasha admiring the sunrise in the distance, and its interlacing with Maggie's epilogue, is telling. Maggie's profound epilogue chronicles the heroic journey of our characters to this point, up to and including Sasha's critical decision, by the end of the episode, to sacrifice herself for the group:

> The decision was made a long time ago. Before any of us knew each other. When we were all strangers who would have just passed each other on the street, before the world ended. And now we mean everything to each other ... You [Rick] were in trouble. You were trapped. Glenn didn't know you, but he helped you. He put himself in danger for you. And that started it all. From Atlanta, to my daddy's farm, to the prison, to here. To this moment now. Not as strangers. As family. Because Glenn chose to be there for you, that day, a long time ago, that was the decision that changed everything. It started with both of you, and it just grew. All of us. To sacrifice for each other. To suffer, and stand. To grieve. To give. To love. To live. To fight for each other. Glenn made the decision, Rick—I was just following his lead. (*TWD*, season 7, episode 16)

Their collective journey started with a single act of self-sacrifice, Glenn's, and culminated with his wife, Maggie—the maternal subject, harbinger of the new seed, and future of the group—taking the role of the heroic leader preparing to fight another good fight. The self-sacrifices of other individuals throughout the series propagate and build an expanding group. It is a beating heart that breathes life into a growing organism, that becomes self-regenerative, capable of regrowing limbs after they have been cut off or exposed to life-threatening trauma. That is the power of hope, and the "life-supporting nature" of hero mythologies professed by Joseph Campbell (1972, p. 12). It is the sun that always rises. It is the breath of new life growing inside the female body, no matter how weary. It is the seed of the ever-expanding and eternal hero organism.

The postapocalyptic setting of *TWD* illuminates with great clarity the endless cycle of heroic leadership and action, hope and despair; the heroic instinct that binds through diversity, suffering, and healing; the selflessness that protects and sustains the vast network of life that is the collection of human hero organisms, allowing it to multiply and flourish, and amalgamating past, present, and future. For that is what heroic leadership is in biological and social terms—the seed that is the ultimate act of love. Allison and Goethals (2017) refer to the germination of this seed as the transformation from selfish egocentricity to selfless sociocentricity. Service to society is the consummate transformative state as described in theories of healthy human lifespan development (Erikson, 1994). *TWD* is saturated with the recognition of the importance of children as hope for the future. As Abraham tells Sasha in flashback in the seventh season finale, "Both of us know if we're going to kick, there sure as hell better be a point to it." Most tellingly, he expresses the exact nature of the "point" shortly after, an observation that may be *TWD*'s guiding principle with regard to societal regeneration: "Maggie ... she's carrying the future."

REFERENCES

Aboitiz, F. (1989). Behavior, archetypes and the irreversibility of evolution. *Medical Hypotheses*, *30*(2), 87–94.

Adams, M. V. (2004). *The fantasy principle: Psychoanalysis of the imagination.* Hove and New York: Brunner-Routledge.

Allison, S. T., & Goethals, G. R. (2011). *Heroes: What they do and why we need them.* New York: Oxford University Press.

Allison, S. T., & Goethals, G. R. (2013). *Heroic leadership: An influence taxonomy of 100 exceptional individuals.* New York: Routledge.

Allison, S. T., & Goethals, G. R. (2014). "Now he belongs to the ages": The heroic leadership dynamic and deep narratives of greatness. In G. R. Goethals, S. T. Allison, R. M. Kramer, & D. M. Messick (Eds.), *Conceptions of leadership: Enduring ideas and emerging insights* (pp. 167–83). New York: Palgrave Macmillan.

Allison, S. T., & Goethals, G. R. (2017). The hero's transformation. In S. T. Allison, G. R. Goethals, & R. M. Kramer (Eds.), *Handbook of heroism and heroic leadership* (pp. 379–400). New York: Routledge.

Allison, S. T., & Setterberg, G. C. (2016). Suffering and sacrifice: Individual and collective benefits, and implications for leadership. In S. T. Allison, C. T. Kocher, & G. R. Goethals (Eds.), *Frontiers in spiritual leadership: Discovering the better angels of our nature.* New York: Palgrave Macmillan (pp. 197–214).

Allison, S. T., Goethals, G. R., & Kramer, R. M. (2017). Introduction: Setting the scene: The rise and coalescence of heroism science. In S. T. Allison, G. R. Goethals, & R. M. Kramer (Eds.), *Handbook of heroism and heroic leadership* (pp. 1–16). New York: Routledge.

Blake, W. (1863). To see a world ... Fragments from *Auguries of Innocence.* Retrieved May 29, 2017 from https://www.poetryloverspage.com/poets/blake/to_see_world.html.

Bynum, T. W. (2010). Philosophy in the information age. *Metaphilosophy*, *41*(3), 420–42.

Byrne, W. F. (2006). Burke's higher romanticism: Politics and the sublime. *Humanitas*, *19*(1/2), 14–34.

Campbell, J. (1949). *The hero with a thousand faces.* Princeton: Princeton University Press.

Campbell, J. (1972). *Myths to live by*. New York: Viking Press.

Corbin, H. (1964, rev. ed. 2011). *Mundus imaginalis or the imaginary and the imaginal*. Retrieved May 29, 2017 from http://hermetic.com/moorish/mundus-imaginalis.

Coyne, R. (1999). *Technoromanticism: Digital narrative, holism and the romance of the real*. Cambridge: MIT Press.

Cranny-Francis, A., Waring, W., Stavropoulos, R., & Kirkby, J. (2003). *Gender studies: Terms and debates*. Basingstoke: Palgrave Macmillan.

Creed, B. (1986). Horror and the monstrous-feminine: An imaginary abjection. *Screen*, *27*(1), 44–71.

Creed, B. (1993). *The monstrous-feminine: Film, feminism, psychoanalysis*. London: Routledge.

Dadoun, R. (1977). Fetishism in the horror film. *Enclitic*, *1*(2), 39–63.

Dubner, A. (2017). 10 things that happen when you get sick. *Ranker*. Retrieved May 29, 2017 from http://www.ranker.com/list/10-things-that-happen-when-you-get-sick/analise.dubner.

Efthimiou, O. (2017). The hero organism: Advancing the embodiment of heroism thesis in the 21st century. In S. T. Allison, G. R. Goethals, & R. M. Kramer (Eds.), *Handbook of heroism and heroic leadership* (pp. 139–62). New York: Routledge.

Erikson, E. H. (1994). *Identity and the life cycle*. New York: W. W. Norton & Company.

Fisher, A. (2017, May 9). Why heroes assemble [Blog post]. *The Hero Forge*. Retrieved May 29, 2017 from https://www.theheroforge.org/blog/2017/5/9/why-heroes-assemble.

Franco, Z. E., Blau, K., & Zimbardo, P. G. (2011). Heroism: A conceptual analysis and differentiation between heroic action and altruism. *Review of General Psychology*, 1–15. doi: 10.1037/a0022672

Franco, Z. E., Efthimiou, O., & Zimbardo, P. G. (2016). Heroism and eudaimonia: Sublime actualization through the embodiment of virtue. In J. Vittersø (Ed.), *Handbook of eudaimonic well-being* (pp. 337–48). Cham, Switzerland: Springer.

Gardiner, P., & Osborn, G. (2006). *The shining ones: The world's most powerful secret society revealed*. London: Watkins Publishing.

Hurley, D. (2013). Grandma's experiences leave a mark on your genes. *Discover*. Retrieved May 29, 2017 from http://discovermagazine.com/2013/may/13-grandmas-experiences-leave-epigenetic-mark-on-your-genes.

Johnson, M. (2008). What makes a body? *The Journal of Speculative Philosophy*, *22*(3), 159–69. doi:10.1353/jsp.0.0046

Kinsella, E. L., Ritchie, T. D., & Igou, E. R. (2015a). Zeroing in on heroes: A prototype analysis of hero features. *Journal of Personality and Social Psychology*, *108*(1), 114–27. doi:10.1037/a0038463.

Kinsella, E. L., Ritchie, T. D., & Igou, E. R. (2015b). Lay perspectives on the social and psychological functions of heroes. *Frontiers in Psychology*, *6*, Article 130, 1–12. doi:10.3389/fpsyg.2015.00130.

Lorenz, M. G., & Wackernagel, W. (1994). Bacterial gene transfer by natural genetic transformation in the environment. *Microbiological Reviews*, *58*(3),

563–602. Retrieved May 29, 2017 from https://www.ncbi.nlm.nih.gov/pmc/articles/PMC372978/.

MacLennan, B. J. (2006). Evolutionary Jungian psychology. *Psychological Perspectives: A Quarterly Journal of Jungian Thought*, *49*(1), 9–28. doi:10.1080/00332920600732968

McCabe, S., Carpenter, R. W., & Arndt, J. (2015). The role of mortality awareness in heroic enactment. *Journal of Experimental Social Psychology*, *61*, 104–9. doi:10.1016/j.jesp.2015.08.001

National Geographic. (2017). *Adaptation*. Retrieved May 29, 2017 from https://www.nationalgeographic.org/encyclopedia/adaptation/.

Rohr, R. (2011). *Falling upward: A spirituality for the two halves of life.* Richmond, VA: Union Theological Seminary.

Rudd, R. (2013). *Gene keys: Unlocking the higher purpose hidden in your DNA.* London: Watkins Publishing.

Sempruch, J. (2007). Desiring death: The defeat of the maternal subject. *Women's Studies*, *36*(5), 333–48.

Shusterman, R. (2006). Aesthetic experience: From analysis to Eros. *The Journal of Aesthetics and Art Criticism*, *64*(2), 217–29.

Zehr, E. P., & Norman, S. (2015). Inside the head of the walking dead: The neurobiology of walker dysfunction disorder. In T. Langley (Ed.), *The Walking Dead psychology: Psych of the living dead.* New York: Sterling (pp. 31–41).

Index

'The chapters in this excellent edited volume illuminate what is often overlooked: leadership's sexual side. From the leaders of the sexual change and transformation movements, to those who inflict their heteronormative biases on others, to the inappropriate, immoral, and illegal sexual missteps of so many leaders, there is much to be gained by examining, explicitly, the sexuality of leadership. Leaders and leadership are fascinating topics, but add a dash of sex, and they become all the more intriguing.'

Donelson R. Forsyth, University of Richmond, USA

'The interplay between sexuality and leadership is a provocative topic that people tend to give a wide berth to, like a gorilla in a room. Not surprisingly, Jim and Scott climb on the gorilla, and bring along some collaborators to show us what can happen when leaders shy away from confronting sexuality-based issues within the group, or misinterpret the sexual intent of a behavior, and draws on real-world events many of us would like to forget. Far from sensational, this volume gives us the opportunity to move past the skittishness and finally address sexuality as an influence on social behavior.'

Craig Parks, Washington State University, USA

'Beggan and Allison's edited book fills the void created by the neglect of scholarship on the links between sexuality and leadership. In this collection of chapters written by social scientists from several fields, authors explore multiple ways in which leadership and sexuality can be related, including, for example, some leaders' sexual abuse of others and the sexuality implications of social dancing. I can't think of an edited book on leadership with a more fascinating and unusual set of chapters.'

Alice Eagly, Northwestern University, USA

Printed and bound by CPI Group (UK) Ltd, Croydon, CR0 4YY

23/04/2025

14660958-0001